TEA AND A SLICE OF ART

TEA AND A

SLICE OF ART

THE LYONS LITHOGRAPHS 1946–1955

CHARLIE BATCHELOR

Published by Artmonsky Arts/
Towner Art Gallery

1

Designed by David Pearson
www.davidpearsondesign.com
Set in 9.5/13 pt Storm John Baskerville

ISBN: 978-0-9551994-2-4

Printed in Great Britain by
Creative Imaging
Unit 29, Bow Enterprise Park
Violet Road
London E3 3QY

EASTBOURNE
Borough Council
www.eastbourne.gov.uk

Contents

Foreword

The Towner Art Gallery in Eastbourne mounted the exhibition *Tea and a Slice of Art – Commercial Lithographs Published by J. Lyons & Co. 1947–55* from 10 July to 12 September 2004. The exhibition was principally drawn from the Towner's permanent collection supplemented by several loans of preparatory material from private collections. It examined the phenomenon of the catering giant J. Lyons & Co. commissioning three series of lithographs from contemporary British artists, including Edward Bawden, David Gentleman, John Minton, John Nash, John Piper and William Scott, for the interior decoration of its famous teahouses in the immediate post-war years.

The Towner Art Gallery has a strong tradition of presenting new displays from its collection and revealing hidden aspects of the collection to an interested public. The development of *Tea and a Slice of Art* was no exception, though the idea was actually formed following the discovery of some piles of rather sad-looking commercial prints in a corner of one of the stores. We are most grateful, therefore, for the swift and decisive offer of financial support offered by the Friends of the Towner that enabled us to conserve and remount all twenty-nine of the Towner's Lyons lithographs. The conservation treatments and remounting were skilfully carried out by Heather Norville-Day.

It is not entirely clear why the lithographs entered the Towner Collection, or indeed why we held twenty-nine of the original forty lithographs. One possible reason for the prints entering the collection is that the artist John Lake, who contributed a work to the first set of prints, was Curator of the Towner at the time of his commission in 1947. However, records show that the prints have been acquired at different times and as recently as the 1970s. The fact that the Towner's set was incomplete seemed to reinforce the ephemeral nature of the prints and encouraged our interest in displaying them.

The exhibition opened appropriately with a tea party including contemporary products of Lyons & Co. The opening was attended by David Gentleman, one of the original artists involved in the scheme, and Peter Bird, the historian of the Lyons company. The exhibition was thoroughly and excellently researched by Charlie Batchelor, then the Exhibitions and Marketing Co-ordinator at the Towner, although the constraints of a regional museum researching and presenting new aspects of its permanent collection at a time when the organisation was involved in an £8.6 million relocation project, meant that no illustrative material could be produced to accompany the exhibition. The Towner was taken aback by the size of the response to the exhibition: it was widely featured in the national press and on radio, which suggested that the exhibition had prompted collective memories of the series and of the benefit of art in everyday lives.

One visitor to the exhibition, Ruth Artmonsky, quickly suggested to the Towner the potential of an illustrated overview of the Lyons lithographs, using the research for the exhibition as a basis on which to build. Her enlightened patronage has enabled Charlie Batchelor to extend her work and produce this publication, which reveals her important research into the Towner Collection that was only partially seen in the exhibition.

Ruth Artmonsky's generous financial commitment and her tireless support in seeing the project realised has resulted in this book celebrating the story of the Lyons lithographs, which represents an often overlooked example of corporate patronage bringing fine art to the people during the late 1940s and 1950s. In a similar way I hope that this publication also reveals one element of a regional gallery's permanent collection to a broad audience.

Matthew Rowe
Curator, Galleries & Museums
Towner Art Gallery

Acknowledgements

The Towner Art Gallery would like to thank the following individuals and organisations for their assistance with this book:

Peter Bird
Anthony Carr
Mr & Mrs Forbes-Robertson
Vincent Freedman
Clifford Frith & Stephanie Britton
David Gentleman
Stuart Henderson
Clarissa Lewis
Norbert Lynton
Chris Mees
John Moynihan
Heather Norville-Day
Joy Plowman
Paul & Karen Rennie
Professor Ian Rogerson
Richard Russell
Elizabeth Sitwell
Alan Sykes
Anne Ullmann
Rob Walker
Valerie West
Ian Weston

David Beevers & Amanda Wilson
Brighton Museum & Art Gallery
Gordon Cummins
The Fry Art Gallery
Patricia Jordan Evans
Bohun Gallery
Sarah Fahmy
Tate Enterprises
Joanna Jones
Atkinson Art Gallery
Elinor Kaye
Ben Uri Gallery
Simon Lawrence
The Fleece Press
Sarah Martin
The Imperial War Museum
Catherine Moriarty
University of Brighton
Jeremy Parrett
Manchester Metropolitan University

Robert Scott & Hester Russellgrant
The William Scott Archive
Sharon Wales & Nicky Balfour
Shell Art Collection

Special thanks to David Pearson and Richard Duguid for their sensitive handling of the design and editing of this book.

Extra special thanks are extended to Ruth Artmonsky for her unwavering support of the author, her research, and her dedication to the project and to the development of 'The Lyons Lithographs' at the Towner Art Gallery.

List of Illustrations

Introduction

On 20 September 1894 J. Lyons & Co. opened their first teashop at 213 Piccadilly, London. More cafés were opened in the years that followed, and with this rapid expansion the Lyons Teashops soon became as famous as they were numerous.

As social places that were recognised and trusted, the teashops were well-patronised and came to represent one of the most significant aspects of the vast Lyons catering empire. In the cafés the company always strove to provide good service in a pleasant and well-maintained environment, and in the inter-war years each individual unit was decorated and updated regularly. However, during the Second World War, a shortage of materials and manpower brought an end to the rolling refurbishment programme and as a consequence the interiors of the two hundred teashops, in both London and the provinces, became uncharacteristically run down.

After the War the regulations of the Utility Scheme[1] and the scarcity of paint continued to prevent any redecoration, but Felix and Julian Salmon (the Lyons directors with responsibility for the teashops) knew they had to improve the war-weary interiors. They recognised that it would be some time before any really substantial structural alterations could be carried out, so in 1946, as a 'quick-fix' solution, they commissioned a series of lithographs, designed by professional artists, to simply make '… the surroundings of the teashops more attractive …'.[2]

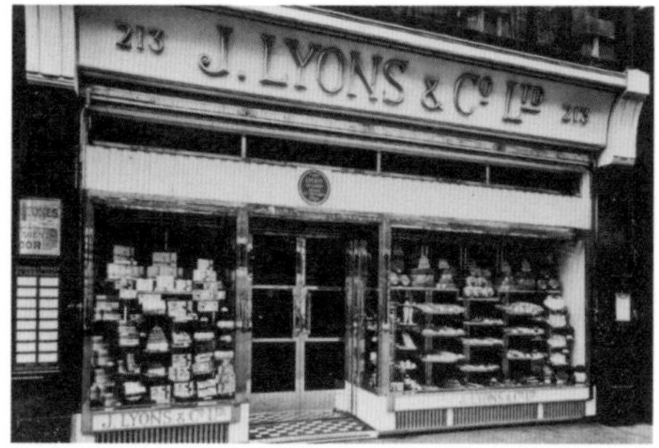

The first Lyons teashop at 213 Piccadilly, London.

1. The Utility Scheme, introduced by the Board of Trade in 1941, rationed the use of valuable resources such as paint, paper, petrol and wood. Only items (including furniture and clothes) that met the pared-down design guidelines of the Scheme could be purchased using special coupons.
2. Letter from Jack Beddington to Barnett Freedman, 12 August 1946 (Lyons Lithograph Archive, Towner Art Gallery).

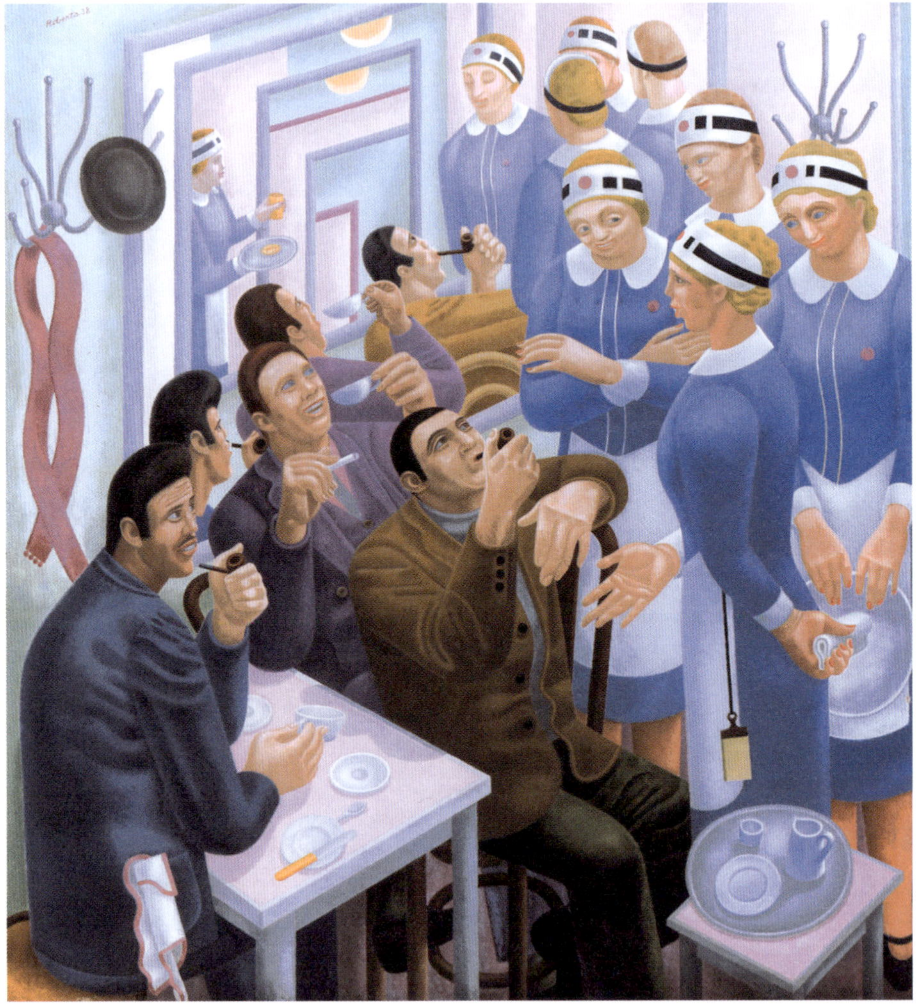

William Roberts (1895–1980), *The Tea Room*, 1938. A bustling scene in a teashop before the War. The waitresses were famously known as 'Nippies' on account of their quick and efficient service.

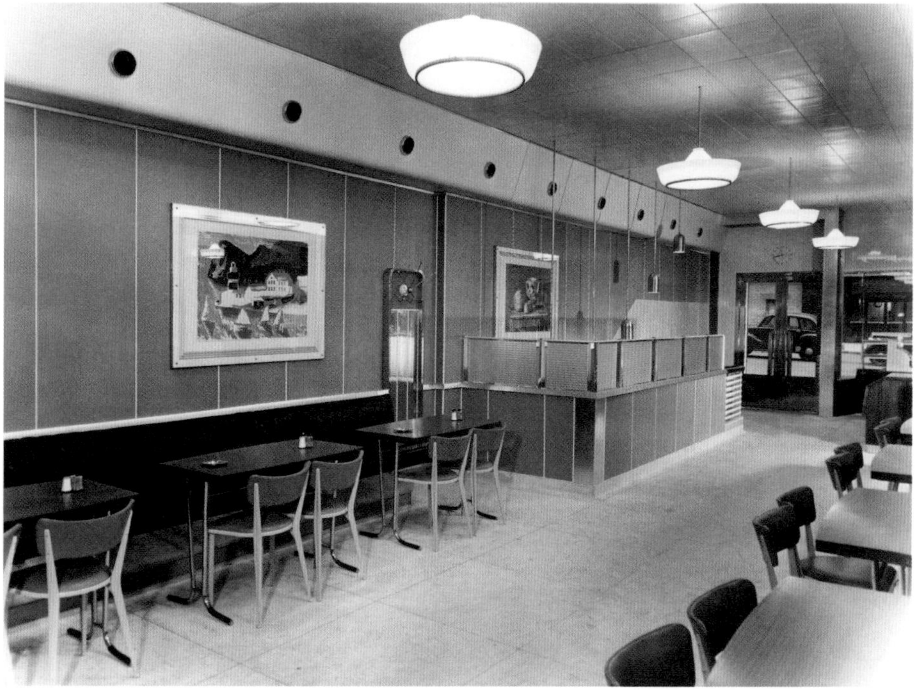

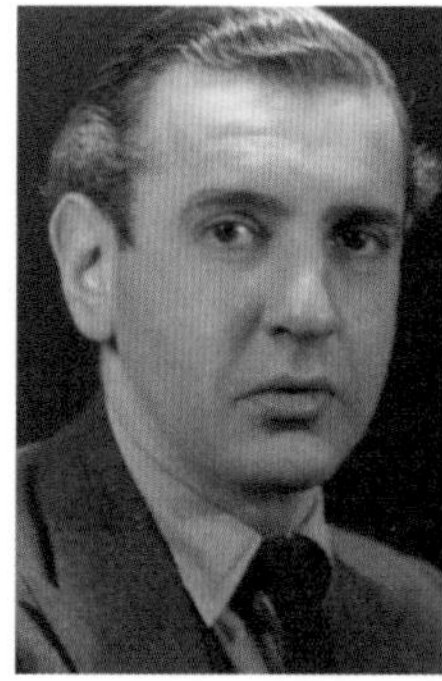

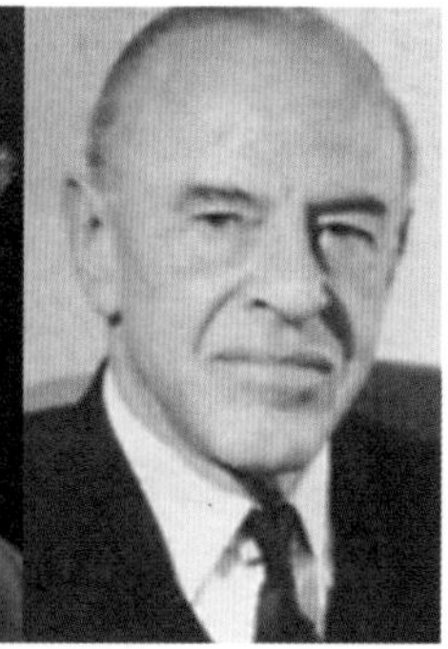

[above, left] Felix Salmon (1895–1980).

[above, right] Julian Salmon (1903–1978).

[left] The first teashop to open in London after the War, Lower Regent Street, photographed in 1951. Within the regulations of the Utility Scheme, Lyons introduced the BA chair (pictured here) in selected cafés. The chair was made from wartime scrap metal and manufactured by Race Furniture Ltd. The interior of this teashop was specially designed by Richard Lonsdale-Hands Associates and included a number of the Lyons lithographs – *Teignmouth* (left) and *Still Life* (right).

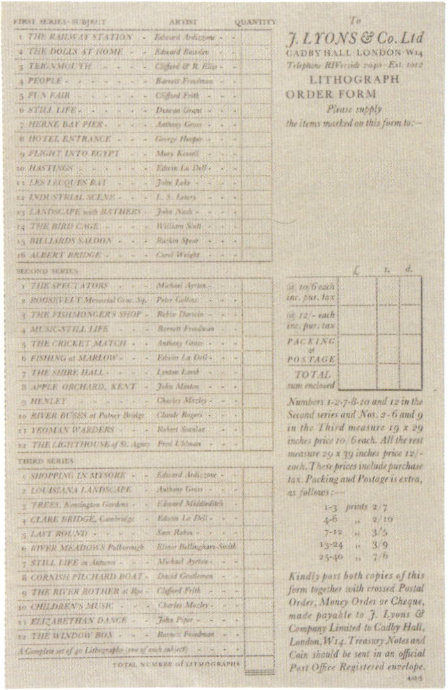

FIRST SERIES · SUBJECT	ARTIST	QUANTITY
1 THE RAILWAY STATION	Edward Ardizzone	
2 THE DOLLS AT HOME	Edward Bawden	
3 TEIGNMOUTH	Clifford & R. Ellis	
4 PEOPLE	Barnett Freedman	
5 FUN FAIR	Clifford Frith	
6 STILL LIFE	Duncan Grant	
7 HERNE BAY PIER	Anthony Gross	
8 HOTEL ENTRANCE	George Hooper	
9 FLIGHT INTO EGYPT	Mary Kessell	
10 HASTINGS	Edwin La Dell	
11 LES LECQUES BAY	John Lake	
12 INDUSTRIAL SCENE	L. S. Lowry	
13 LANDSCAPE with BATHERS	John Nash	
14 THE BIRD CAGE	William Scott	
15 BILLIARDS SALOON	Ruskin Spear	
16 ALBERT BRIDGE	Carel Weight	
SECOND SERIES		
1 THE SPECTATORS	Michael Ayrton	
2 ROOSEVELT Memorial Grov. Sq.	Peter Collins	
3 THE FISHMONGER'S SHOP	Robin Darwin	
4 MUSIC-STILL LIFE	Barnett Freedman	
5 THE CRICKET MATCH	Anthony Gross	
6 FISHING at MARLOW	Edwin La Dell	
7 THE SHIRE HALL	Lynton Lamb	
8 APPLE ORCHARD, KENT	John Minton	
9 HENLEY	Charles Mozley	
10 RIVER BUSES at Putney Bridge	Claude Rogers	
11 YEOMAN WARDERS	Robert Scanlan	
12 THE LIGHTHOUSE of St. Agnes	Fred Uhlman	
THIRD SERIES		
1 SHOPPING IN MYSORE	Edward Ardizzone	
2 LOUISIANA LANDSCAPE	Anthony Gross	
3 TREES, Kensington Gardens	Edward Middleditch	
4 CLARE BRIDGE, Cambridge	Edwin La Dell	
5 LAST ROUND	Sam Rabin	
6 RIVER MEADOWS Pulborough	Elinor Bellingham-Smith	
7 STILL LIFE in Autumn	Michael Ayrton	
8 CORNISH PILCHARD BOAT	David Gentleman	
9 THE RIVER ROTHER at Rye	Clifford Frith	
10 CHILDREN'S MUSIC	Charles Mozley	
11 ELIZABETHAN DANCE	John Piper	
12 THE WINDOW BOX	Barnett Freedman	
A Complete set of 40 Lithographs (one of each subject)		
TOTAL NUMBER of LITHOGRAPHS		

To
J. LYONS & Co. Ltd
CADBY HALL · LONDON · W14
Telephone RIVerside 2040 · Est. 1012
LITHOGRAPH
ORDER FORM
Please supply the items marked on this form to:—

	£	s.	d.
@ 10/6 each inc. pur. tax			
@ 12/- each inc. pur. tax			
PACKING & POSTAGE			
TOTAL sum enclosed			

Numbers 1-2-7-8-10 and 12 in the Second series and Nos. 2-6 and 9 in the Third measure 19 x 29 inches price 10/6 each. All the rest measure 29 x 39 inches price 12/- each. These prices include purchase tax. Packing and Postage is extra, as follows:—

1-3	prints	2/7
4-6	„	2/10
7-12	„	3/5
13-24	„	3/9
25-40	„	7/6

Kindly post both copies of this form together with crossed Postal Order, Money Order or Cheque, made payable to J. Lyons & Company Limited to Cadby Hall, London, W14. Treasury Notes and Coin should be sent in an official Post Office Registered envelope.

An order form for the Lyons lithographs, 1955. Copies of the lithographs could be purchased by the general public from the Publicity Department of Lyons. The price of the prints changed with the publication of each series.

The 'Lyons Lithographs', as they subsequently became known, were therefore conceived as a practical response to a potentially long-term situation. However, by deciding also to publish the prints, the Salmons were offering demonstrable support for British artists and, in turn, were consciously establishing Lyons as a corporate patron of the visual arts. Copies of the prints were made available for sale to the general public 'at a price within reach of the slenderest purse',[3] which meant that while the project was undoubtedly laced with genuine philanthropic intention, it was also accompanied by an element of commercial savvy which became increasingly important with the production of further prints in 1951 and 1955.

Publishing a series of fine art prints was an ambitious undertaking in the difficult post-war period. Yet at the same time the enterprise was a perfect expression of the practical and progressive approach to business which had characterised J. Lyons & Co. since its foundation. Furthermore, by selling the prints to the public at a reasonable price, the lithographs reflected the particular 'brand values' of the teashops, which themselves sold good quality food at affordable prices.

Lyons was by no means the first commercial concern to commission art, in particular lithographs, to display in busy 'everyday' places, quite distinct from the hushed and reverential surroundings of a gallery. The Underground division of London Transport, for instance, had been commissioning artists to produce posters, printed as lithographs, since the 1920s. These prints were consistently bold and bright, and because the publicity manager, Frank Pick (1878–1941), displayed them in prominent locations he had 'effectively turned every Underground station ... into a venue for constantly changing exhibitions of modern art'.[4]

Other high-profile industrial firms with products and services to sell, notably the regional railway operators and Shell-Mex, had employed artists to produce

3. P. Hendry, *Lithographs by Contemporary Artists – First and Second Series* (London, J. Lyons & Co./Arts Council of Great Britain (printed by the Curwen Press), 1951), p. 3.
4. O. Green, *Underground Art*, 2nd edn (London, Laurence King, 2001), p. 12.

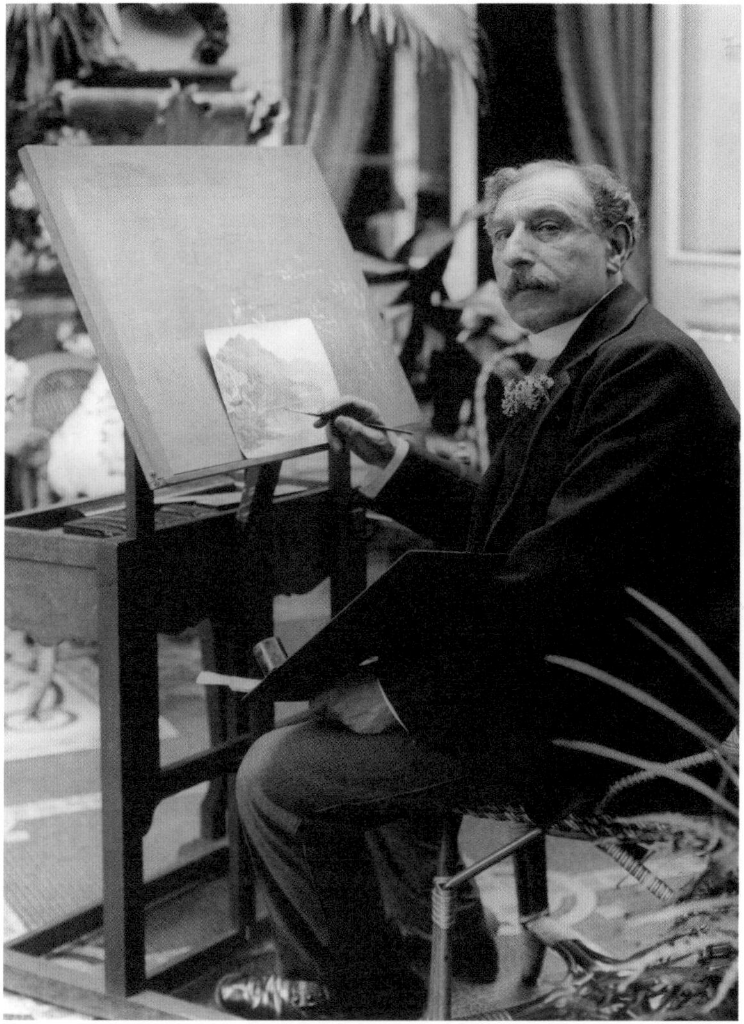

Joseph Lyons (1847–1917), 1907. Lyons (a keen amateur painter) established J. Lyons & Co. in 1887, with his relatives Montague and Isidore Gluckstein and Barnett Salmon. The business first supplied catering services at large-scale civic exhibitions but quickly grew into a formidable enterprise operating hotels, teashops and restaurants, as well as manufacturing own-brand goods, such as tea and, famously, Battenburg cake.

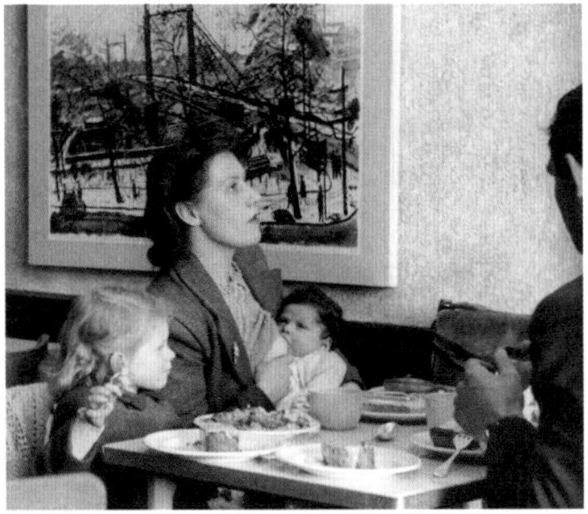

The 'everyday' environment of a Lyons teashop, 1950, showing the Lyons lithograph *Albert Bridge*.

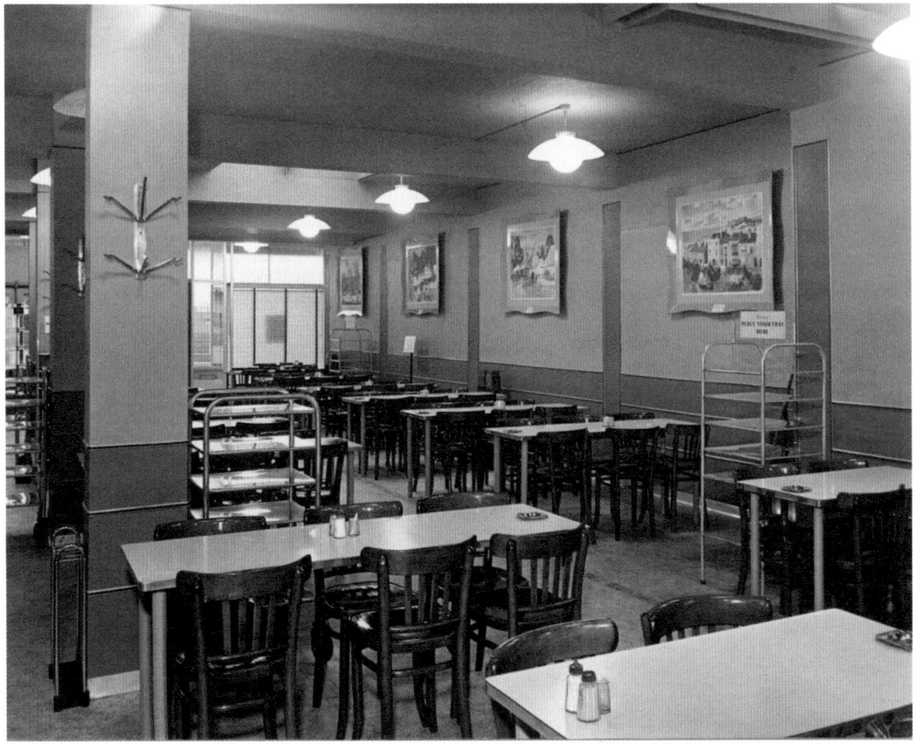

The interior of a teashop, post 1947, including the lithographs *Hastings*, *Fun Fair*, *Teignmouth* and *Flight into Egypt*.

high-quality publicity posters, and these had always been as much about the promotion of art and artists as they had been about 'marketing'. Similarly, lithographs created for schemes such as *Everyman Prints* (1940) and *School Prints* (1946/7) had been commissioned and designed specifically to hang in homes, canteens and schools and were indicative (as were the teashop lithographs) of the mid-century drive to make art accessible to a wide audience – so-called 'Art for All'. Initiatives such as *Contemporary Lithographs* (1937/8) had also promoted lithography as a versatile print medium.[5]

All of these various schemes and series were broadly similar in their overall appearance, but because they were each developed for a different purpose and audience they were ultimately all defined by their own unique qualities. The Lyons lithographs, for instance, certainly adopted the general aesthetic of the *School Prints*, but because there was no advertising other than the Lyons name in very small type they were essentially quite different from the graphic 'soft-sell' posters published by the likes of London Transport and Shell-Mex.

Lithography was developed in Europe at the end of the eighteenth century. Deriving from the Greek words *lithos* and *graphos*, the term literally translates as 'to draw on stone'. By the time Lyons commissioned their first prints, lithography had become a dominant commercial printing method, as numerous variations of the technique had been developed (such as photo-lithography) that had helped to increase the productivity of the medium. Stone had been replaced by metal, and machine production had also long since been introduced. As a result, the teashop lithographs were printed on zinc plates and on Crabtree two-colour offset presses, which meant the images were printed onto a rubber blanket before they were transferred to paper (Chariot cartridge from Grosvenor Chater) and the artists therefore did not have to draw their work in reverse.

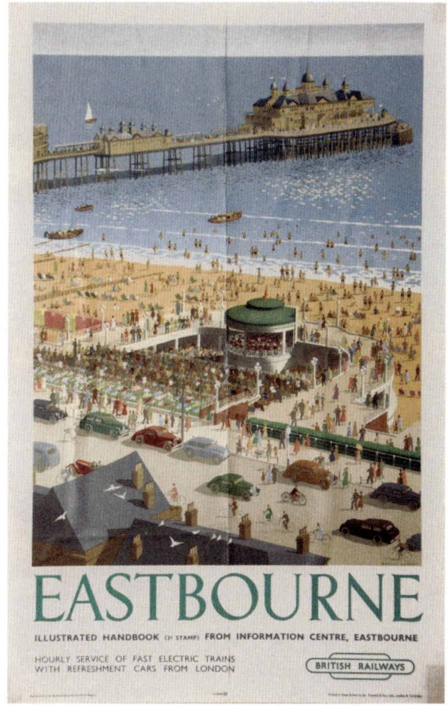

Eastbourne, Ronald Lampitt, *c.*1940s. Published by the Railway Executive (Southern Region).

5. *Contemporary Lithographs* was founded in 1936 by the artist John Piper and Robert Wellington, director of the Zwemmer Gallery. The aim of the scheme was to publish artists' lithographs that were distributed to schools simply to promote aesthetic awareness. A first series was published in 1937 followed by a second in 1938.

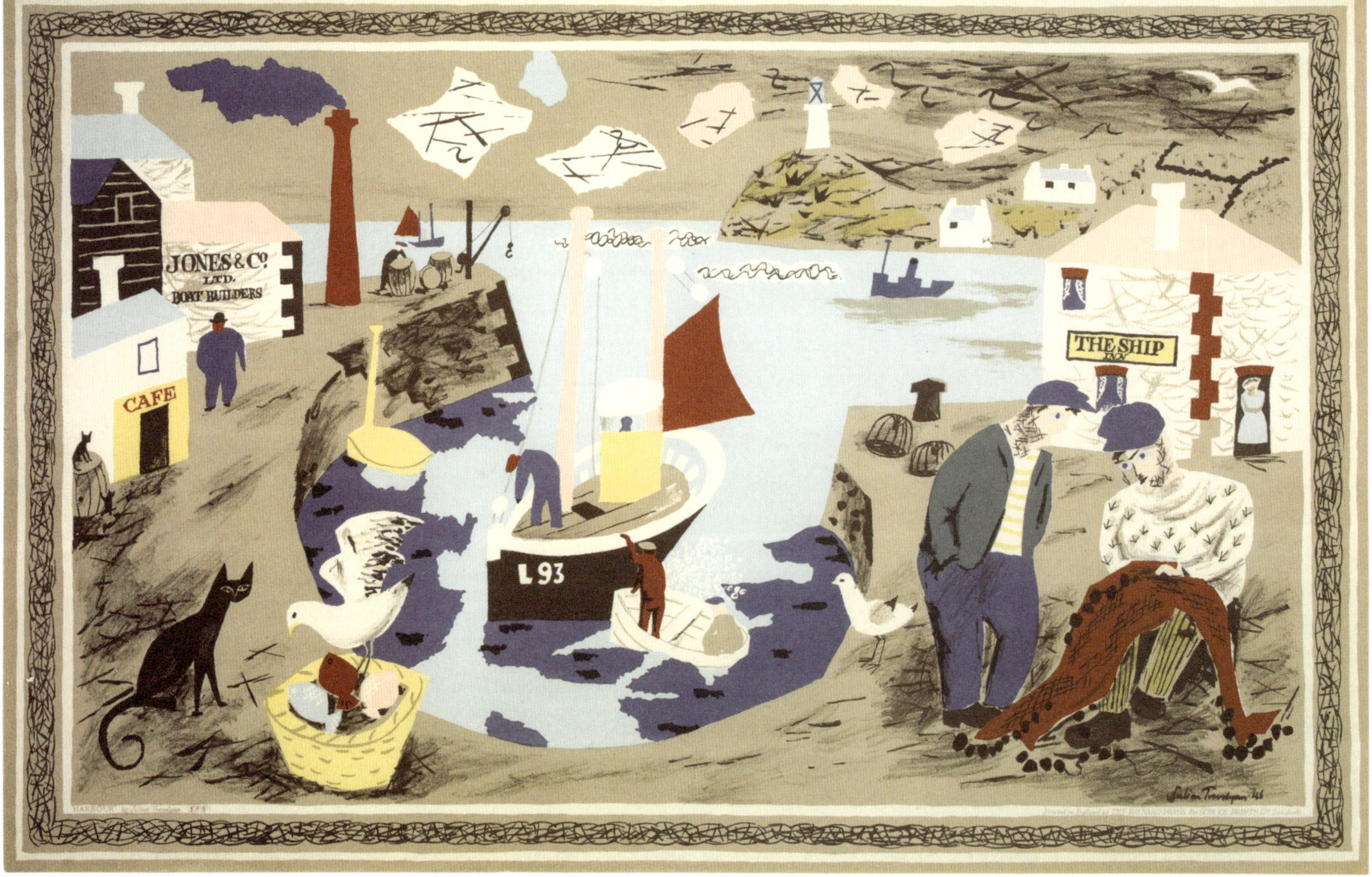

Julian Trevelyan (1910–1988), *Harbour*, 1946, *School Prints*, First Series.

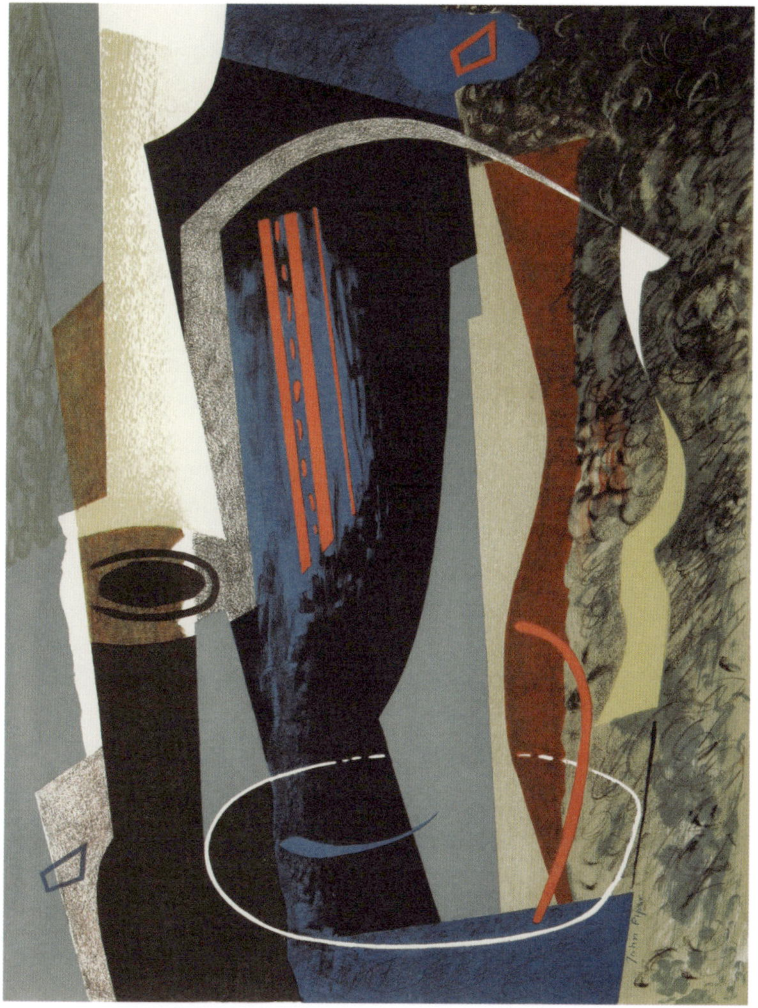

John Piper (1903–1992), *Abstract Composition*, 1938, *Contemporary Lithographs*, Second Series.

Auto-lithography allows artists to take complete responsibility for the design and transfer of their work to the printing plates, which means that each print they produce is arguably an 'original' work of art. Yet, despite being able to achieve a great range of tones and clarity in detail it is to this day widely acknowledged by artists as a 'damn tricky'[6] medium and one for which, at the time of the tea-shop project, many did not have the patience or necessary skills. Most, therefore, relied on highly trained interpretive technicians working at commercial printing companies to transpose their designs into lithographs.

However, those artists who did experiment with colour auto-lithography frequently became strong advocates of the medium and chose to use and re-use it at various points in their career. Eric Ravilious (1903–1942), for example, believed that lithographic printing ink was 'beastly stuff'[7] but in 1937 contributed *Newhaven Harbour*, as an auto-lithograph, to the first series of *Contemporary Lithographs*. A little later, in 1941, he then became completely absorbed in the complexities of auto-lithography during the production of his seminal prints documenting life on-board a military submarine.

Although some British artists were thus familiar with and enjoyed experimenting with lithography and auto-lithography, during the 1930s and 1940s the field of high-end artistic print production was relatively small. Consequently, the names of the same artists and printers often appear in relation to the histories of various prints produced before, and indeed after, the first of the teashop lithographs in 1947. A number of the artists who were commissioned for the Lyons lithographs, such as Edward Bawden (1903–1989), Edwin La Dell (1914–1970) and Charles Mozley (1914–1991), also contributed to a mixture of other schemes including *School Prints* and *Contemporary Lithographs*, as well as to advertising campaigns for

6. Letter from Eric Ravilious to Diana Tuely, 1 April 1941, quoted in A. Ullman (ed.), *Ravilious at War* (Upper Denby, the Fleece Press, 2002), p. 147.
7. Letter from Eric Ravilious to Diana Tuely, 4 January 1941, quoted in Ullman (ed.), *Ravilious at War*, p. 140.

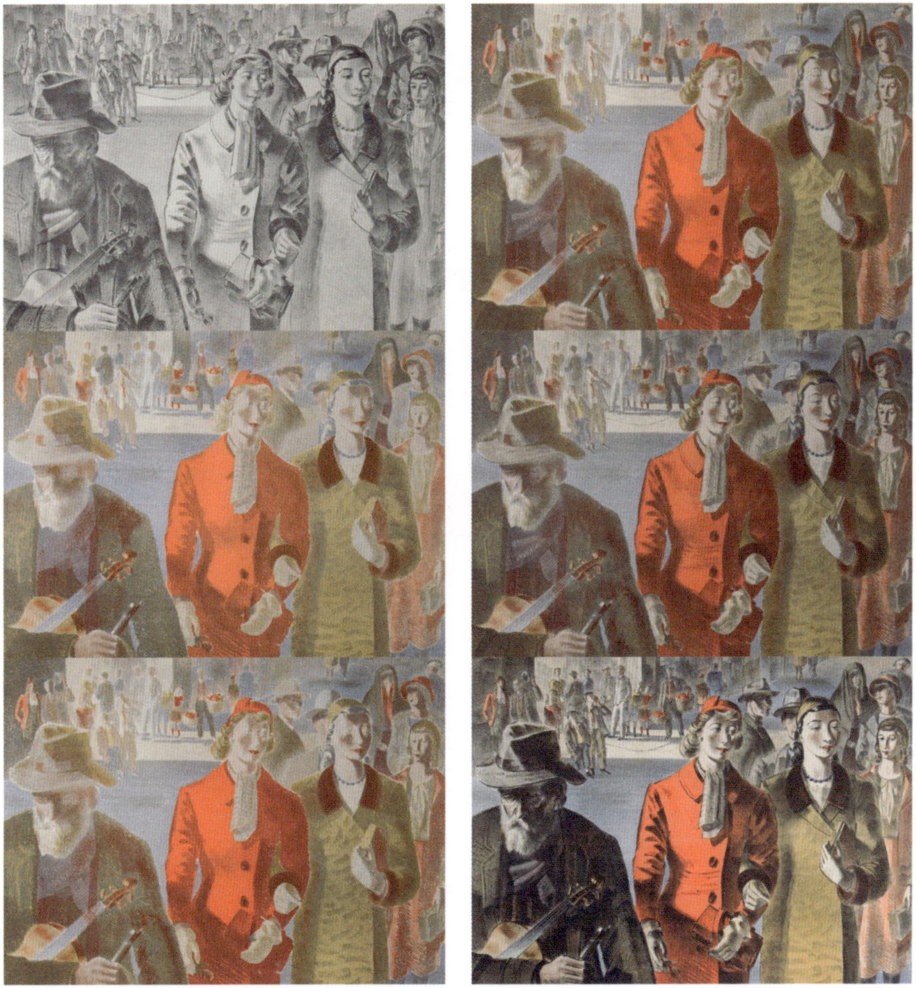

Progressives showing the development of *People*, Barnett Freedman's first auto-lithograph for the teashops, *c.* 1946.

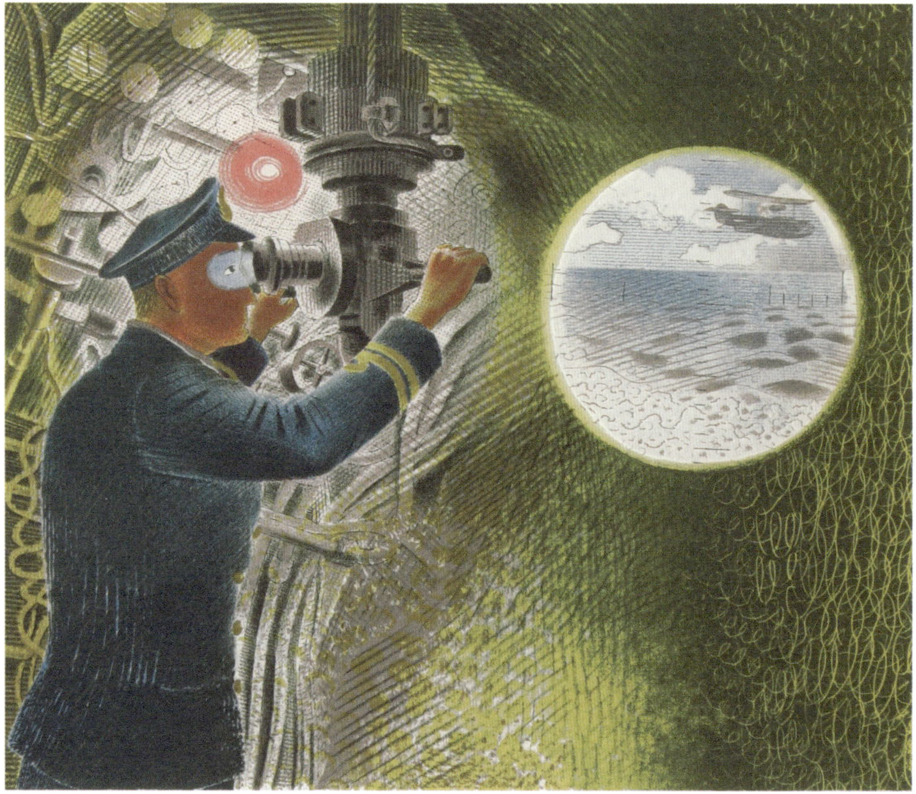

Eric Ravilious (1903–1942), *Commander Looking Through the Periscope*, Auto-lithograph printed at W. S. Cowell (Ipswich), 1941.

companies such as Shell-Mex and London Underground. However, despite being designed by significant artists and having once been displayed in two hundred teashops and being printed in large editions of 1,500 copies, the Lyons lithographs have frequently been overlooked in the wider context of twentieth-century British printmaking.

Tea and a Slice of Art now tells the story of these particular lithographs and reveals how a post-war necessity was developed into a prudent and worthwhile artistic enterprise by a small team of strong and influential characters. As a prominent British company with a thirst for quality, Lyons was in a position to employ leading creative professionals to assist them. As a result, they turned to the advertising guru Jack Beddington (1893–1959) for the overall creative direction, to the artist Barnett Freedman (1901–1958) for technical guidance, and to Frank Oppenheimer and his printing firm, Chromoworks Ltd, for the print production.

The Creative Team

Jack Beddington

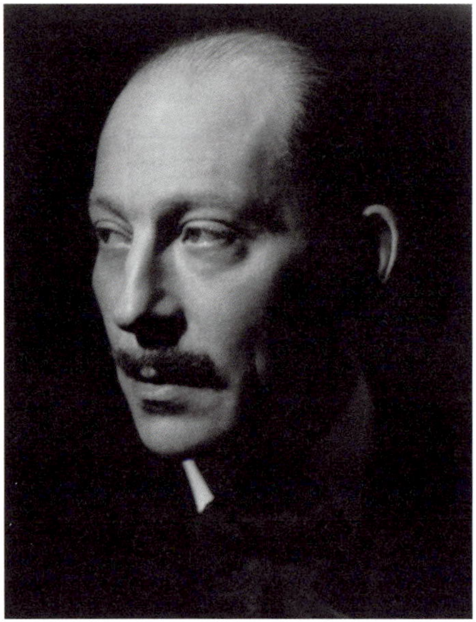

Jack Beddington by Howard Coster, 1938.

During a long and prestigious career in the advertising industry, Jack Beddington performed 'miracles of coordination'[8] through a variety of projects that successfully united creativity and commerce. He demonstrated this most notably through the high-profile publicity campaigns he masterminded for Shell-Mex during the 1930s, but he also brought the same knowledge and skills to the post-war teashop project.

In 1919, after studying at Oxford University, Beddington began his professional career in Shanghai working as a management trainee for the Shell Petroleum Company. He returned to London in 1928 and, after boldly criticising Shell's advertising for being rather dull, in 1929 took up a new position as publicity manager for Shell-Mex UK.

Since 1920 the company's advertising had been an in-house operation, focusing almost exclusively on the promotion of Shell-Mex products through coordinated campaigns appearing both as newspaper advertisements and as posters (known as 'lorry bills') attached to the firm's delivery vehicles. Beddington immediately ushered in significant changes in the publicity department and took on responsibility for the production of the lorry bills himself, reorienting them away from the promotion of Shell-Mex products towards marketing Shell-Mex the company. He introduced a standard graphic format for the lorry bills, which were printed lithographically, and created memorable slogans, such as 'Everywhere You Go You Can Be Sure of Shell'. In doing so, he established a distinctive house style that quickly became completely synonymous with Shell.

8. P. Rotha, obituary of Jack Beddington, *The Times*, 17 April 1959.

Importantly, Beddington commissioned British artists to design the lorry bills. Some, such as Duncan Grant (1885–1978) and Paul Nash (1889–1946), already had established professional reputations, but many more were talented young artists, such as Charles Mozley, to whom he was particularly keen to offer avuncular yet business-like support. He was quick to dismiss art which he deemed to be of bad quality or pretentious, but he did 'really understand artists and continually sought new means of patronage'.[9] In fact, John Moynihan, the son of the artists Rodrigo Moynihan (1910–1990) and Elinor Bellingham-Smith (1906–1988), remembers his mother describing Beddington as 'a veritable saint, issuing bonhomie and cheques from his office on the Thames Embankment'.[10]

In 1940, in a move necessitated by the Second World War, Beddington became Head of the Films Division at the Ministry of Information and in 1943 was awarded a CBE for his contribution. After the War, with the full encouragement of Shell-Mex, he joined the advertising firm of Colman, Prentis & Varley, where, by the time of his death in 1959, he held the position of deputy chairman.

Jack Beddington was a formidable character who 'emanated power and, so, was rather frightening to meet'.[11] Yet he was also as vivacious as he was generous in his support of British artists, and when he became involved with the Lyons lithographs he was at the peak of his professional influence.

For Lyons he flexed his skills as a project manager and shaped the aesthetic aspect of the lithographs by selecting suitable artists to take part in the scheme, as well as appropriate subjects for the prints. The Salmons required a well-connected and decisive individual to coordinate the project, and, as *the* figure in the industrial patronage of artists, Beddington was exactly the man for the job.

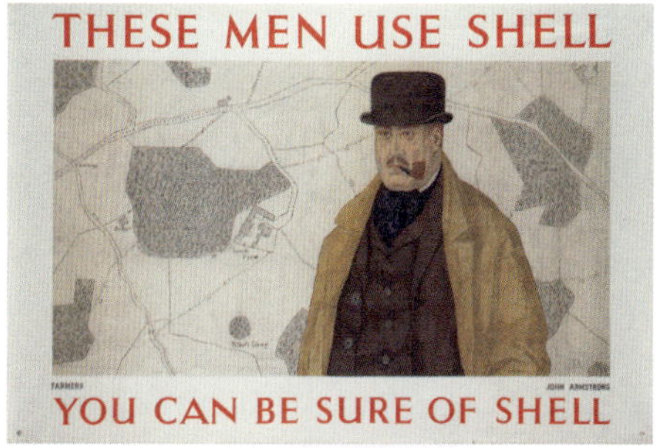

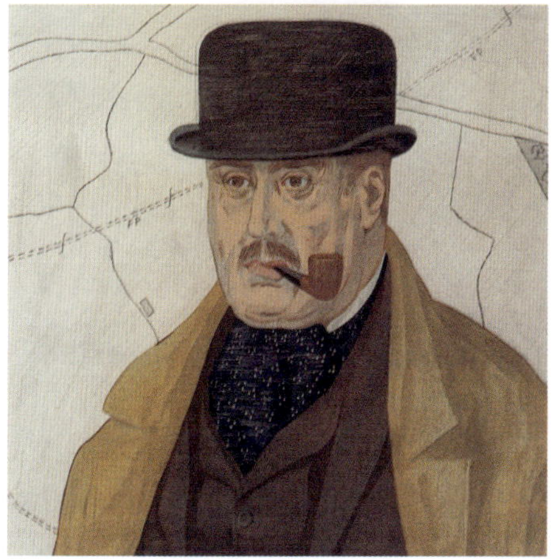

Farmers Use Shell, John Armstrong, 1939. A portrait of Jack Beddington.

9. James Gardner, *The ARTful Designer* (London, self-published, 1993), p. 82.
10. John Moynihan, *Restless Lives* (Bristol, Sansom & Company, 2002), p. 37.
11. Gardner, *The ARTful Designer*, p. 82.

Barnett Freedman

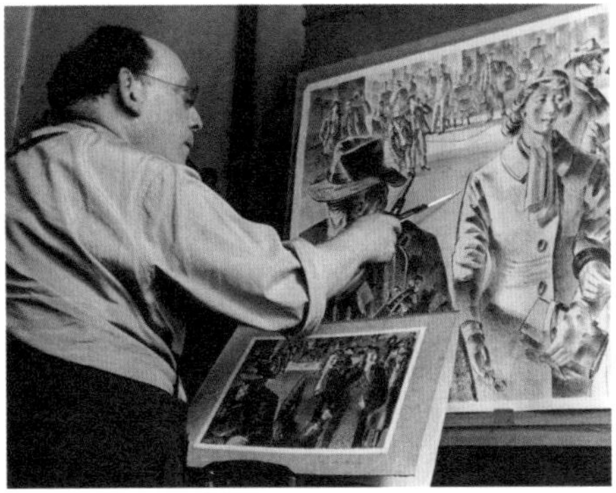

Barnett Freedman working on *People* in his studio.

In Jack Beddington, Lyons employed an adept coordinator who possessed an address book bulging with all the right contacts. In Barnett Freedman they employed an influential and skilled proponent of lithography who was well versed in the art of commercial print production.

Freedman trained at Saint Martins School of Art and in the Painting School at the Royal College of Art; he also enjoyed a more technical 'apprenticeship' at the Baynard Press. There he was exposed to the rigours of auto-lithography by Thomas Griffits,[12] and he displayed such an aptitude for the medium that Griffits later described him as the best pupil he had ever taught.

Freedman was somewhat unusual in this dual training and was one of only a relatively small number of artists who received a formal fine art education as well as a more practical art-based apprenticeship under a professional printer. This was because, at the time, stringent rules imposed by the trade unions governed the printing trade. These guidelines were designed to protect the professionalism and specialist skills of commercial lithographers working in the field, and it was therefore often quite difficult for fine artists to gain access to print works to experiment with techniques such as auto-lithography.

Having seized the opportunity to learn the art of colour auto-lithography himself, Freedman adopted the medium for most of his career and quickly became an expert in the production of auto-lithographs for machine printing. He wrote extensively about lithography in various journals, but also recognised how difficult it was for artists to experiment with the medium. As a result, he was generous with his knowledge and expertise and was particularly noted for stretching out 'a generous hand of comfort and rescue to successive generations of students'[13] at the Royal College of Art.

12. Thomas Griffits (1883–1957) was one of the most skilled lithographic artists/printers working in Britain in the 1920s and 1930s. He served his apprenticeship with the printer Vincent Brooks and later set up a respected printing workshop at the Baynard Press.

13. The Royal College of Art, Convocation 1956, Principal's Address (Barnett Freedman Archive, Manchester Metropolitan University Special Collections, FRE/1/1/327).

Freedman made his greatest artistic contribution through numerous illustrations for the interiors and jackets of books published by established and leading companies such as Faber & Faber. At the same time he designed and lithographed an array of prints for high-profile schemes, including one for *Contemporary Lithographs*. In 1940, Sir Kenneth Clark, then Chairman of the War Artists' Advisory Committee, recommended him for work as an official war artist, and Freedman subsequently served with the RAF and the Admiralty during the Second World War.

From his days at the Royal College of Art and the time he spent as a war artist, Freedman was well acquainted with many artists (such as Edward Bawden), prestigious printers and discerning patrons, becoming a close friend of Beddington, for example, after being commissioned by him to design a range of advertising material (including lorry bills) for Shell-Mex.

Freedman made hanging lithographs in the teashops a reality. He was entirely responsible for the technical execution of all forty prints, guiding the artists through the process and liaising with Frank Oppenheimer at Chromoworks. He also undertook the design of the catalogues, invitations, posters and exhibitions which accompanied the prints, and contributed one auto-lithograph to each series. These works were often much admired for their technical execution and overall composition, and in a letter written in July 1951 Felix Salmon said that *Music – Still Life* [p. 113], Freedman's contribution to the second series, 'is by far the best, it really is the tops'.[14]

Barnett Freedman's working alliance with Lyons and their artistic publishing scheme was, at all times, convivial and beneficial to all the various parties involved. The Salmons knew that their project was in the very best technical hands, and being passionate about his craft, Freedman allowed his enthusiasm to percolate into every aspect of the process.

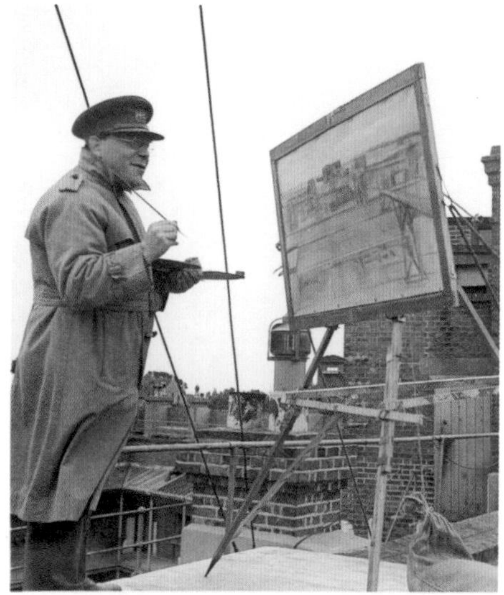

Barnett Freedman working as an Official War Artist in France, *c.* 1940.

14. Letter from Felix Salmon to Barnett Freedman, 3 July 1951 (Barnett Freedman Archive, Manchester Metropolitan University Special Collections, FRE/1/1/251).

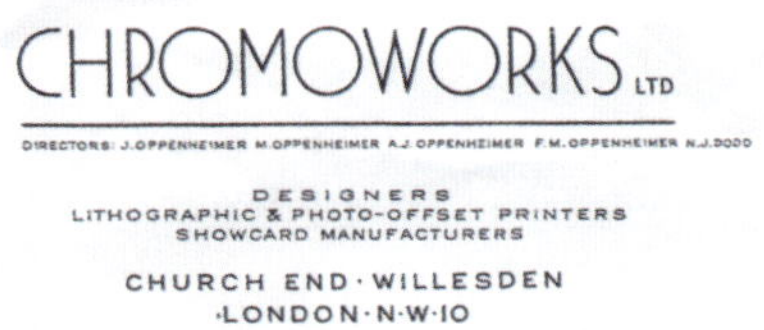
CHROMOWORKS LTD

DIRECTORS: J. OPPENHEIMER M. OPPENHEIMER A.J. OPPENHEIMER F.M. OPPENHEIMER N.J. DODD

DESIGNERS
LITHOGRAPHIC & PHOTO-OFFSET PRINTERS
SHOWCARD MANUFACTURERS

CHURCH END · WILLESDEN
· LONDON · N · W · 10

The Chromoworks Ltd letterhead, as used during the period 1947–1955.

Frank Oppenheimer and Chromoworks Ltd

All forty of the teashop lithographs were printed by the Willesden printing firm Chromoworks Ltd. Frank Oppenheimer, the managing director, took a personal interest in the scheme, and the ease and grace which characterised the whole printing process really stemmed from his genial nature and fastidious attention to detail. Everyone was impressed by his 'hands-on' approach, and in a letter to Barnett Freedman, Anthony Gross (1905–1984) stated, 'I must say that work on the lithograph went very smoothly owing to the trouble Frank Oppenheimer took with it from the start.'[15]

Chromoworks had been established by Julius Oppenheimer in 1908 and, as the 'chromo' in their name suggests, were largely concerned with the production of quality colour print for commercial use. They did, for instance, at one time hold the contract to print the distinctive coloured labels for Heinz Baked Beans, but they became particularly well known for lithographic printing incorporating photography.

They had undertaken some art-based jobs, such as printing a number of Shell lorry bills and the Puffin Picture Books,[16] but by 1946 they had gained only limited experience of working with artists on the production of a particular series of prints. This was probably partly because of the craft restrictions surrounding the professional print trade, but also because these schemes were quite an undertaking, with as much at stake, in terms of reputation, for the printer as for the artists involved.

15. Letter from Anthony Gross to Barnett Freedman, 28 January 1951 (Barnett Freedman Archive, Manchester Metropolitan University Special Collections, FRE/1/1/169).
16. Puffin Picture Books were the brainchild of Noel Carrington (1894–1989) – a one-time editor at *Country Life* – and were first published by Penguin Books in 1940 to provide British children with informative books designed and illustrated by professional artists.

In agreeing to print the Lyons lithographs, which from the outset involved some of the artists auto-lithographing their own design and thus creating potential problems with the unions, 'Frank Oppenheimer showed both initiative and courage'.[17] Chromoworks, however, charged a substantial fee for the project, and the only real elements of risk associated with the venture were the technical reputation of the company, and the potential risk of upsetting the unions. For Oppenheimer, who had great faith in his firm and confidence in his own personal skills of negotiation, being involved with the project was a sound commercial move which, in short, was very good for business.

Twenty-two of the forty teashop prints were eventually produced as auto-lithographs. The remaining prints were translated from the artists' originals by a team of lithographers at Chromoworks. These technicians were, importantly, also involved with the production of the auto-lithographed prints and 'went to great lengths preparing the colours'[18] and graining the plates for the commissioned artists.

Frank Oppenheimer was already acquainted with both Felix Salmon and Barnett Freedman before the teashop project got underway. Although there is no concrete evidence to determine who suggested lithographs might be the answer to the decoration dilemma, it is possible that he actually proposed the idea to Felix on hearing him 'bemoaning ... the difficulty of redecorating the tatty and often war-damaged walls ...'.[19]

Frank Oppenheimer and Chromoworks played an integral and essential role in this graphic scheme, and with Beddington and Freedman also in place the attention of the creative triumvirate turned to the artists and the product – the Lyons lithographs.

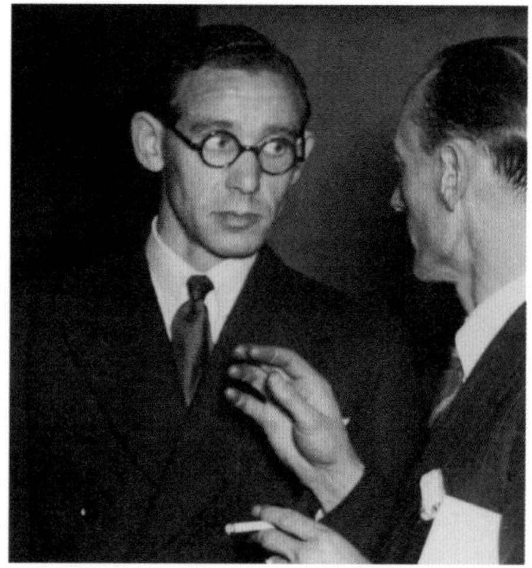

Frank Oppenheimer, 1947.

17. Noel Carrington, 'Art in the Teashops', *Penrose Annual*, Vol. 47, 1950, p. 50.
18. Letter from Gross to Freedman, 28 January 1951.
19. Carrington, 'Art in the Teashops', p. 50.

The First Series, 1946–1947

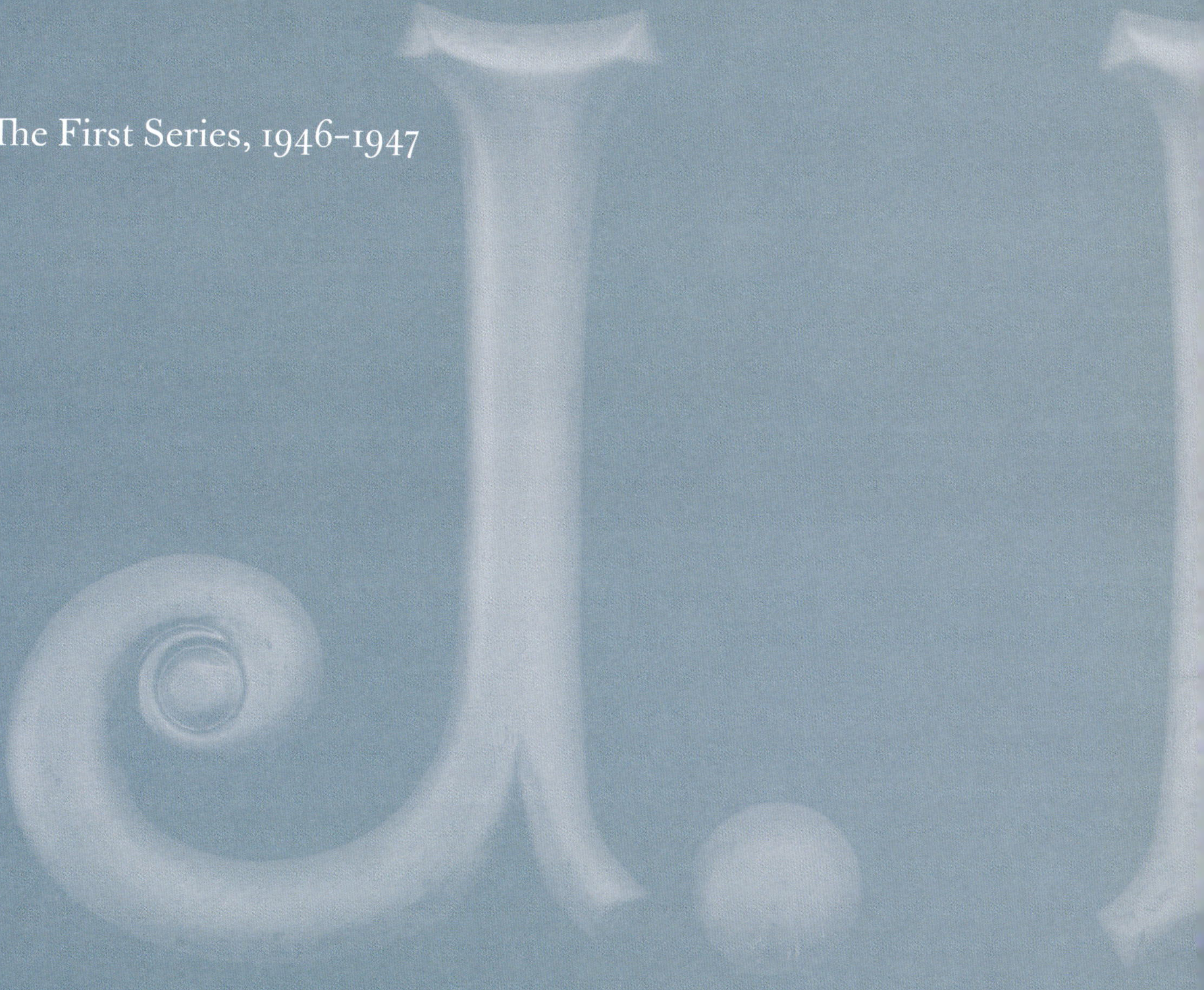

Getting Started

The notion of displaying lithographs in the teashops was first mooted in January 1946. Later that year, artists were approached to take part in the project, and by October 1947 sixteen artist-designed lithographs were on show in at least thirty of the decoratively distressed and bomb-damaged London teashops. By today's fast-paced working standards this might seem like a rather protracted turnaround for a project, but with Britain just emerging from the disruption of the Second World War it was an achievement even for a company as large and ambitious as Lyons.

Less than a week after meeting the Salmons for the first time, Jack Beddington sent a letter to Julian setting out his initial ideas for the scheme and proposing what were to become four touchstones of the project: the prints should be a mixture of those auto-lithographed by artists and those fabricated by the printers from original paintings; the artists should be paid a commission fee as well as a royalty on each print sold; the scheme should have no connection with advertising; and the whole project should receive wide publicity.

A number of other proposals were eventually modified as the project evolved, but the letter set the tone for an open and direct style of professional correspondence that was to characterise the entire scheme. Any changes followed intervention from Barnett Freedman and Frank Oppenheimer over practical matters or from Lyons over issues concerning the company's image. Beddington, for instance, initially suggested that 'no rigid rule should be made as to size',[1] but when the commission letters were sent to the artists it had been decided that the lithographs

1. Letter from Jack Beddington to Julian Salmon, 24 January 1946 (Barnett Freedman Archive, Manchester Metropolitan University Special Collections, FRE/1/1/251).

would be printed at Quad Crown, which measured a standard, yet substantial, 30" x 40". Settling on one size, of course, made the production of the lithographs more straightforward but, rather significantly, also meant that the prints would physically reflect the strictly regulated operation of the teashops and that, given their large scale, they would cover a great deal of the 'tatty' décor.

Artists

In the everyday environment of a Lyons teashop, customers seeking a cup of tea rather than cultural instruction were naturally going to respond to the subject matter of a lithograph before they responded to the names of specific artists. For the sake of good business the teashop prints thus needed to depict subjects that provoked admiration but never sparked outrage from the clientele. For Beddington the key to achieving this, of course, lay in the selection of artists who could produce appropriate designs, leaving the matter of subject and style to come later.

In his first letter to Julian, Beddington enclosed a list of twenty-nine artists he considered to be appropriate for the scheme, putting a star beside the names of nine to denote his 'first choices' but welcoming any 'addition or subtractions'[2] from the two directors.

The starred artists were Edward Ardizzone (1900-1979), Clifford Ellis (1907-1985), Barnett Freedman, Mary Kessell (1914-1977), L. S. Lowry (1887-1976), Dodie Masterman (b. 1918) Henry Moore (1898-1986), John Piper (1903-1992) and Carel Weight (1908-1997). Of those, Ardizzone, Ellis with his wife Rosemary (1910-1998), Freedman, Kessell, Lowry and Weight were commissioned to each produce a lithograph; Piper undertook a later commission for the third series, but Masterman and, more significantly, Moore were not included.

Other notable artists also appeared on the list, such as Cedric Morris (1889-1982), Matthew Smith (1879-1959) and Graham Sutherland (1903-1980), but ultimately none of these contributed lithographs. Naturally, names would have

2. ibid.

been both added to and dismissed from the list for a whole host of reasons that may never have been fully documented, but in some cases a removal had a self-evident explanation: Paul Nash, for instance, was included but died in July 1946, just six months after the list had been compiled. It is also possible that some of the artists Beddington approached actually declined the commission.

Of the artists who were mentioned but not starred, Duncan Grant, Anthony Gross and John Nash contributed, and the roll call for the first series was then finalised with the addition of Edward Bawden, Clifford Frith (b. 1924), George Hooper (1910–1994), Edwin La Dell, John Lake (1903–1975), William Scott (1913–1989) and Ruskin Spear (1911–1990), none of whom were mentioned on the original list.

Determining how many prints would make up the set and, therefore, how many artists should be commissioned, was not a straightforward process. Beddington originally recommended that the scheme should be initiated by 'buying eighteen pictures expecting to print from twelve',[3] while keeping the remaining six for possible use in the future. However, there is nothing to suggest that they did purchase eighteen works of art and decide to print sixteen of them, saving the extra two for a potential following series.

Constructing a definitive list of exactly who and what was being commissioned became easier on seeing how different images might, or might not, work together. On his original list Beddington cited a number of artists who had previously worked for him at Shell-Mex, such as Morris and Sutherland, but as the project evolved he seems to have consciously avoided selecting from just those artists, to ensure the teashop prints had a sufficiently distinct character.

Those whom Beddington did commission were neither from one artistic group nor united by the exploration of a common theme or style in their work. Many were friends from the Royal College of Art, and nearly all (including

3. ibid.

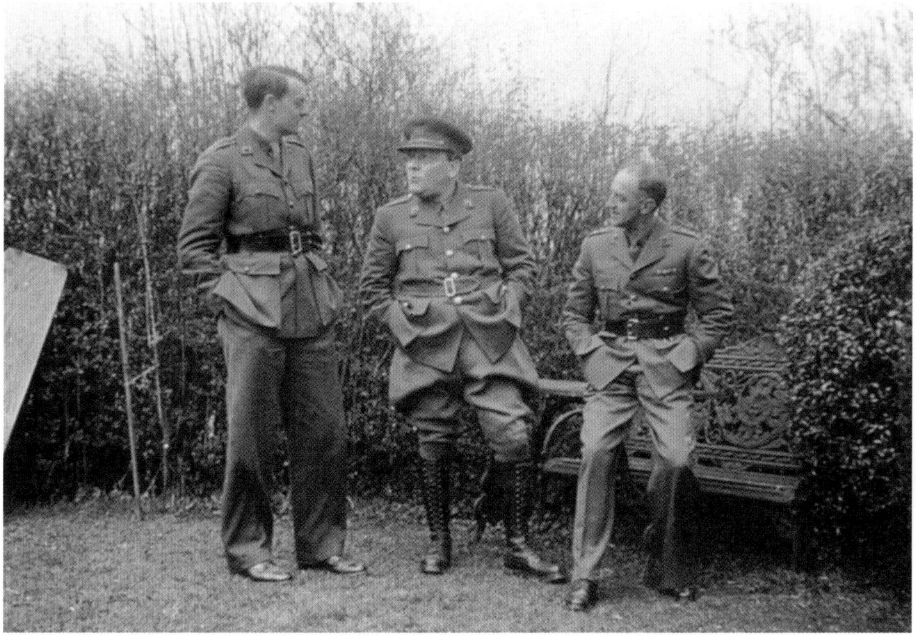

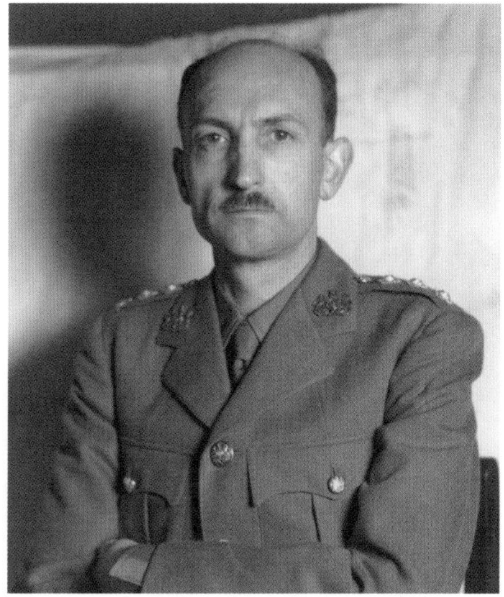

[left] Eric Ravilious, Barnett Freedman and John Nash in military uniform, April 1940.

[above] Captain Anthony Gross, 28 March 1941. Anthony Gross served as an Official War Artist between 1941 and 1946 and was posted to the Far and Middle East and Africa.

Mary Kessell) had served as official war artists or had received special commissions from the War Artists' Advisory Committee. Some were also professional colleagues who were familiar to one another from teaching at various art schools (Scott, for instance, was teaching at the Bath Academy of Art at Corsham Court with Ellis), while others held administrative positions in cultural organisations – John Lake was appointed Curator of the Towner Art Gallery in the year that the prints were published.

These professional networks, coupled with Beddington's energy for visiting galleries and attending exhibitions in search of fresh artistic talent, helped him to bring together a range of commercial and fine artists of both 'fame and

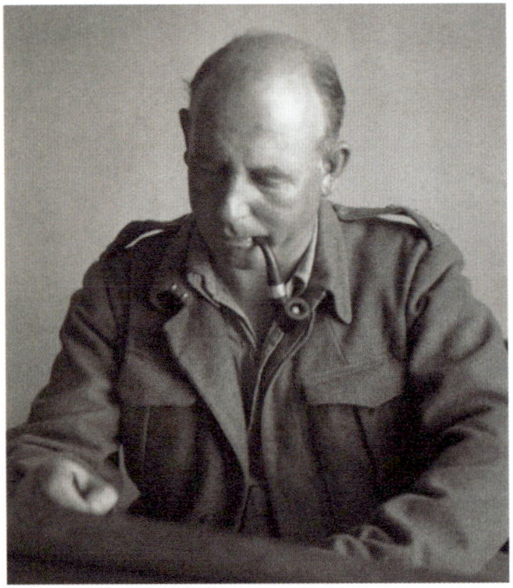

[above] Edward Ardizzone, 21 October 1943. Ardizzone served as an Official War Artist in Europe and North Africa.

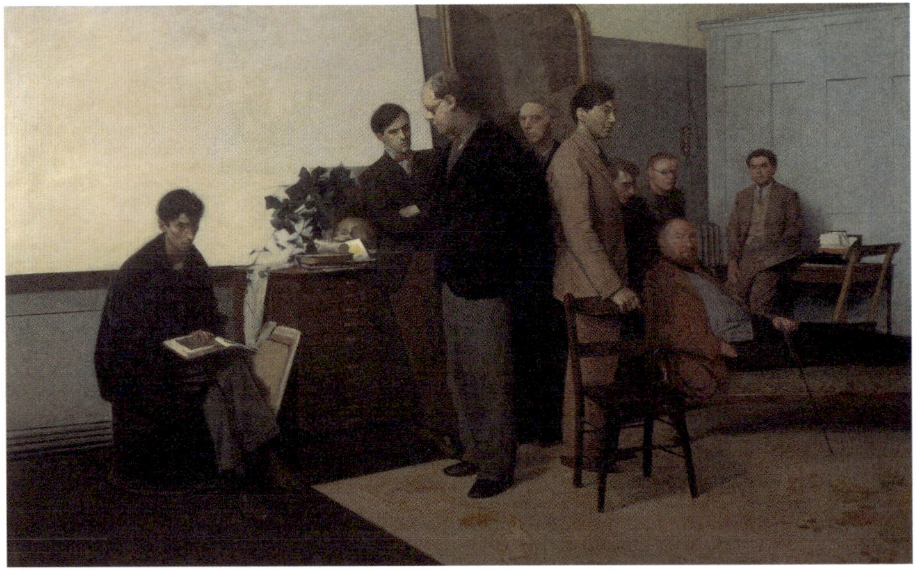

[above, right] Rodrigo Moynihan, *Portrait Group*, 1951. This painting depicts the staff of the painting school at the Royal College Art. From left to right the figures are: John Minton (seated/Lyons contributor) Colin Hayes, Carel Weight (standing centre/ Lyons contributor), Rodney Burns, Robert Buhler, Charles Mahoney, Kenneth Rowntree (*Everyman* and *School Prints*) Ruskin Spear (on chaise longue/Lyons contributor) and Rodrigo Moynihan.

promise'.[4] This, of course, created a balanced selection of work but, at the same time, was also something of a practical measure to help satisfy the broad tastes of the all-important teashop customers.

4. N. Bentley, 'Lithographs for Lyons', *Alphabet and Image*, May 1948, no. 7, p. 54.

Different Approaches to the Commission

Being ambitious businessmen always striving for the best, at first the Salmons were keen for all the artists to undertake their own lithography, but Beddington opposed the idea on the grounds that the scheme 'would suffer very considerably (a) from delay because many would have to be taught the craft (b) from many of the best artists refusing the work'.[5] Through his experience at Shell-Mex, Beddington understood that many artists did not have the time, patience or necessary artistic skill to try their hands at the rather involved medium of auto-lithography. To ensure that the teashop project had a broad but realistic scope he therefore strongly recommended that the artwork for the first series be a blend of auto-lithographs, reproductions of commissioned paintings, and reproductions of paintings not commissioned but bought on sight. Each artist initially submitted a sketch or fully realised painting and it was these works ('the originals') which Lyons purchased and, wherever possible, later exhibited alongside the finished lithographs. The originals (a number of which are reproduced in this book) ranged from collages (for example Edward Bawden's *The Dolls at Home*, [p. 62]) to watercolours (*Hotel Entrance* by George Hooper [p. 74]).

Just under half of the first prints were designed and lithographed by the artists themselves: Ardizzone, Bawden, Freedman, Gross, La Dell, Nash and Scott, all of whom were already familiar with lithography or had undertaken a variety of previous commissions. The remaining lithographs were worked up at Chromoworks from the originals and, for the most part, appear to have actually been painted in response to the teashop commission and were not already existing works of art.

5. Letter from Beddington to Salmon, 24 January 1946.

Clifford Frith, for example – at just 23 the youngest artist to be commissioned for the series – remembers that when he painted *Fun Fair* [p. 69] he 'really didn't consider the technical implications of lithography', and because he 'knew very little about the process ... went ahead and painted the work that [he] wanted to do'.[6]

Frith exhibited regularly at Wildensteins Gallery in Bond Street (run by Jack Beddington's brother, Fred), and it was here that Beddington had first seen examples of his work. In response to the commission Frith painted a gentle image of a travelling fair. He remembers that his original painting had a 'sketch-like quality' and that it was 'entirely the skill of Chromoworks in the translation that made it successful'.[7]

In the case of George Hooper's *Hotel Entrance* [p. 75], Beddington was attracted to an example of the artist's work depicting the Cricketers pub in Brighton, and he commissioned Hooper to produce a lively, yet different, image of the same subject for the teashops. Hooper prepared a number of sketches, but before submitting a final design he was asked to remove any beer glasses and to give the work the title *Hotel Entrance*, as Lyons did not think it was entirely appropriate to hang an image of a pub on the walls of their genteel teashops.[8] Interestingly, this is the only recorded instance of 'editorial control' being exerted on the first series by the company, yet it was an early indicator of how the Salmons themselves would become increasingly involved in the development of the second and third series.

Undertaking an auto-lithograph for the first series was also not necessarily a straightforward process and, as a result, even some of the relatively experienced artists who were commissioned to produce their own prints sought technical advice before embarking on their designs. In January 1947, for example, Edward

6. Clifford Frith, e-mail to Ruth Artmonsky, 29 January 2005 (Lyons Lithograph Archive, Towner Art Gallery).
7. ibid.
8. J. Beechey, *George Hooper* (London, Hooper Gallery, 1995) pp. 35–6.

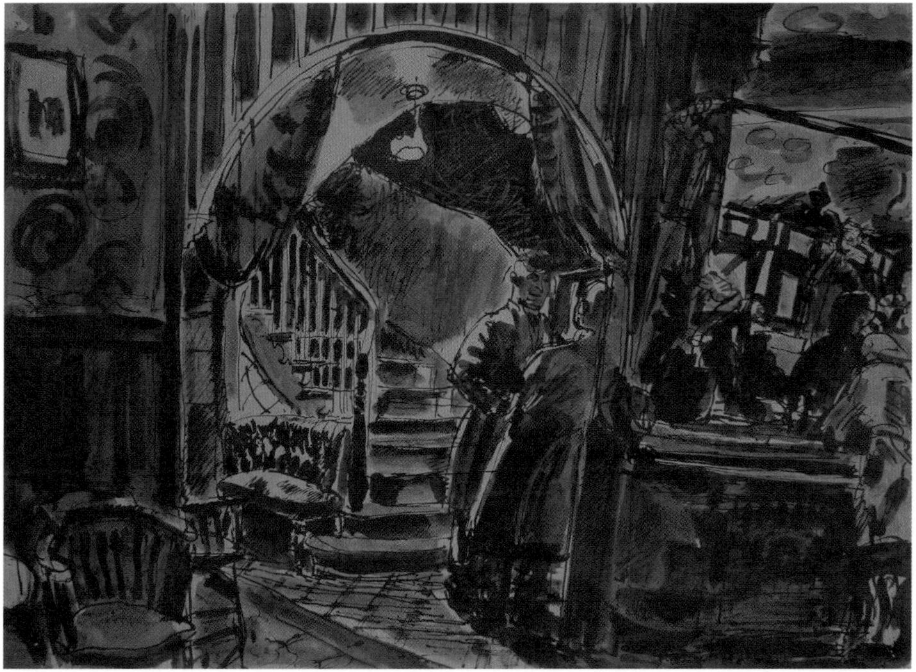

George Hooper, sketch for *Hotel Entrance*, *c.*1946, pen & wash, 47.5cm x 62cm. A preparatory study for the lithograph.

Bawden wrote to Freedman (whom he already knew well) to ask for his guidance on how best to compose a lithograph in six separate colours and where he might obtain transfer paper in an appropriate size. (Two months later, however, work on *The Dolls at Home* was still not complete, the artist having had a septic finger amputated 'because an inch of bone, including the terminal joint, underwent complete decay – a horrible sight'.[9])

9. Letter from Edward Bawden to Barnett Freedman, 7 March 1947 (Barnett Freedman Archive, Manchester Metropolitan University Special Collections, FRE/1/1/251).

Bawden, of course, did eventually finish his lithograph and proclaimed in one of his charming letters to Freedman that it was 'an enjoyable job to do'.[10] However, reality is also ever apparent, and it is important to remember that while many artists may have enjoyed their work for commercial commissions, it also often constituted the real 'bread and butter' of their existence and was a job that paid the bills as well as bringing artistic satisfaction. Bawden, for instance, asked Freedman if on seeing the proofs he 'could touch Beddington for an advance payment or the whole sum, something at least to offset doctors' bills and other debts which at the moment seem to be flying home like a cloud of pigeons'.[11]

Jack Beddington was a professional art connoisseur who could readily source both art and artists to contribute to the scheme. It is not clear how many of the first lithographs he commissioned from paintings bought on sight (*Les Lecques Bay* [p. 81] by John Lake is perhaps such an example), but what is clear is that each lithograph was commissioned in a different way and was dependent on the individual artists, how they worked and what was pertinent in their work at the time. Despite this being a rather mixed approach, the end result was sixteen lithographs produced in a timely fashion and to a comparable standard.

10. Letter from Edward Bawden to Barnett Freedman, undated (Barnett Freedman Archive, Manchester Metropolitan University Special Collections, FRE/1/1/251).
11. ibid.

Treatment

For the first series (and only for the first series), the subject matter of the lithographs was left largely to the artists' discretion. Yet despite this 'free hand', the prints do focus on a number of recognisable themes. Scenes drawn from everyday life, for instance, such as *People* [p. 67], and representations of the English coast, as illustrated by *Teignmouth* [p. 65], dominate the series. There is nothing sensational or controversial embodied in any of the lithographs. As decorative objects there was no need for the prints to draw attention to themselves through contentious subject matter; far better for them to be of interest simply because of the recognisable imagery. Beddington, therefore, required artwork that had 'a known quantity' and was readily accessible in both subject and style, and for that reason the lithographs do not mark a moment of great departure for any of the artists. William Scott, for example, had initially explored the subject of a figure and a birdcage in a 1946 oil painting entitled *Robert with Birdcage* [right], and he simply adapted the idea for his teashop lithograph *The Bird Cage* [p. 87]. Familiar scenes of life in London dominated Carel Weight's work, and his contribution of *Albert Bridge* [p. 91] is thus a wholly characteristic example of his broader creative oeuvre.

Likewise, in its focus on the smoky Greater Manchester landscape pictured from a high viewpoint and in horizontal bands of activity, *Industrial Scene* [p. 83] by L. S. Lowry is typical of the artist's work. This format also meant that it particularly suited the large-scale of the Lyons lithographs.

With its 'gritty' subject matter, Lowry's piece was visually linked to George Hooper's rather nocturnal *Hotel Entrance* and Ruskin Spear's dark and brooding *Billiards Saloon* [p. 89]. In contrast, *Fun Fair* by Clifford Frith, *Herne Bay Pier* [p. 73] by Anthony Gross, *Hastings* [p. 79] by Edwin La Dell and *Landscape with Bathers*

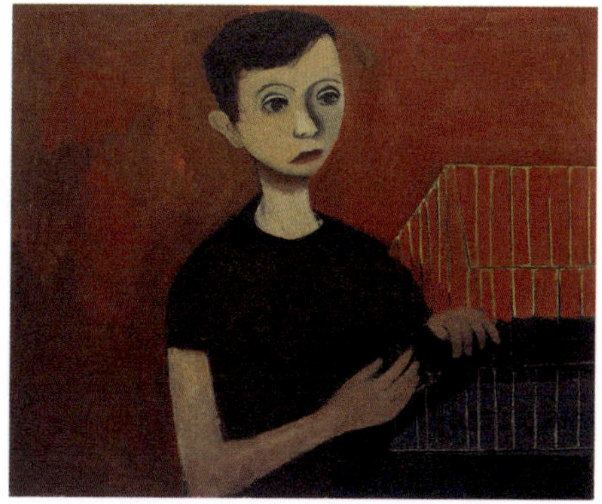

William Scott, *Robert with Birdcage*, *c.* 1946, oil on canvas, 50.8 cm x 61 cm.

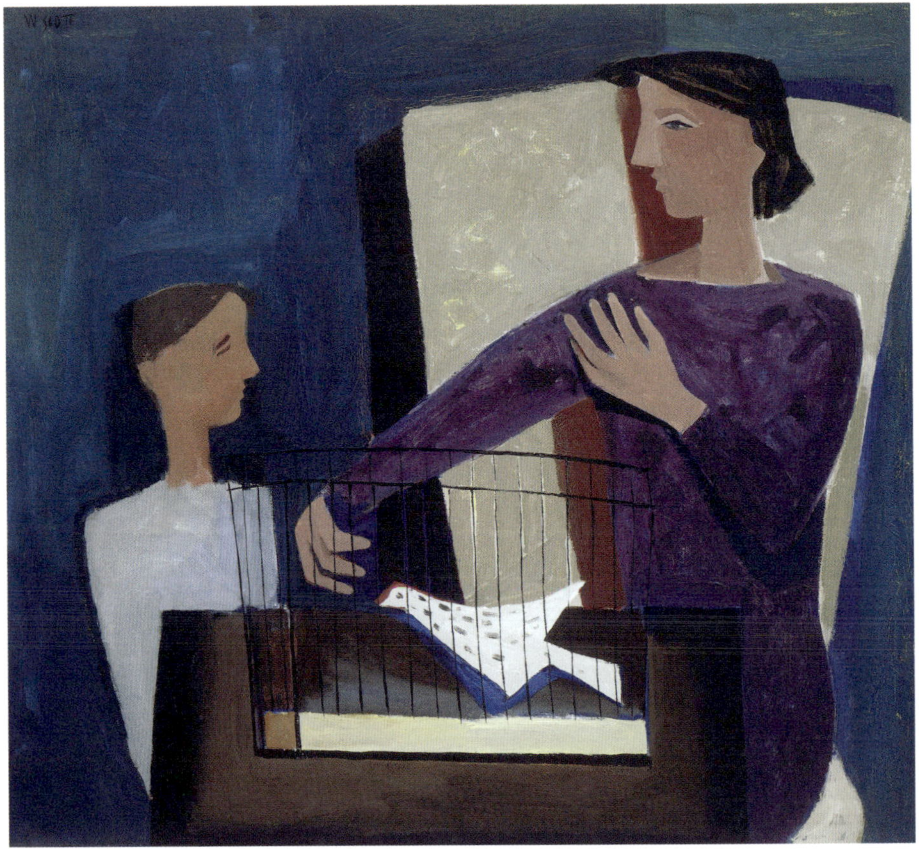

William Scott, *Boy and Birdcage*, 1947–8, oil on canvas, 58.5cm x 76.1cm. Scott further developed the motif of a figure and a birdcage in this larger oil painting, adopting the composition of his teashop lithograph but modifying the colours.

[p. 85] by John Nash focused on leisure activities associated with holidays and warm summer days in the English landscape. These lithographs were naturally very British in character, but Beddington gave a nod to the influence of both an art and a life beyond the English Channel through Duncan Grant's *Still Life* [p. 71], with its obvious debt to the work of the French Post-Impressionists, and John Lake's serene *Les Lecques Bay*, which expressed 'just a soupçon of Dufy'.[12]

The Dolls at Home by Edward Bawden was more concerned with artistic expression than a specific subject, and in comparison with the other lithographs was really an exercise in graphic composition. But while it may have therefore been more challenging to the general public than some, there were others that had less success in gaining broad acceptance. In both its biblical subject matter and its rather sketchy style, *Flight into Egypt* by Mary Kessell [p. 77] was one of the least successful contributions to the scheme. It was also 'most disliked by staff and customers',[13] and its inclusion represents a momentary lapse of judgement by Beddington, who, without doubt, had selected the artist on the strength of her excellent work documenting refugees in Berlin at the end of the War. This image, however, simply did not translate effectively from a painting into a large-scale lithograph.

A mistake such as this did not matter greatly, as the series was evaluated as a whole, with some pictures inevitably more successful than others in reflecting what critics regarded as the 'spirited and healthy condition of contemporary English art'.[14]

It should be said that in both subject and style the Lyons lithographs, despite being new commissions, were not examples of provocative 'contemporary' art, with all the meaning that that word now carries. The fact that Beddington nominated the septuagenarian William Nicholson (1872–1949) but not his more active son Ben Nicholson (1894–1982), who had been exploring abstraction in his work since the 1930s, helps to demonstrate that the avant-garde really had no place in the first lithographs, or indeed in any of the prints that were to follow in the 1950s.

12. G. S. Whittet, 'Teashop Lithographs', *The Studio*, September 1948, p. 74.
13. *Comments on Lithographs Displayed in Teashops* (Barnett Freedman Archive, Manchester Metropolitan University Special Collections).
14. Bentley, 'Lithographs for Lyons', p. 54.

Of course, this was a perfect reflection of the traditional corporate identity of J. Lyons & Co. and of the fact that their teashops were an established institution patronised because they were the reliable choice. To hang works of art on the walls of the cafés was something new in itself, and to display contentious new works just simply would have not been in keeping.

The only image that proved to be even slightly controversial and which caused 'minor outrage' on account of its overall style was *The Bird Cage*. This was distinguishable from the other lithographs because it was rendered in a bold artistic style of simple shapes and blocks of flat colour, leading one customer to tersely remark that it was 'very good as it was painted by a child of eight years old'.[15]

In comparison to the other fifteen lithographs in the series, *The Bird Cage* represents a bold choice by Beddington and a brave endorsement by Lyons. Yet, at the same time, its inclusion also perfectly embodies the elements of the accidental and the experimental that appear in the first series; elements that were essentially eradicated in the second and third series as various agendas, not just the need for decoration, were attached to the lithographs.

The overall aim for the first lithographs was to function as 'a novel and intriguing method of decoration ... with no other purpose in mind than that of giving the teashops themselves an interesting and homely appearance'.[16] Beddington's global choice of both artists and subjects achieved exactly that.

15. *Comments on Lithographs*.
16. J. Lyons & Co., press release, 1955 (J. Lyons & Co. Archive at the London Metropolitan Archives, ACC/3527).

Money Matters

In June 1947 an internal Lyons memo estimated a total cost (including printing fees, tax, catalogues, etc.) for the first series of approximately £15,500, which in 1947 was a vast amount of money and demonstrates just how serious the firm were about the undertaking.

Beddington truly respected the professionalism of British artists and pushed to properly and fairly remunerate those he selected to contribute to the scheme. He ensured that all of the artists were paid a fee for their commission of between £50 and £150 (Beddington believed that 'there should be no reason for all to get the same'[17]), with 'one quarter ... paid for the rough design and three-quarters if ... accepted, but not otherwise'.[18] There appear to be no official records of exactly how much each artist was eventually paid on this sliding scale, or of what criteria helped to determine an individual artist's fee. In total, however, the company paid £1,530 to the sixteen artists; approximately 10 per cent of the overall cost.

It was, of course, a perfectly normal practice to pay artists for their work, but by further paying them a sixpence royalty for each copy of their print that was sold, the teashop scheme was unusually generous. In contrast, in a letter written in 1946 by Brenda Rawnsley (a director of *School Prints*) inviting Barnett Freedman to submit a sketch for the schools scheme, artists were being offered 'an inclusive standard fee of £85 plus a royalty of £5 per 1000 copies sold to education authorities ... and £10 [per 1000 copies] sold to the general public'.[19] Beddington

17. Letter from Jack Beddington to Barnett Freedman, 12 August 1946 (Lyons Lithograph Archive, Towner Art Gallery).
18. ibid.
19. Letter from Brenda Rawnsley to Barnett Freedman, 26 June 1946 (Barnett Freedman Archive, Manchester Metropolitan University Special Collections, FRE/1/1/344).

[right] The first post-war teashop to open in London, Lower Regent Street, photographed in 1951. For flagship teashops in Central London a number of the lithographs were framed for display. Here it is possible to see, from left to right, *Hotel Entrance*, *Les Lecques Bay* and *Fun Fair*.

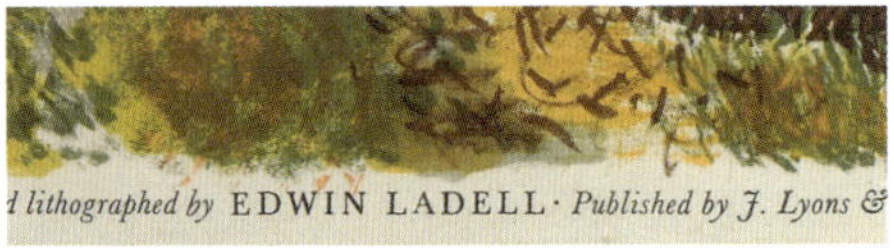

[above] The imprint from the Lyons lithographs, printed along the bottom edge of the paper surround on each lithograph. The name of the artist, title of the work and details of how the lithographs had been produced appeared on each print. For those that were auto-lithographed the imprint read 'designed and lithographed by'. For those translated at the printers the imprint simply read 'painted by'. J. Lyons & Co. were given as the publishers and Chromoworks Ltd recorded as the printers. Each print was also allocated a number which appeared in the bottom right-hand corner.

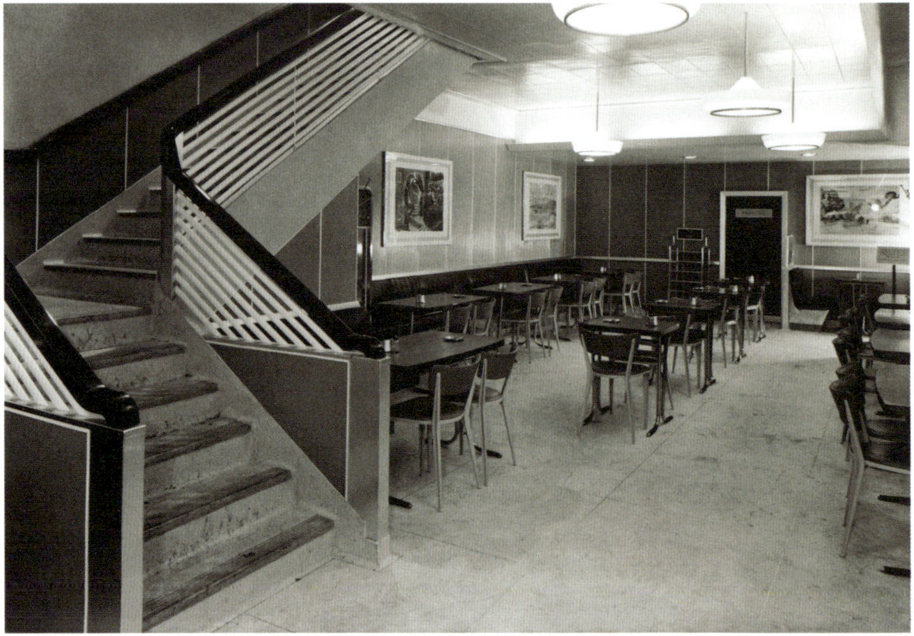

believed that the teashop project was the only one of its kind which paid artists, alongside their initial fees, a royalty for every copy sold, and saw it as solid evidence of a commercial firm genuinely wanting 'to do their best for artists'.[20] It also proved to be popular with the commissioned artists because, as Clifford Frith remembers clearly, Lyons 'sold an enormous number of prints. I know because I received sixpence royalties on every sale and I received a couple of hundred pounds!'[21]

20. Letter from Jack Beddington to Kenneth Clark, 8 November 1954 (Barnett Freedman Archive, Manchester Metropolitan University Special Collections, FRE/1/1/251).
21. Frith, e-mail to Artmonsky, 29 January 2005.

However, the scheme was not just an exercise in spending as much money as possible, and in some cases pre-emptive measures were taken to curb any unnecessary expenditure. Each lithograph, for example, was printed with a plain paper surround, which meant that they did not necessarily need to be displayed in frames but could be pasted directly on to the walls and mirrors in the cafés. A number of the lithographs were professionally framed for a handful of high-profile teashops in central London, but because the company chose not to frame the majority of the prints they were freed from bearing a large extra cost. While this was a prudent decision, in some cases the lack of a real frame did little to enhance the appearance of the lithograph: one critic noted that 'some of the artists have not kept in mind that these prints were for decoration in crowded teashops ... with no frames to isolate them from their surroundings.'[22]

Incidentally, at the end of Beddington's first letter he stated that neither '... Barnett nor I know what to suggest for our own fees'.[23] The Salmons responded by paying them each £400, which, for a single project, was a handsome but well-merited sum.

22. Noel Carrington, 'Art in the Teashops', *Penrose Annual*, Vol. 47, 1950, p. 52.
23. Letter from Beddington to Salmon, 24 January 1946.

Publicity

Jack Beddington believed the teashop scheme should be widely publicised through exhibitions and press coverage, but also 'that the venture should be presented … to popularise British artists and not to sell service, goods or anything else'.[24]

From the outset, then, he was clear that the project should not be a vehicle for overt advertising and for that reason did not warrant the production of commercial posters akin to those he had produced for Shell-Mex. Having noted that, at the time, there was 'much more widespread and informed interest in music, literature, the arts and matters of the mind generally',[25] he was confident that the teashop clientele would appreciate a series of artist-designed lithographs, unadorned by advertising slogans, as works of art in their own right.

In reality, the lithographs were an exceptionally public solution to an internal management problem and were seen by an enormous number of consumers passing through the teashops. While on paper the scheme was genuinely not conceived as a 'marketing' campaign, it was, perhaps inevitably, still perceived by some as an attempt to boost the firm's advertising, which up to that point had sometimes not been 'marked so much by the common touch … as by a touch of the commonplace'.[26]

Beddington, however, was firm in his stance that the lithographs were not to be saddled with advertising and equally adamant that it was imperative to draw attention to the higher, artistic *raisons d'être* of the project. Having staged exhibitions of the work he commissioned for Shell-Mex, he had a keen understanding

24. ibid.
25. ibid.
26. Bentley, 'Lithographs for Lyons', p. 54.

of just how valuable a gallery-based exhibition of art, commissioned for a commercial purpose, could be, and he proposed that Lyons host such an event to mark the publication of the first lithographs.

Thus on 20 October 1947 the chairman and directors of the company presided over a private showing of the lithographs at the Trocadero in London in the presence of Her Majesty, Queen Mary. The following day they hosted a cocktail party and a preview of the exhibition for the press, the artists and all those who had been involved with the project.

The exhibition included all the lithographs hung above their corresponding original oil painting, watercolour or sketch, which Beddington had purchased, along with the copyright, for the commission. In the newspaper clipping showing Queen Mary at the Trocadero [right] it is just possible, for example, to see the lithograph and the small collage of *The Dolls at Home* on the far left, and the lithograph and original painting of *Teignmouth* on the far right.

Sir Stafford Cripps, the President of the Board of Trade, was due to open the exhibition but at the last minute was unable to attend, and the celebrated actor and keen painter Sir Ralph Richardson stepped into the breech. Freedman designed an illustrated catalogue [p. 57], and this contained a supportive foreword penned by Philip Hendy – the director of the National Gallery charged with implementing its post-war recovery – in which he claimed that the lithographs were 'something more than good news', and that in 'the midst of utility, each of them is something existing in its own right; made … for pleasure; mass produced, but retaining the germ of human personality.'[27]

Support from the higher echelons of society, including royalty, was not difficult for Lyons to solicit and bears testament not only to the company's elevated commercial position but to the sound status, contacts, skills and general appeal of Beddington, Freedman and Oppenheimer. Beddington personally invited

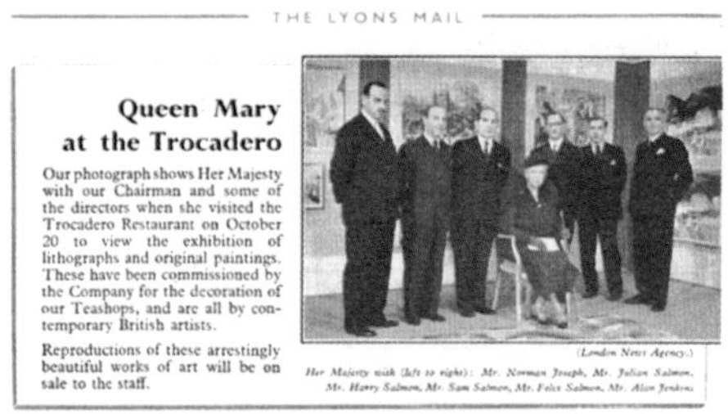
THE LYONS MAIL

Queen Mary at the Trocadero

Our photograph shows Her Majesty with our Chairman and some of the directors when she visited the Trocadero Restaurant on October 20 to view the exhibition of lithographs and original paintings. These have been commissioned by the Company for the decoration of our Teashops, and are all by contemporary British artists.

Reproductions of these arrestingly beautiful works of art will be on sale to the staff.

(London News Agency.)

Her Majesty with (left to right): Mr. Norman Joseph, Mr. Julian Salmon, Mr. Harry Salmon, Mr. Sam Salmon, Mr. Felix Salmon, Mr. Alan Jenkins

Queen Mary and the Lyons directors at the Trocadero, 20 October 1947. This photograph appeared in the Lyons in-house magazine, *The Lyons Mail*.

27. P. Hendy, *A Catalogue of Lithographs* (London, J. Lyons & Co., printed at the Shenval Press, 1947), p. 2.

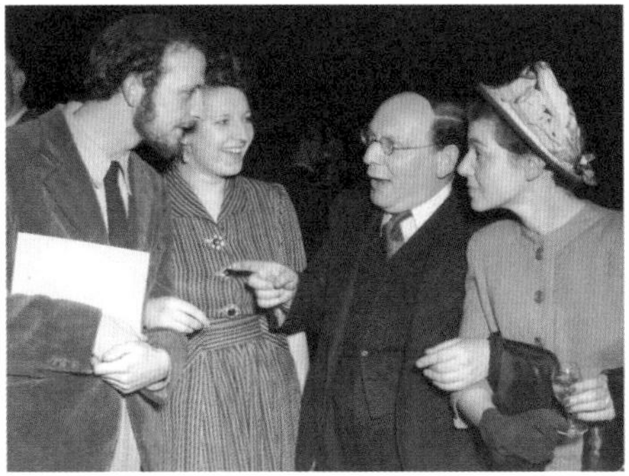

[above] Clifford Frith (left) and his wife Toni being introduced to Mrs Felix Salmon (right) by Barnett Freedman at the Trocadero, 21 October 1947.

[right] The Chromoworks Ltd dinner at the Trocadero, 21 October 1947. Frank Oppenheimer is on the right, wearing glasses.

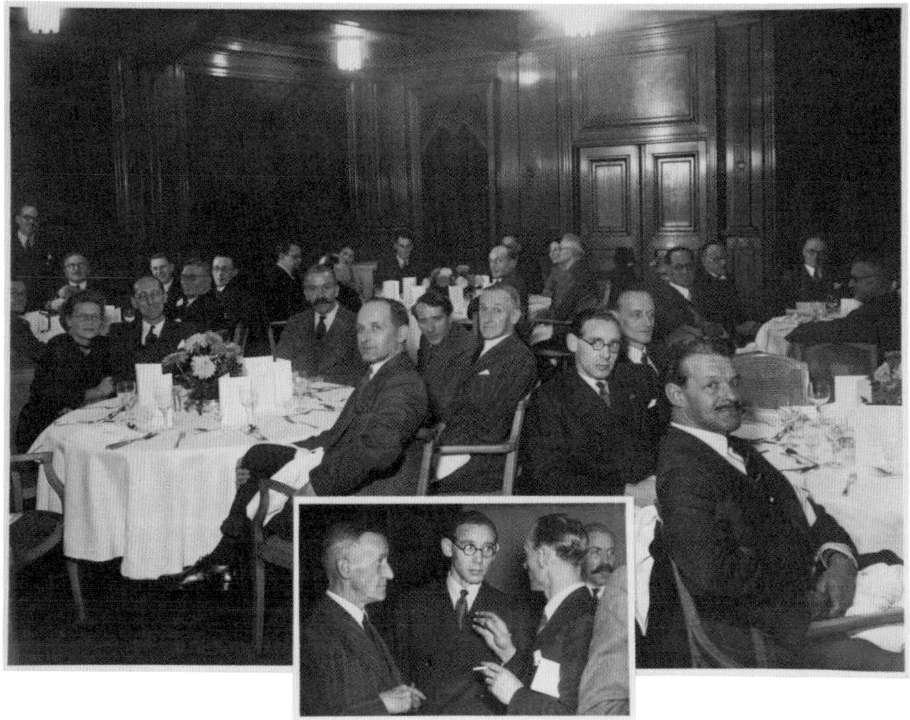

over one hundred journalists from the national press, trade journals and the BBC to the exhibition and put the business of publicising the lithographs firmly at the top of his agenda.

Publicity was further drawn to the lithographs by the Salmons themselves, who were keen for the prints to be distributed to museums, public institutions and large corporations. In an internal report produced after the publication of the first series, it was, for example, proudly noted that the 'Director of the Victoria and Albert Museum has ... written for two sets of the Lithographs to be added to the collection'.[28] At the same time, a list was drawn up of 'Various Purchasers of Lithographs', and this included institutions ranging from the National Gallery of Scotland and the British Council, to Oxfordshire County Council and Gloucester Education Committee. With national museums and institutions choosing to purchase, rather than waiting for copies of the lithographs to be donated, the teashop project was instantly given greater credence.

Copies of the prints were made available for sale in America through Rudolf Lesch Fine Arts in New York. These were accompanied by an illustrated pamphlet, again designed by Freedman, and this touted the prints as being 'lively and colourful and designed to bring warmth and interest into the room in which they are hung'.[29]

J. Lyons & Co. were quick to exploit the commercial potential of any product, and it is entirely fitting that the Salmons sought ways to distribute the prints beyond the teashops in order to achieve publicity simply through exposure. However, the fact that the lithographs were so well received by a broad spectrum of high-ranking people, ranging from senior politicians to art critics, was not because they were widely distributed, but because the project was undertaken and, more importantly, realised in the austere period immediately after the War.

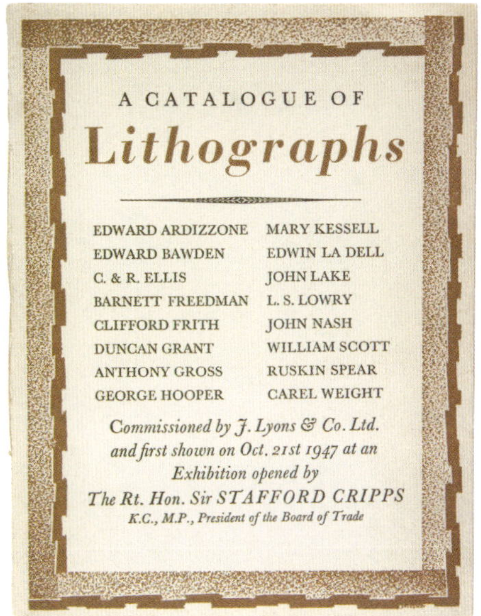

The front cover of the 1947 exhibition catalogue, designed by Barnett Freedman and printed at the Shenval Press.

28. Internal J. Lyons & Co. memo, 1947 (J. Lyons & Co. Archive at the London Metropolitan Archives, ACC/3527), p. 3.
29. *The Lyons Lithographs* – USA sales catalogue (London, J. Lyons & Co., printed at the Shenval Press, 1947).

When a large and successful business such as Lyons needed to make improvements to their teashops as a direct result of the War, it was symptomatic of how everything needed to be improved in post-war Britain. In reality, the lithographs were only a small demonstration of how this could be achieved, but because they were produced by a well-respected company and displayed in an arena as public as the Lyons teashops they became a high-profile demonstration of how 'Britain could make it'.[30]

It is, therefore, entirely understandable that individuals, such as Philip Hendy, who were charged with finding ways to boost war-weary Britain, were keen to be publicly associated with this enterprising project. In turn, this then drew the general public's attention to the lithographs and made the whole undertaking something of a success.

30. In 1946 what proved to be an extremely popular exhibition entitled 'Britain Can Make It' was held at the Victoria & Albert Museum. It was staged by the Council of Industrial Design (a body established in 1944 to improve and promote British design) to serve as a tribute to the recovery of British manufacturing in the immediate post-war period.

The Lyons Lithographs - First Series

Unless otherwise stated, lithographs measure 30" x 40".

1. The Railway Station

Designed and lithographed by Edward Ardizzone

When Edward Ardizzone saw the first proof of his lithograph he was quick to telephone Chromoworks and request that he be allowed to '… redraw the yellow plate, add additional work to the dark grey plate and probably alter the shade of green'.*

* Letter from Frank Oppenheimer to Barnett Freedman, 27 March 1947 (Barnett Freedman Archive, Manchester Metropolitan University Special Collections, FRE/1/1/87).

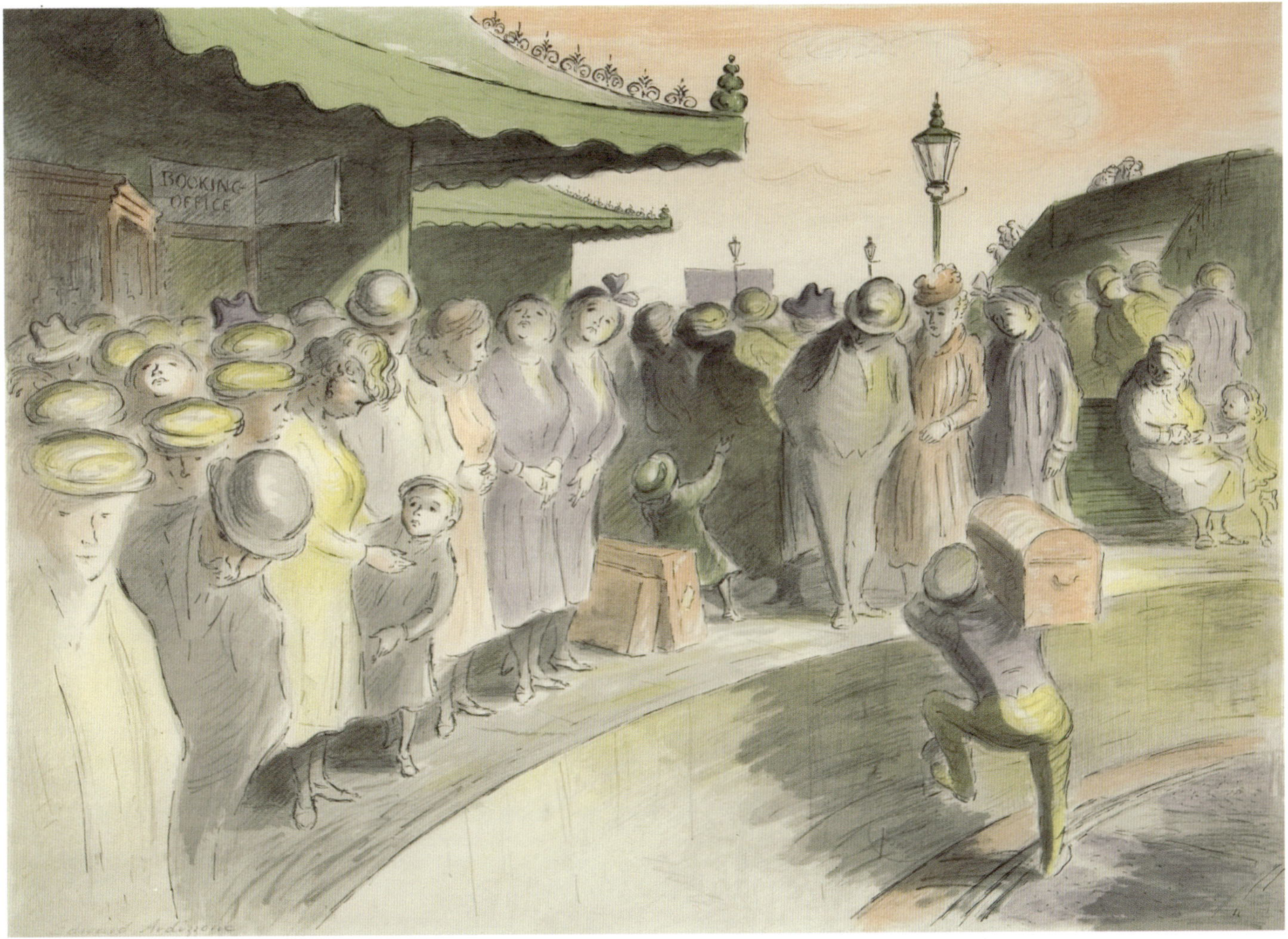
BOOKING
OFFICE

2. *The Dolls at Home*

Designed and lithographed by Edward Bawden

Here the original collage of *The Dolls at Home* is pictured alongside the finished lithograph. The original is much smaller than the 30" x 40" print, and while the two are certainly similar in their overall composition, there are a number of notable differences in the detail which serve to make it clear that the auto-lithograph is a work of art defined by its own qualities, rather than a mere imitation of the original painting.

The image was drawn from the artist's memory and features a doll's house with ceramic figures that had been in Bawden's London home before the Second World War.

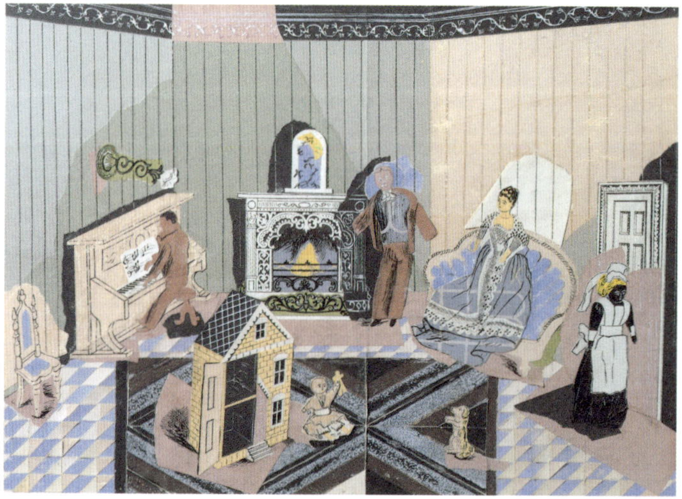

Edward Bawden, *The Dolls at Home*, 1947 (original), watercolour and collage, 35.5cm x 48.5cm.

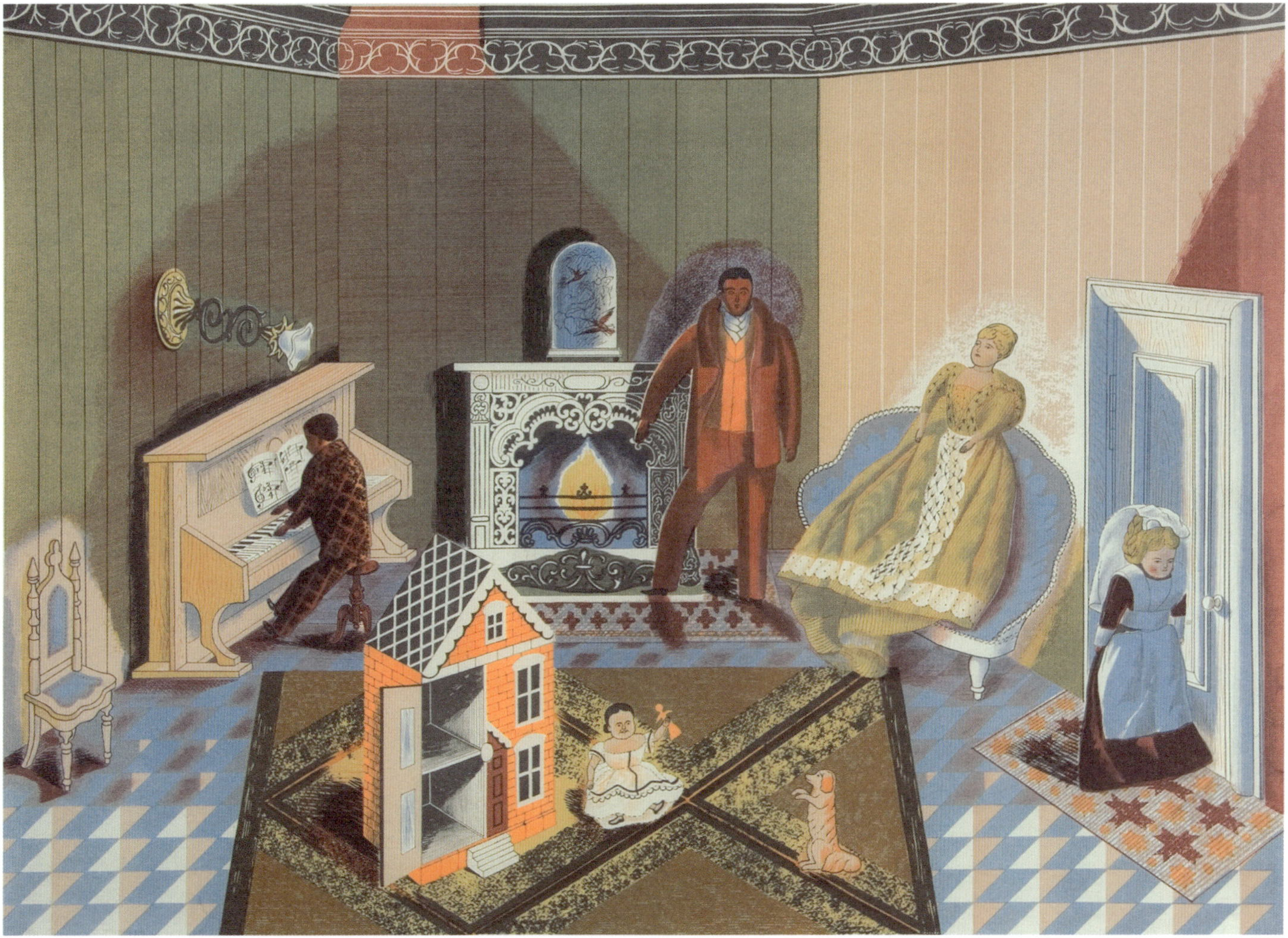

3. *Teignmouth*

Painted by Clifford and Rosemary Ellis

For the lithographs worked up at Chromoworks from originals, Freedman's input at the proofing stage was crucial. In response to his comments about the proof of *Teignmouth*, for example, Oppenheimer noted at the printers that they would '… try a light grey printing over the sails etc … alter the colour of the light brown high light in the hills in printing [and] … make the colour of the sky and sea slightly warmer'.*

* Letter from Frank Oppenheimer to Barnett Freedman, 15 July 1947 (Barnett Freedman Archive, Manchester Metropolitan University Special Collections, FRE/1/1/87).

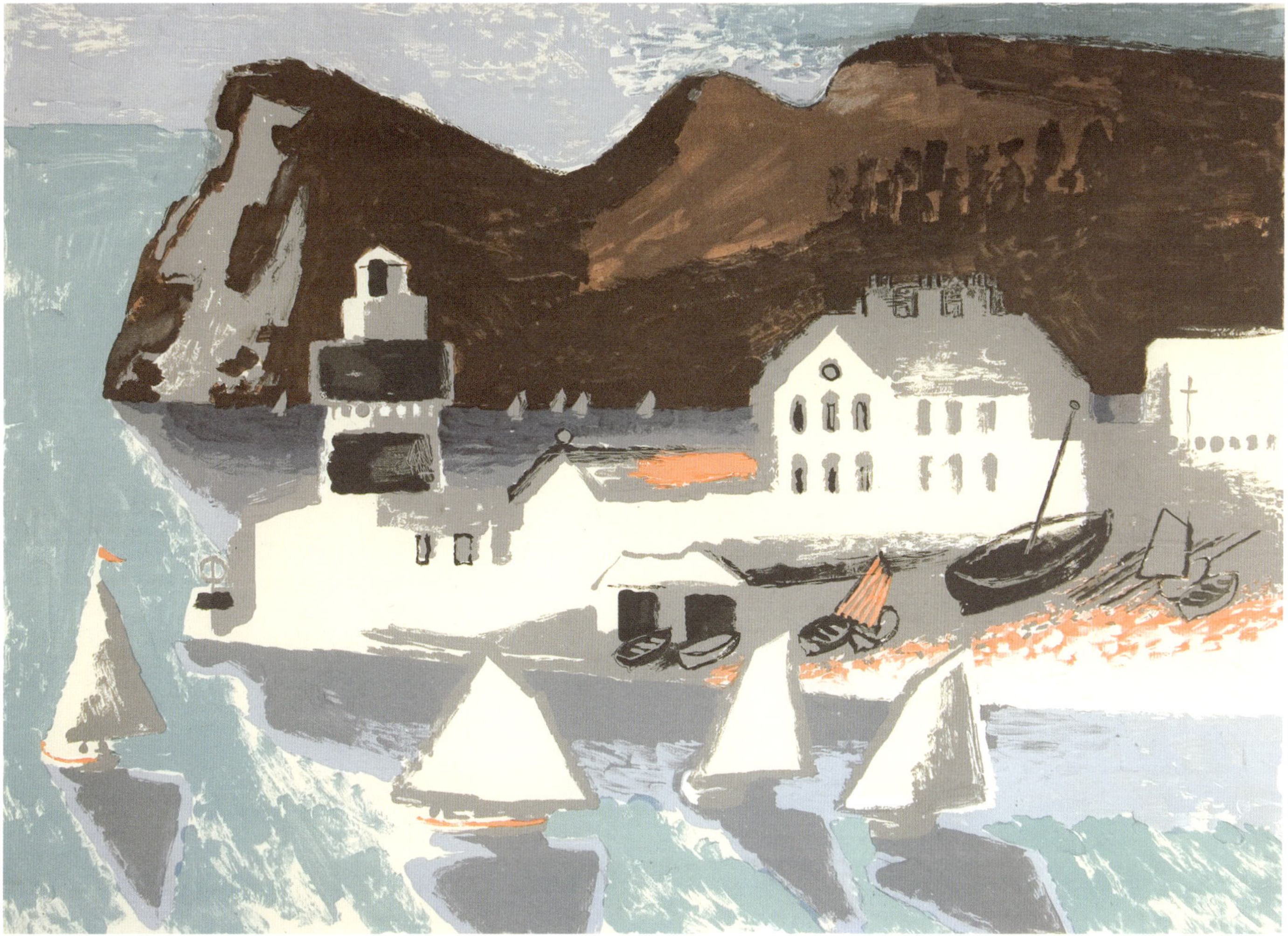

4. People

Designed and lithographed by Barnett Freedman

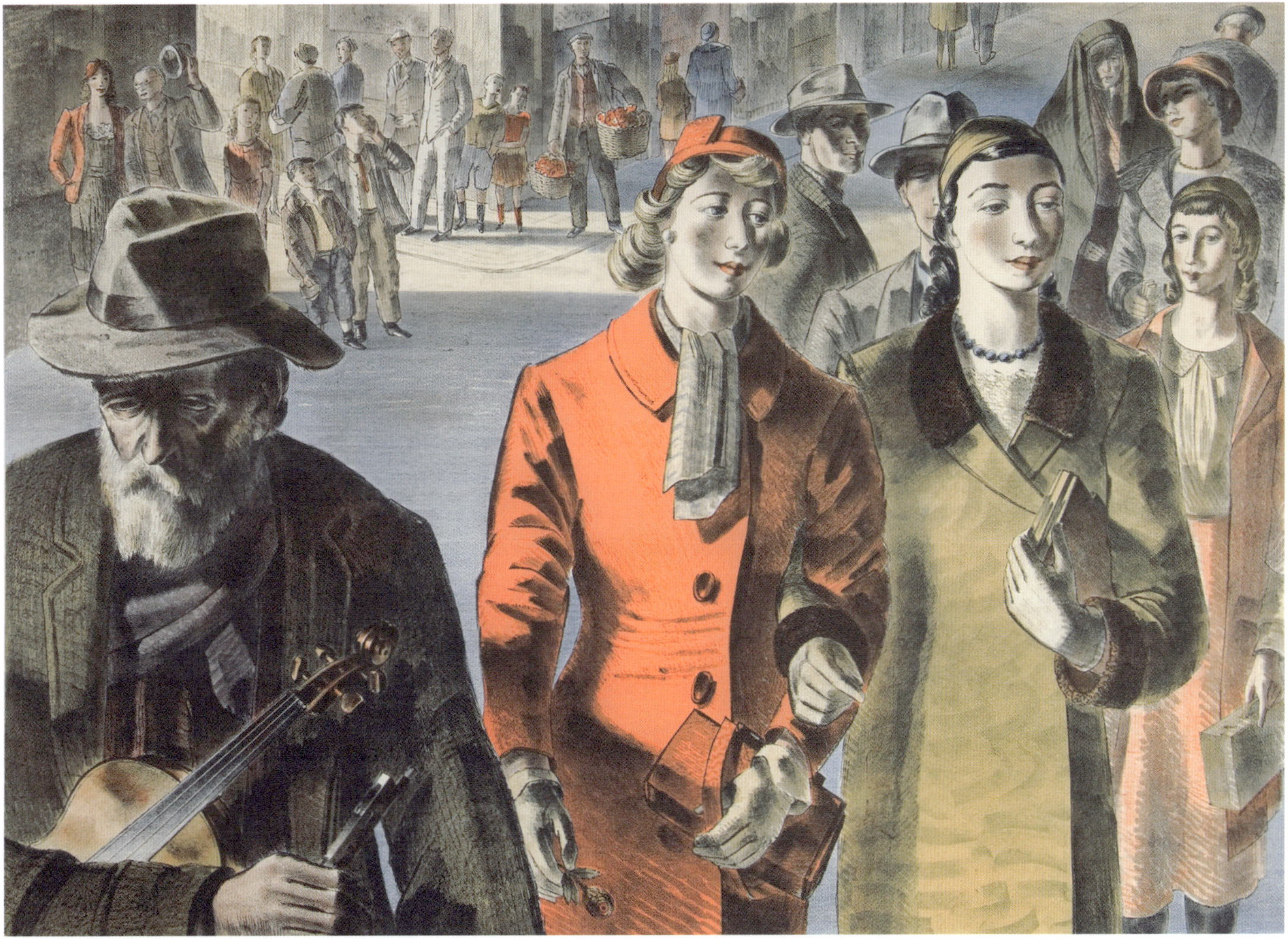

5. *Fun Fair*

Painted by Clifford Frith

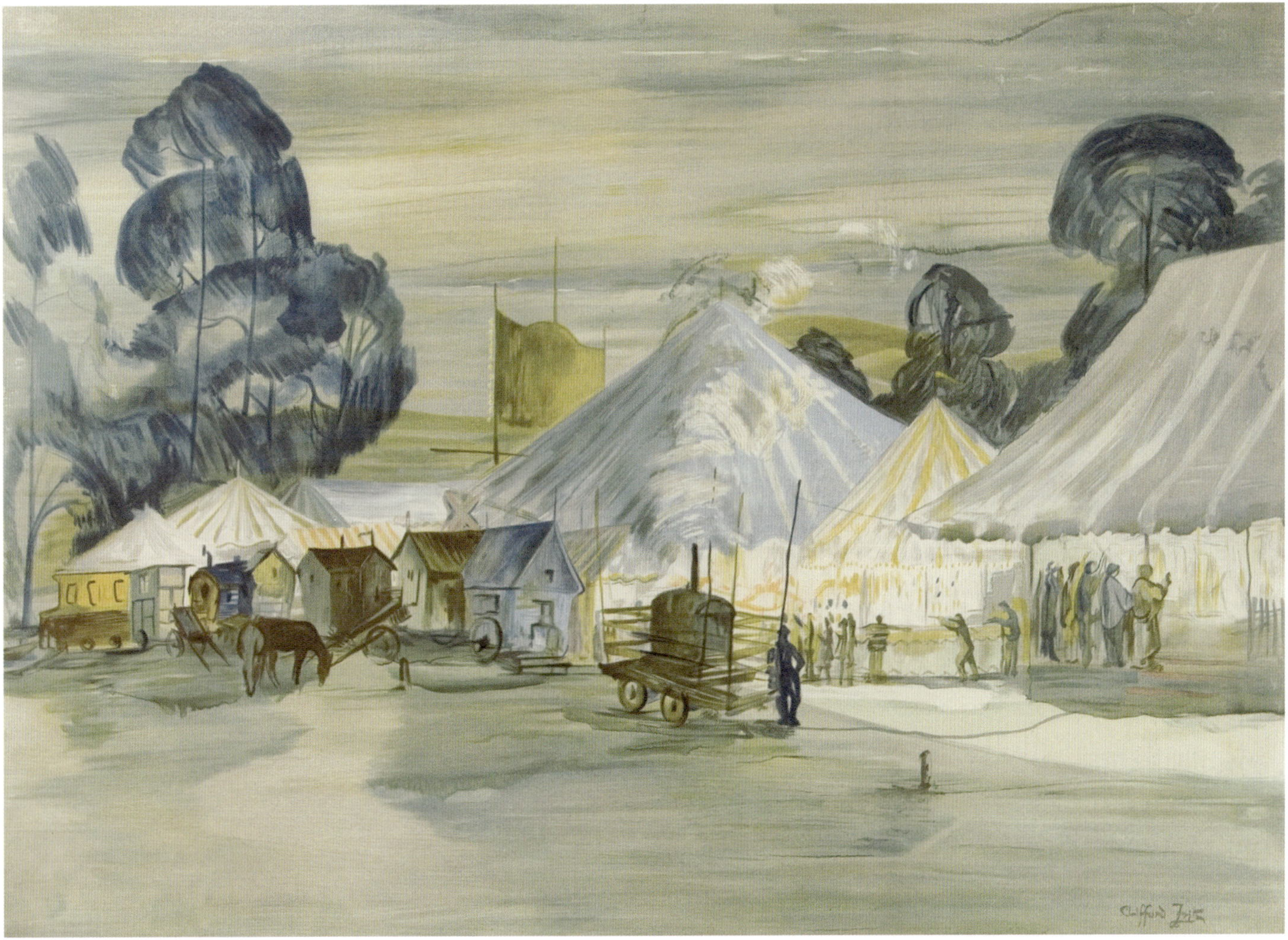

6. Still Life

Painted by Duncan Grant

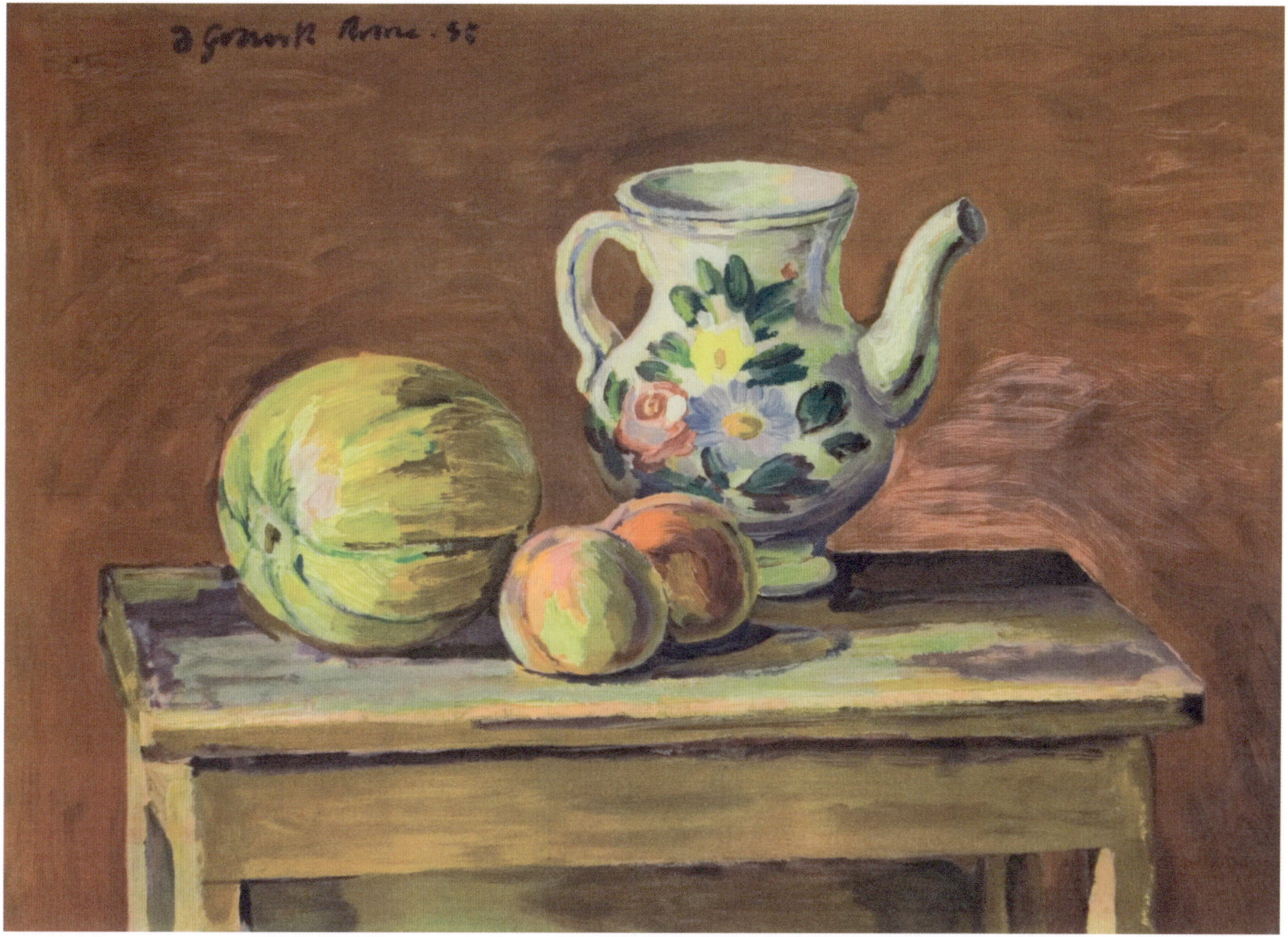

7. Herne Bay Pier

Designed and lithographed by Anthony Gross

In a 1948 review *Herne Bay Pier* was described as being '... as bracing and breezy as Anthony Gross can make it ...'.* By 1955 it was declared 'the best-seller'† and in 1962 was used as a dressing on the set of *Carry on Cruising*. By illustrating the original alongside the finished lithograph it is possible to see how Gross slightly modified his design for printing but remained committed to translating much of the detail and atmosphere of his initial work.

Anthony Gross, *Herne Bay Pier*, 1947 (original), watercolour, black ink and chalk, 69.2 cm x 94 cm.

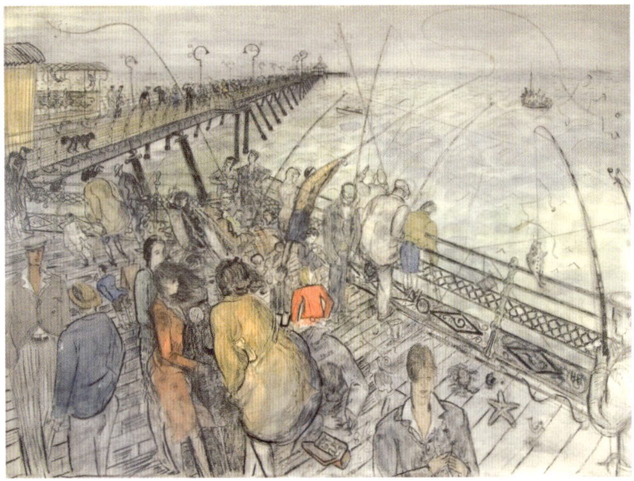

* G. S. Whittet, 'Teashop Lithographs', *The Studio*, September 1948, p. 72.

† *The News Chronicle*, 11 March 1955 (press cuttings held in the J. Lyons and Co. Archive at the London Metropolitan Archives, ACC/3527).

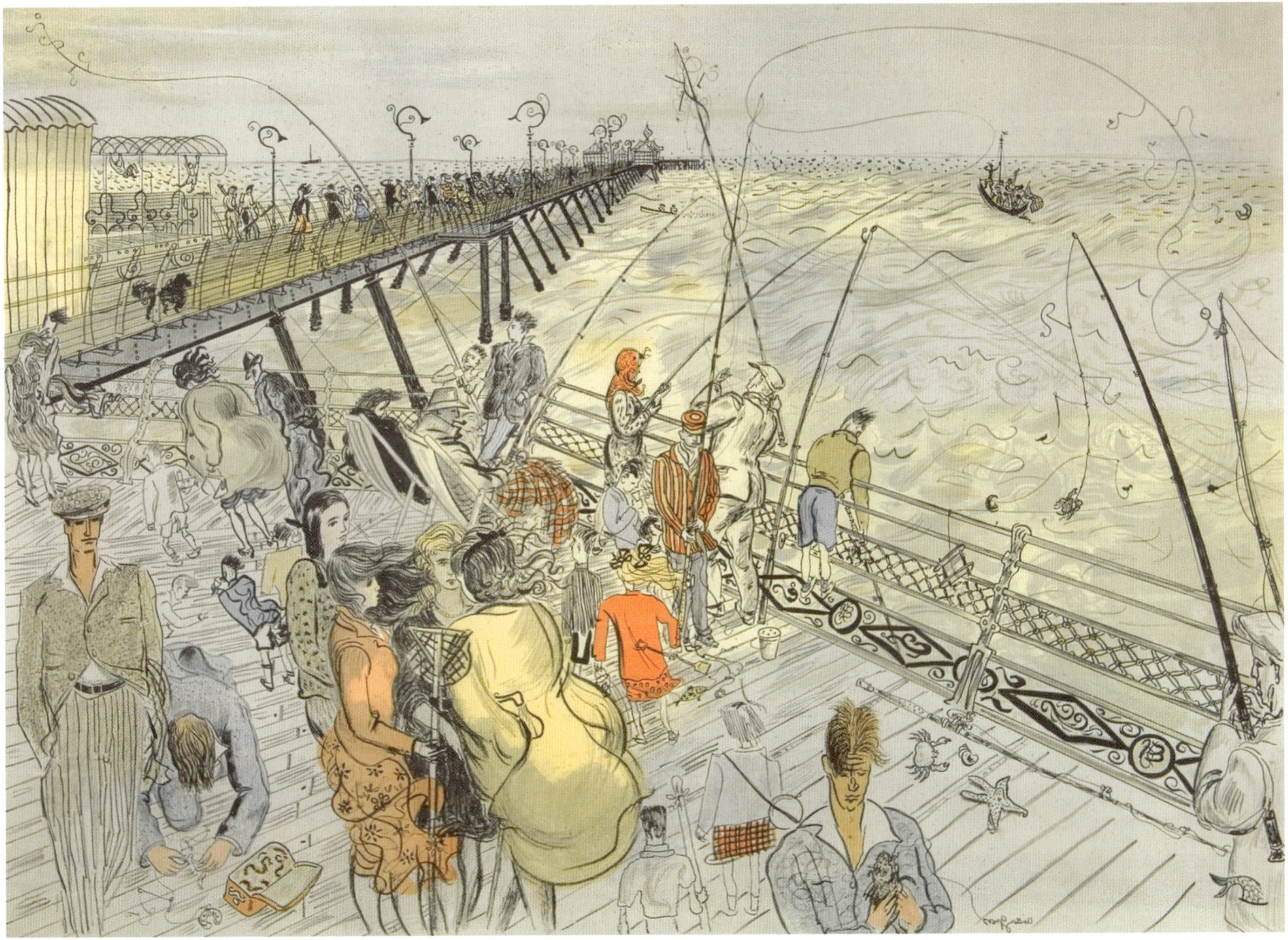

8. Hotel Entrance

Painted by George Hooper

When Freedman saw the first proof of *Hotel Entrance*, in his capacity as technical supervisor he noted that 'the colours are too clean especially the green. The ceiling is too dark and in many other places also. There is not enough work on the plates, giving the effect of flatness and lack of graduation.'* As a result, the printing plates were completely revised.

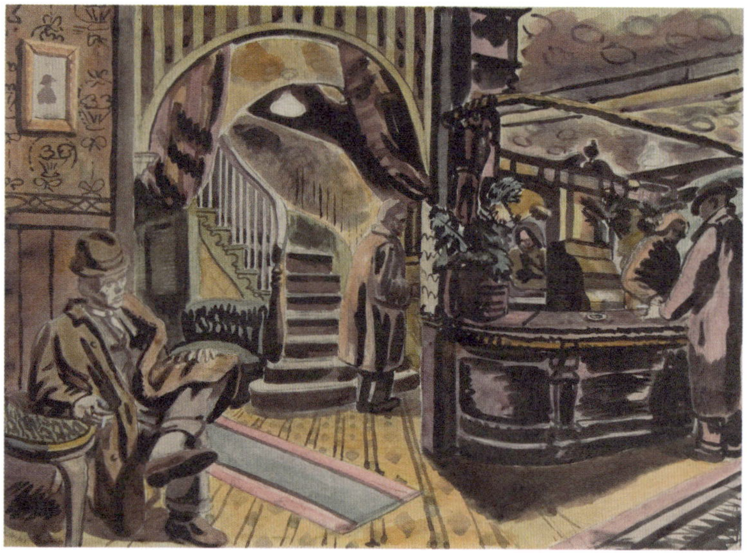

George Hooper, *Hotel Entrance*, *c.* 1946 (original), watercolour on paper, 72.5cm x 97.8cm.

* Letter from Frank Oppenheimer to Barnett Freedman, 15 July 1947 (Barnett Freedman Archive, Manchester Metropolitan University Special Collections, FRE/1/1/87).

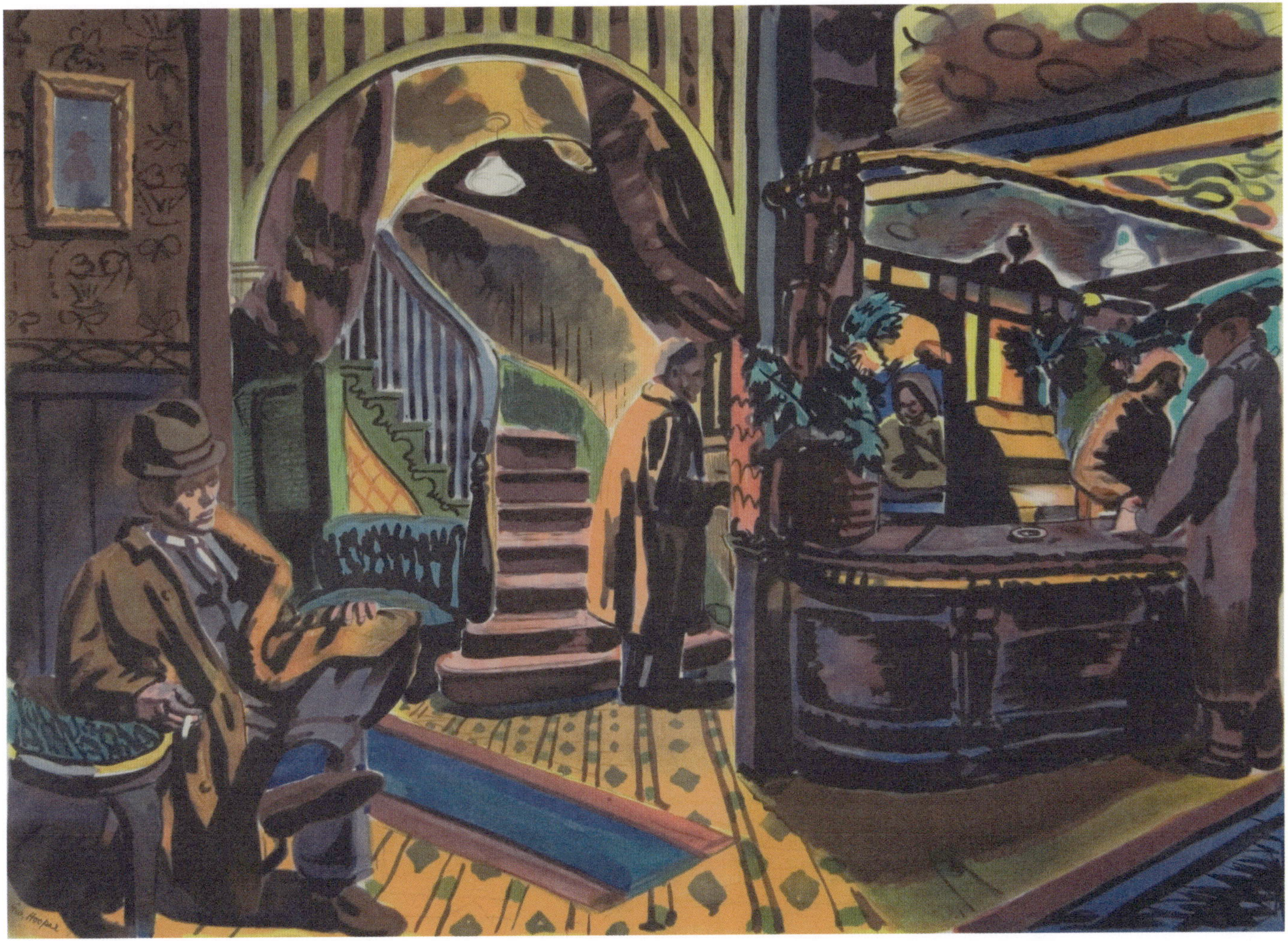

9. *Flight into Egypt*

Painted by Mary Kessell

When the Lyons lithographs were first published they were not displayed (in the teashops or elsewhere) as 'precious' fine art objects in controlled conditions. Copies of Lyons lithographs that come to light now, sixty years after they were first published, therefore often show obvious signs of 'wear and tear', and this copy of *Flight into Egypt* has been included to illustrate this. During the 1940s and 50s this print probably hung in an office or a corridor at the Towner Art Gallery (the Lyons lithographs were only later accessioned into the permanent collection) and would have been subject to strong and fluctuating light levels. The colours have faded as a result, and while Kessell's design was always 'sketchy', originally the print was a stronger shade of blue/green.

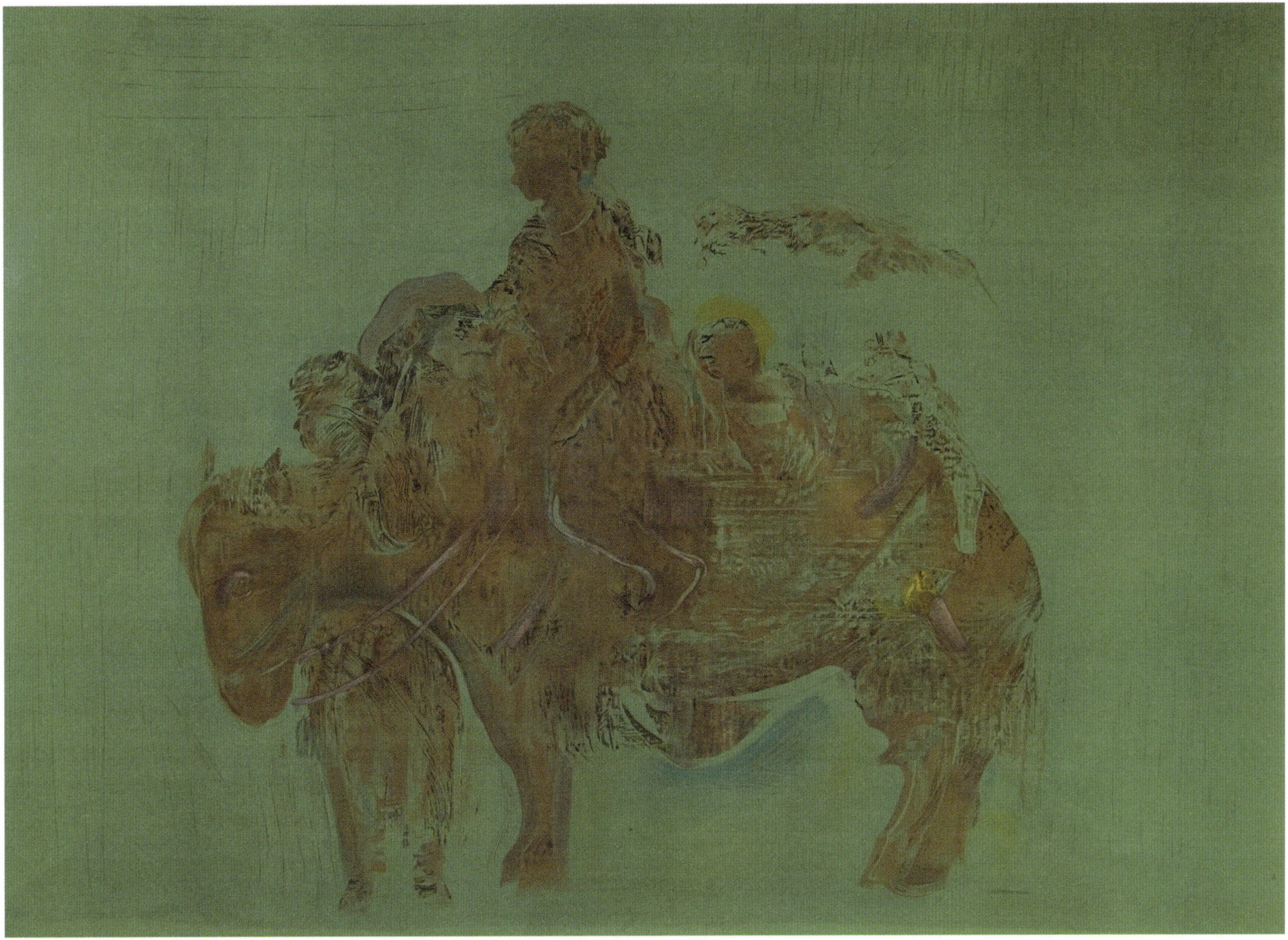

10. Hastings

Designed and lithographed by Edwin La Dell

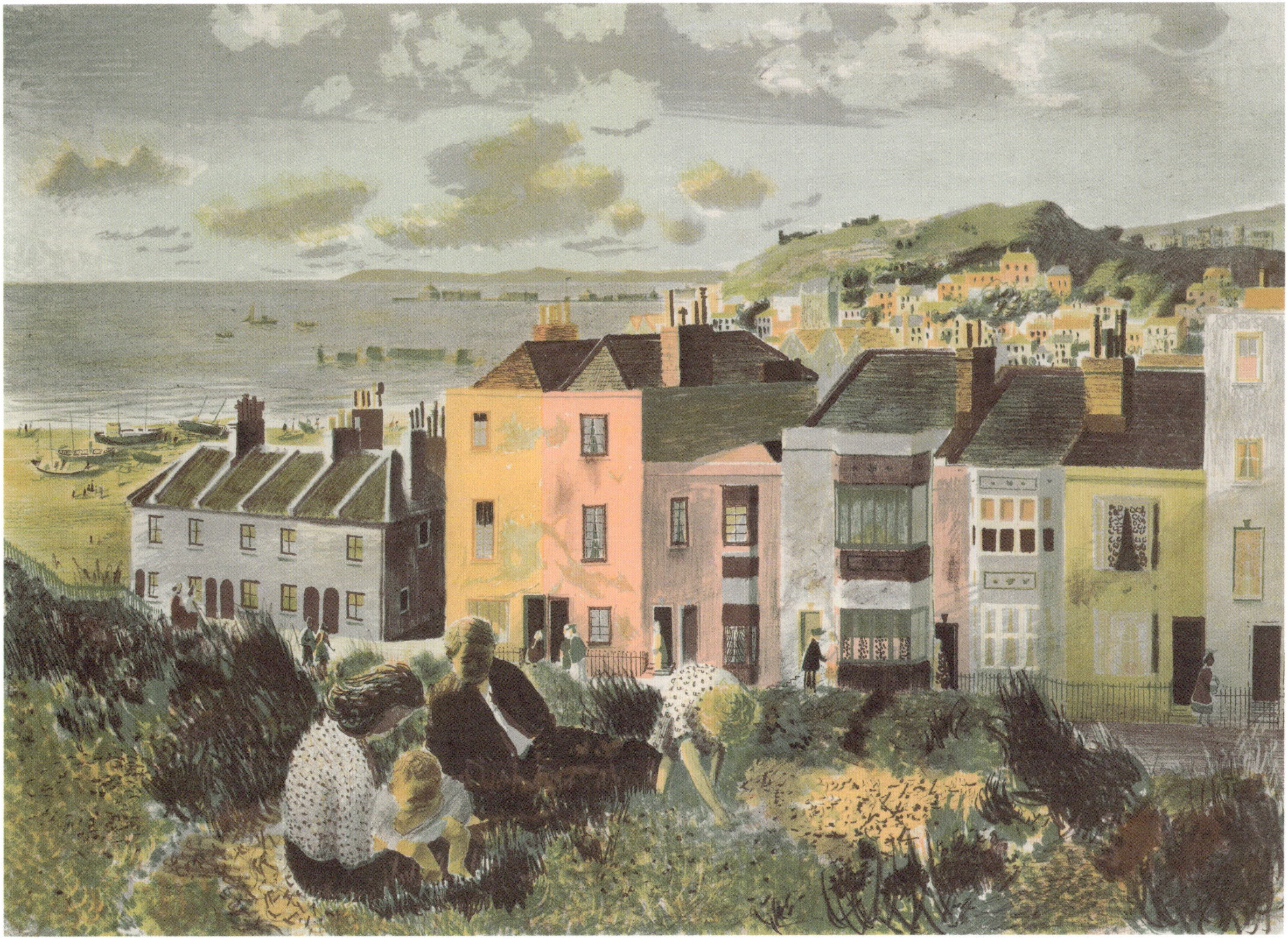

11. Les Lecques Bay

Painted by John Lake

In 1947 Lake was appointed Curator of the Towner Art Gallery in Eastbourne. In the same year he undertook his commission for the teashops, and the gallery subsequently acquired various copies of the lithographs. Select examples of the *School Prints*, and designs produced for the General Post Office and Shell-Mex, are also held in the permanent collection.

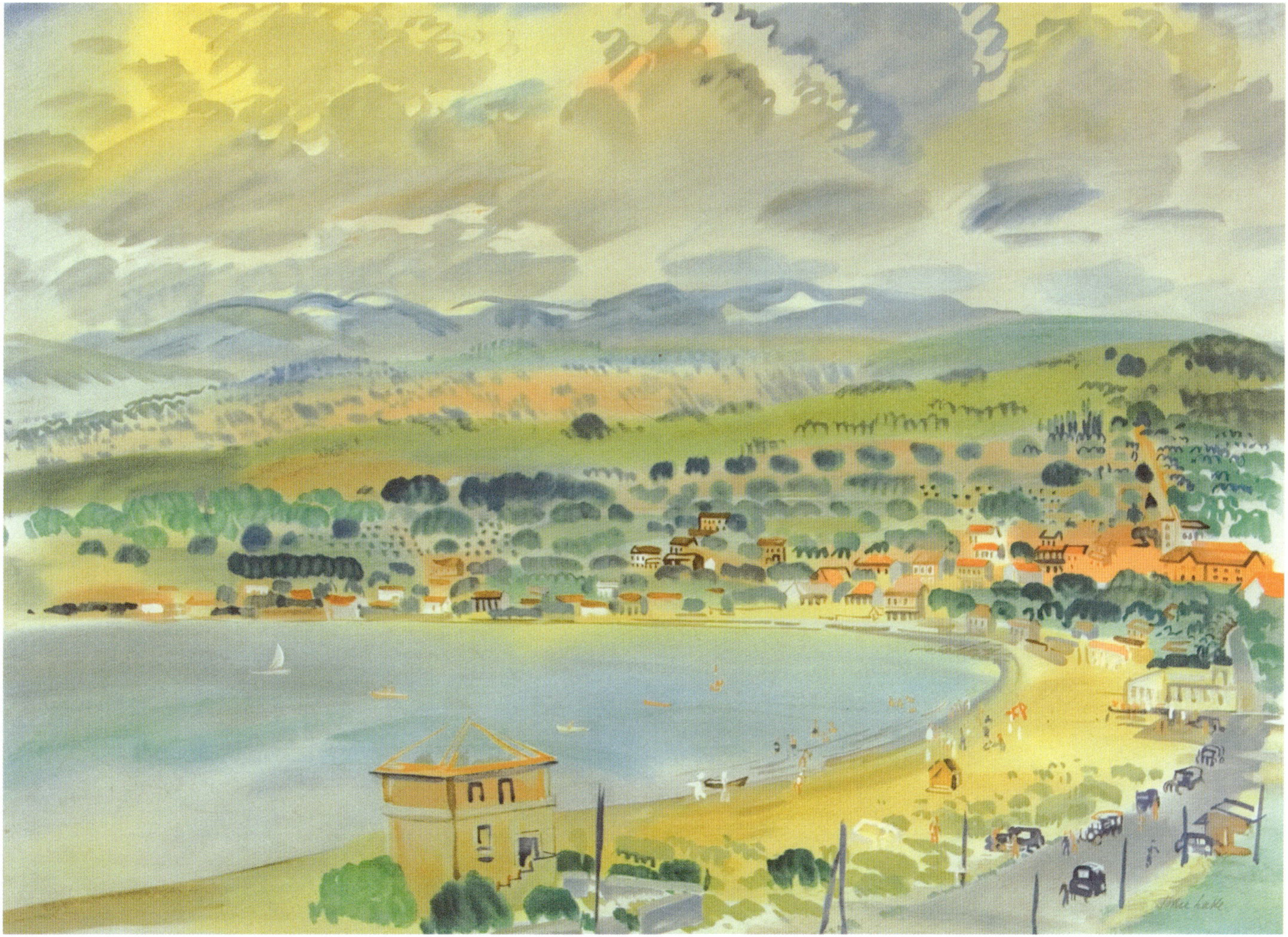

12. Industrial Scene

Painted by L. S. Lowry

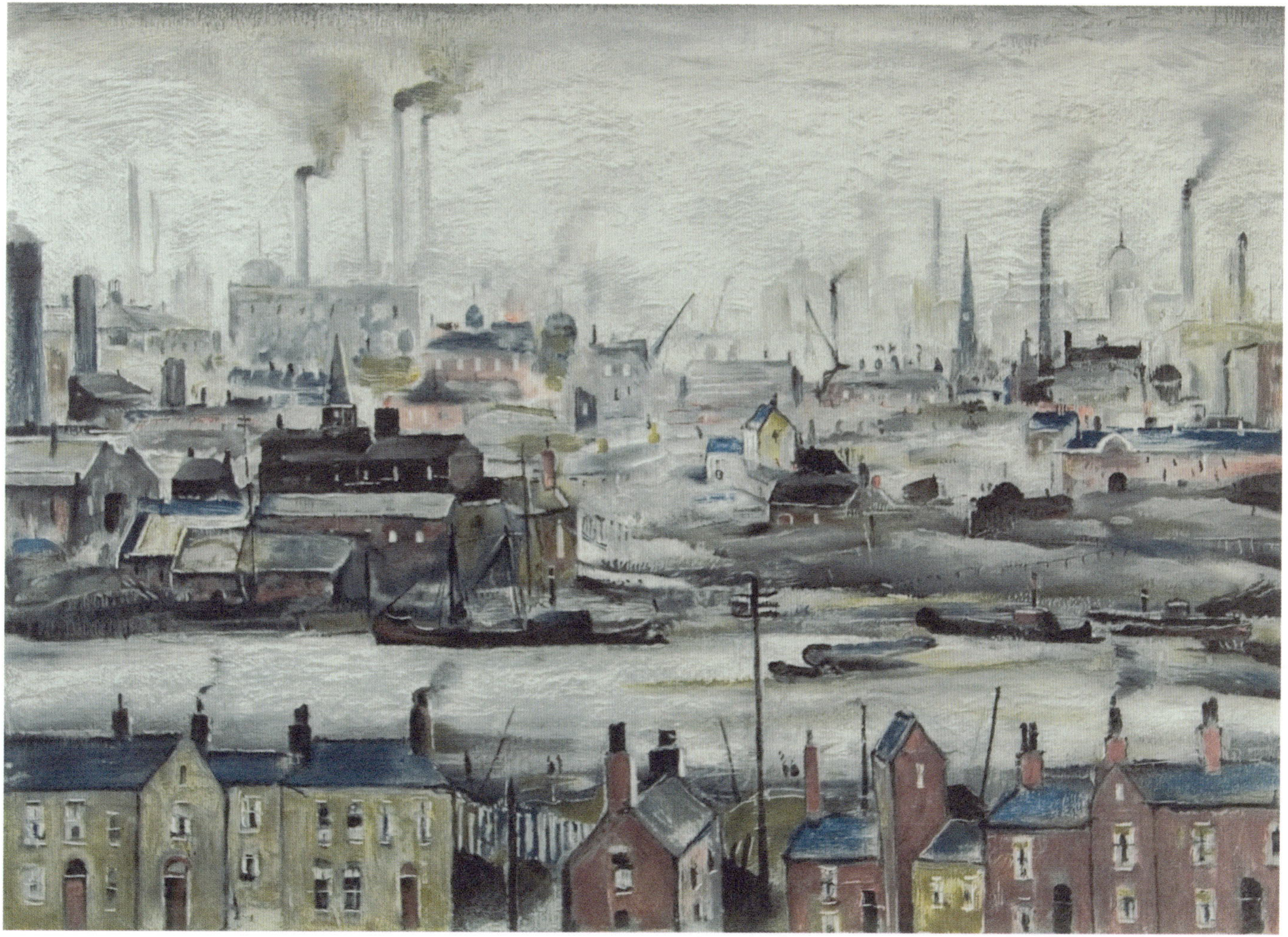

13. Landscape with Bathers

Designed and lithographed by John Nash

Here it is possible to see the modifications Nash made between the original and his finished lithograph. Interestingly, the sketch is squared for transfer from the paper to the printing plates and is also annotated with details of the different colours he intended to use for the lithograph; it is very much a 'working' document. The two figures in the centre of the picture are thought to be the artist's wife, Christine, and Bernard Meninsky's wife, Nora. The male figure, sitting quietly fishing in the right-hand corner, is thought to represent the artist himself.

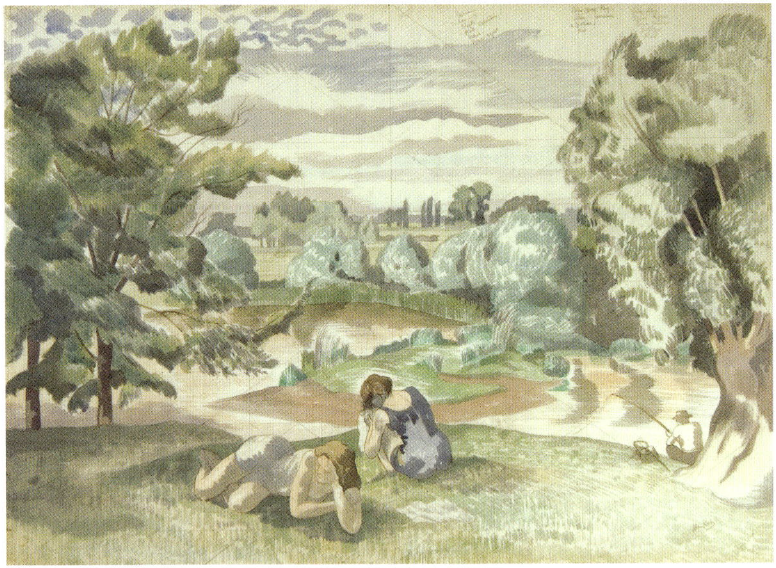

John Nash, *Landscape with Bathers*, *c.* 1946–7 (original), watercolour, 75.5 cm x 56 cm.

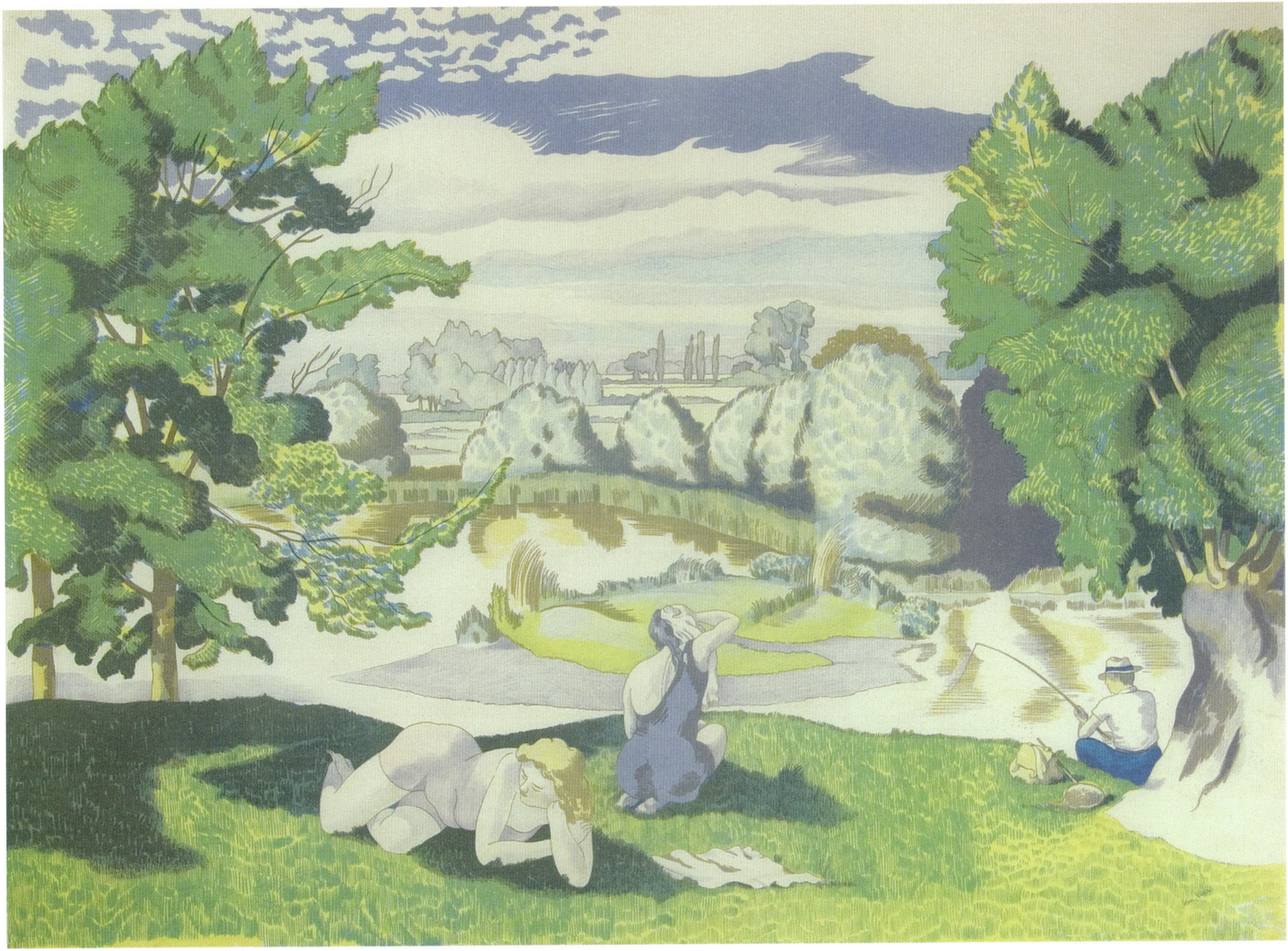

14. The Bird Cage

Designed and lithographed by William Scott

William Scott, *The Bird Cage*, 1947 (original), gouache and chalk on paper, 53.3 x 48.2cm.

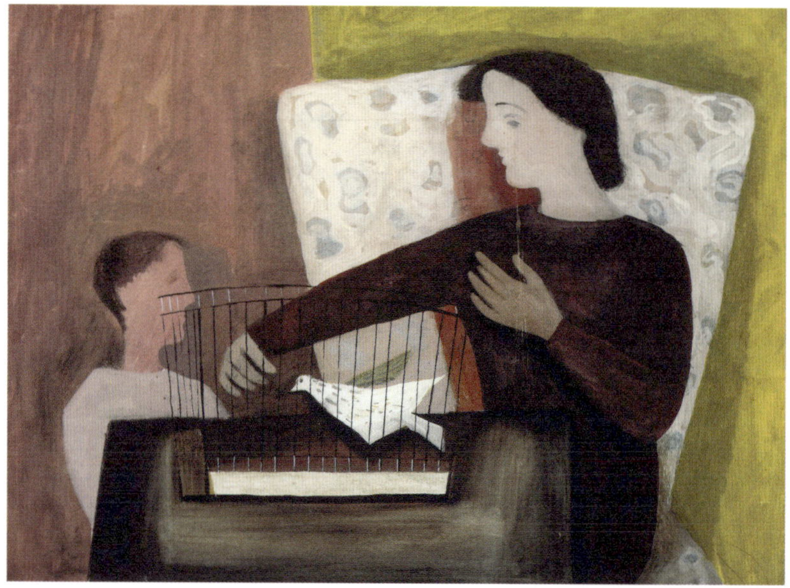

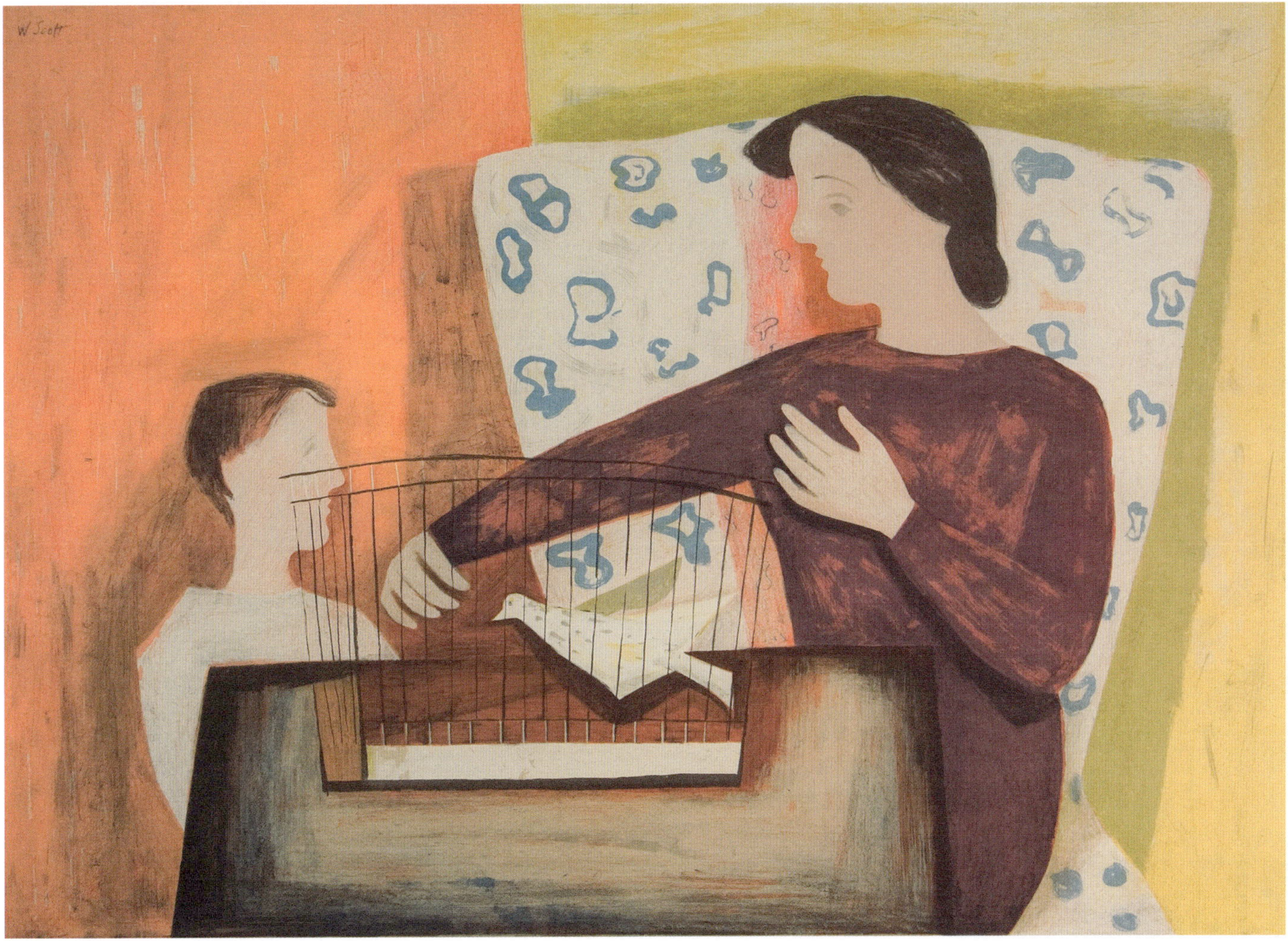
W. Scott

15. Billiards Saloon

Painted by Ruskin Spear

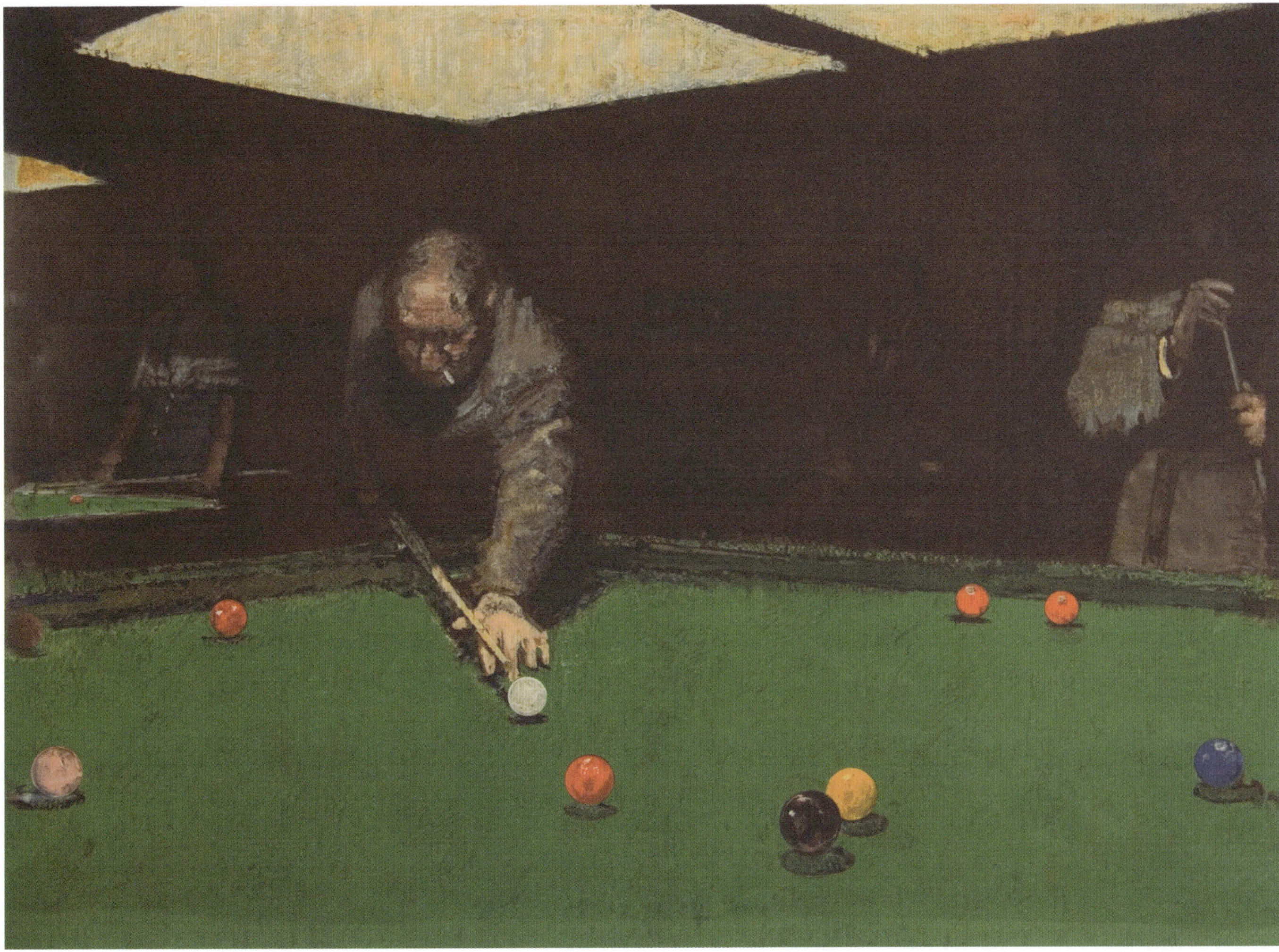

16. Albert Bridge

Painted by Carel Weight

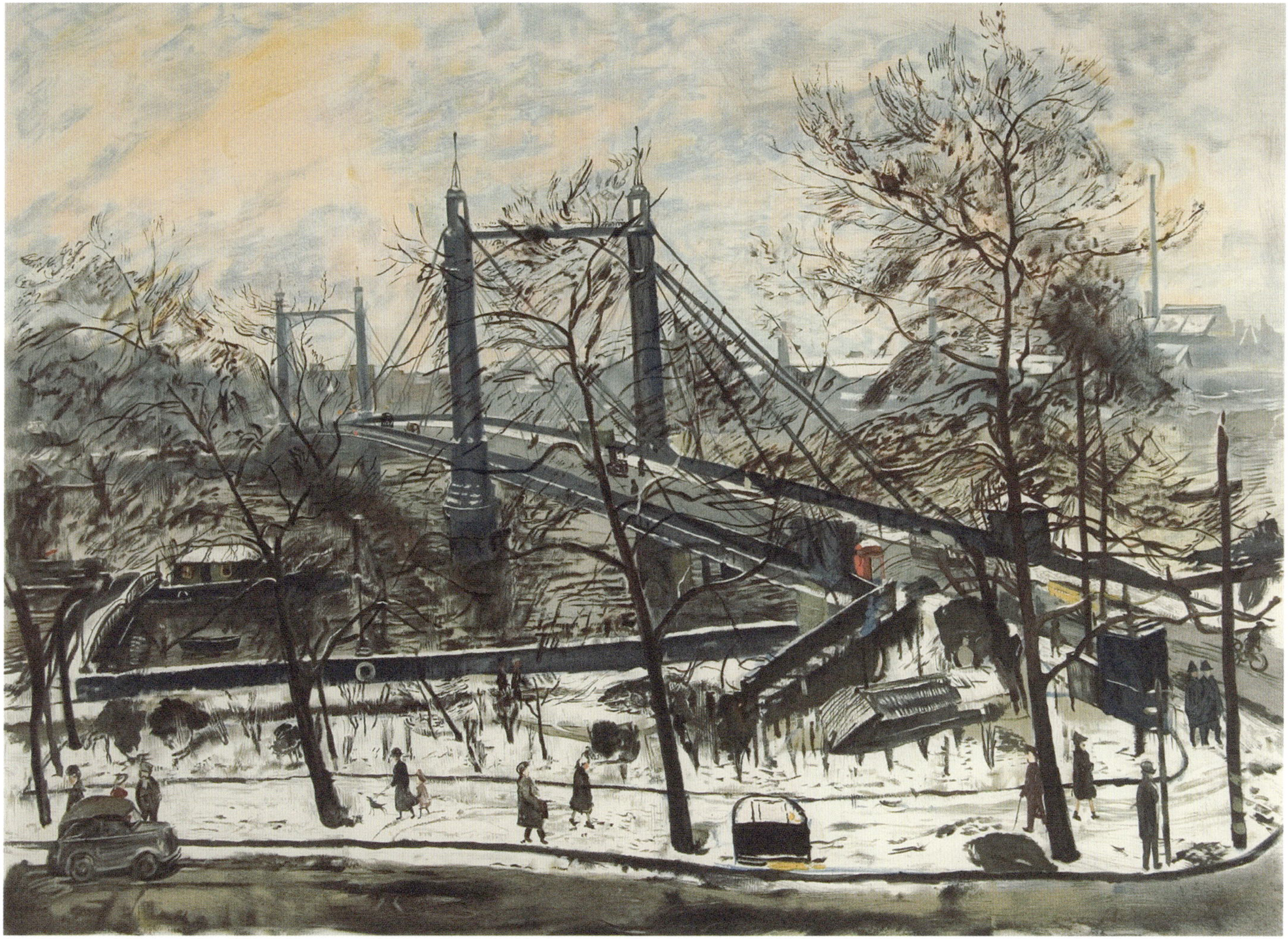

The Second Series, 1949–1951

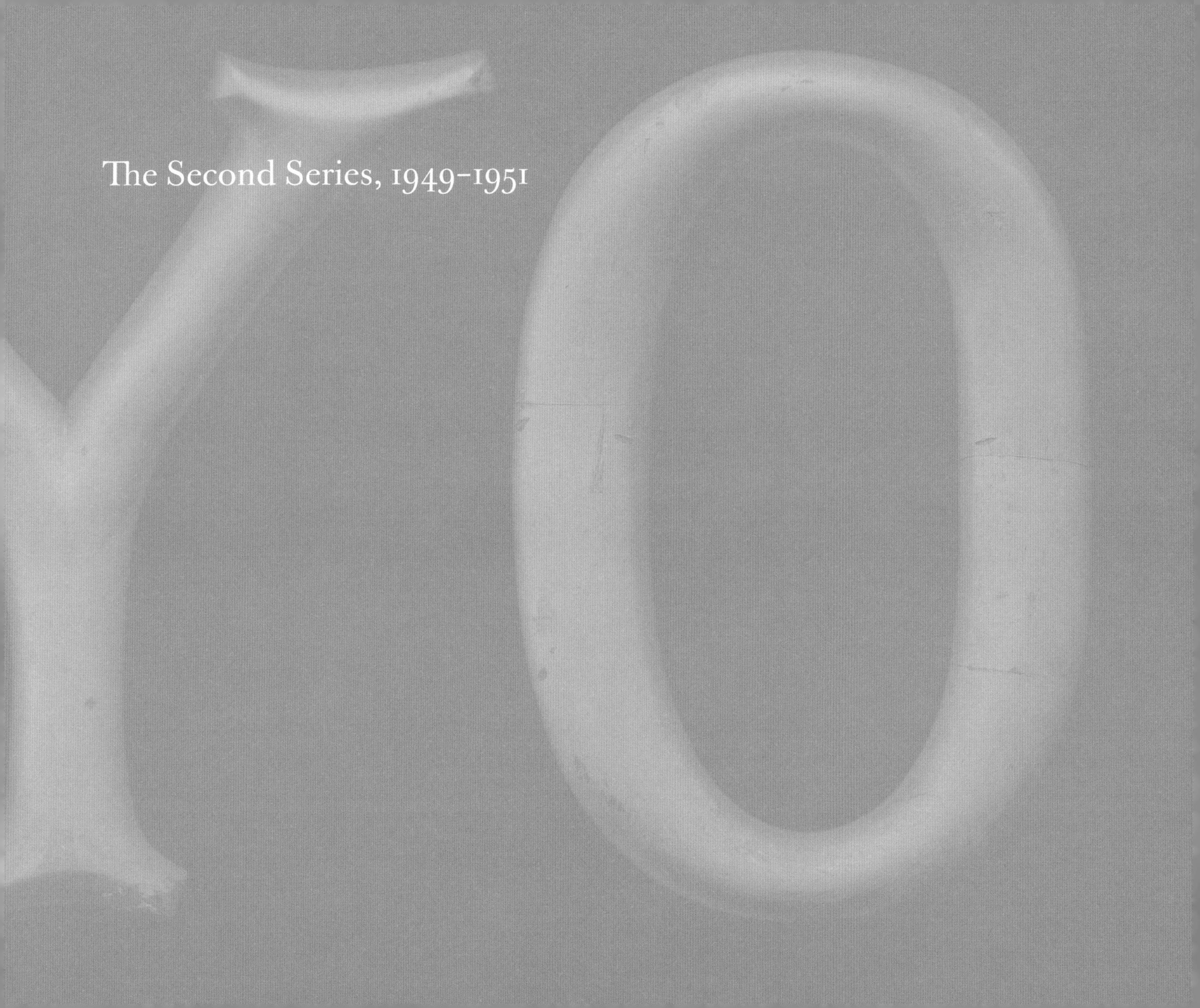

Deciding to Publish a Second Series

The Salmons and Beddington always hoped that the teashop lithographs would be something more than just a 'one hit wonder'. Yet, because the first prints were still 'performing well' two years after they had first been displayed, there was no particular impetus to produce a further edition. However, in the late 1940s, plans were announced to stage the Festival of Britain, and because of the broad remit of the proposed event it was collectively felt that there was now a justifiable and important reason to publish another series.

In June 1949, Julian Salmon wrote to Gerald Barry, Director General of the Great Exhibition Centenary Committee, asking if the authorities would support a second series 'by providing a Show of the Lithographs on the South Bank - or elsewhere in London - and whether the Arts Council ... would hold an Exhibition, or send such an Exhibition on tour'.[1]

This was, of course, a bold request, and in order to make it altogether more appropriate Julian stated that the new lithographs would be entitled 'The British Scene'. Any profit made from the sale of the prints 'would be used to launch subsequent Editions by Artists of excellence'.[2]

Offering demonstrable support for British artists through 'an artistic venture of some importance'[3] was now a priority for Lyons, and while there was still a need to decorate the cafés, it was no longer the sole motivation to produce further lithographs. As astute businessmen, the Salmons realised that by being associated

1. Letter from Julian Salmon to Gerald Barry, 7 June 1949 (Barnett Freedman Archive, Manchester Metropolitan University Special Collections, FRE/1/1/251).
2. ibid.
3. ibid.

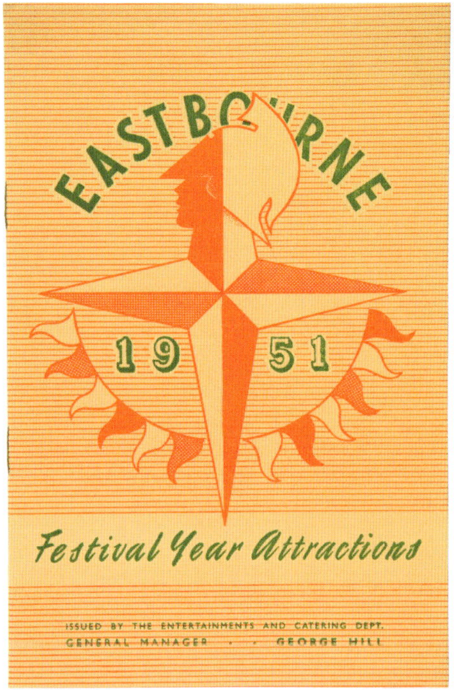

A pamphlet advertising official Festival of Britain events taking place in Eastbourne, 1951. The Festival of Britain was designed to offer a 'tonic to the nation' in the aftermath of the Second World War. There was particular focus on London's South Bank, which had been developed for the Festival, but musical and entertainment events took place throughout Britain in 1951.

with the Festival they could not only extend the presence and impact of their publishing scheme beyond the teashops but could also raise the profile of J. Lyons & Co. as a corporate patron of visual art.

However, although Barry himself thought the scheme should receive official recognition, initially the exhibition committee decided that they would not support the publication or display of further prints as part of the Festival. This might seem a little mean spirited, but it is perhaps understandable in the light of official plans that were already being made for 'sixty artists to paint a large work, not less than 44 by 60 inches, on a subject of their own choice',[4] for an ambitious exhibition entitled *Sixty Paintings for '51*, which was to be shown in London and the provinces.

The project specified large-scale artworks because the show was also being designed specifically to offer 'the new collective patrons of the future ... an opportunity [to] exercise their patronage'.[5] Further to this, numerous other significant artistic projects were being commissioned (murals, public sculptures, etc.), so the Festival was already not only going to incorporate British visual art, and on a grand scale, but would also be promoting corporate patronage. While the teashop enterprise would clearly complement these activities, there was essentially nothing new about the lithographs, and 'newness' was at the very core of the Festival of Britain.

Nevertheless, despite this rejection, at the end of 1949 the Salmons decided to go ahead and publish a new set of lithographs to coincide with the 1951 celebrations, as a way of taking advantage of the increasingly receptive cultural climate. Once again, they turned to Beddington, Freedman and Oppenheimer for creative assistance.

4. P. James, Foreword to *Sixty Paintings for '51* (London, Arts Council of Great Britain, 1951).
5. ibid.

Developing the Series

From the outset, the impetus for the second series was thus quite different from the first, and taking this into account Beddington proposed, in a letter written to Felix in December 1949, a number of changes that would make the second series noticeably different from the first. The most important change was that he believed that any future prints should, where possible, be auto-lithographed.

As individual works, the first lithographs were still taking up a great deal of wall space and successfully covering the shabby décor of the teashops. Yet it was their large scale that had often deterred those artists who were not comfortable with auto-lithography from using the medium and who, as a result, had chosen the expensive option of submitting a painting to be copied into a lithograph at Chromoworks. When nine of the first sixteen prints had been produced in this way the financial impact had been quite substantial, and reducing the production cost of the second series quickly became a point of particular importance.

As cultural awareness developed in the post-war years, the lithographs needed to have an added dimension, beyond their purely decorative role. By commissioning an entire series of auto-lithographs Beddington knew he could not only reduce production costs but also elevate the artistic status of the prints and the project as a whole. To achieve this aim he proposed to print just twelve (rather than sixteen) lithographs, with six measuring a rather less daunting 20" x 30" as opposed to 30" x 40", as a way of encouraging more, if not all, of the selected artists to try their hand at auto-lithography.

Eventually only Robin Darwin (1910–1974), Barnett Freedman, Anthony Gross, Edwin La Dell, Lynton Lamb (1907–1977), Charles Mozley and Robert Scanlon (1908–1997) produced auto-lithographs for the series, while Michael

Ayrton (1921-1975), Peter Collins (b.1923), John Minton (1917-1957), Claude Rogers (1907-1979) and Fred Uhlman (1901-1985) still submitted originals to Chromoworks. Six of the lithographs were printed at 20" x 30" (as Beddington had hoped), but of this smaller size only *The Shire Hall* [p. 119] was actually auto-lithographed, and even then there were a number of problems during its production [see p. 118].

Modifying the size of the lithographs also influenced how much each artist was paid for their commission, with Beddington now offering set fees of '100 guineas for the six small … and 125 guineas for the six large'.[6] If any artists were considered 'not capable of putting their design on the plates'[7] they were to be restricted to the large size and paid 75 guineas, but all of the originals were eventually produced as smaller prints and the artists were presumably paid a fee which reflected this. Beddington did, however, urge the Salmons to continue paying a sixpence royalty for each print that was sold, on account of him 'constantly hearing about this system and the artists themselves [being] simply delighted'.[8]

6. Letter from Jack Beddington to Felix Salmon, 9 December 1949 (Barnett Freedman Archive, Manchester Metropolitan University Special Collections, FRE/1/1/251).
7. ibid.
8. ibid.

Artists and Treatment

The selection of artists was, at first, guided by the need to employ practitioners who were comfortable with auto-lithography. The inclusion of Freedman, Gross and La Dell, for example (all of whom had produced auto-lithographs for the first series), represents a natural choice for Beddington. If this was playing it a little safe, it was perhaps a justified decision: Freedman's *Music – Still Life* [p. 113] was showered with accolades on account of its 'great technical mastery'[9] and helped to project the overall standard of the scheme.

Many of the artists commissioned were, once again, friends and colleagues. Ayrton and Minton had, for instance, at one time shared a studio; and by 1951 Minton was teaching at the Royal College of Art under the principal and fellow teashop artist, Robin Darwin. La Dell and Mozley were related by marriage.

All twelve artists were established professionals in their thirties and forties, but none, as yet, had achieved the artistic stature of either Duncan Grant or L. S. Lowry, who had been commissioned for the first series. Ayrton was, however, well known as an art critic and broadcaster and, incidentally, was also the only artist cited on Beddington's original 1946 list who was not commissioned for the first series but took part in both the second and third. Interestingly, Ayrton, Lamb, Minton and Rogers also had work included in *Sixty Paintings for '51*, and Rogers' submission *Miss Lynn* was even one of five works purchased by the Arts Council.[10]

9. P. James, *Lithographs by Contemporary Artists – First and Second Series* (J. Lyons & Co. Ltd/Arts Council of Great Britain, printed at the Curwen Press, 1951), p. 4.
10. *The Island* by Elinor Bellingham-Smith was another of the five paintings selected; Bellingham-Smith later contributed to the third series of teashop prints.

In commissioning, among others, Mozley, Scanlon and Uhlman, Beddington demonstrated that he was not afraid to include artists who were associated more closely with the commercial fields of book illustration and poster design than with fine art. These artists were, however, a wise inclusion, because they were accustomed to producing work for a clear purpose. With its direct illustrative style and lively use of colour and composition, Scanlon's *Yeoman Warders* [p. 127] perfectly fitted the brief to produce a design that would both brighten up the teashops and represent something demonstrably British – the 'imposed' theme of the second series. Similarly, because of its pared-down graphic style, *The Lighthouse of St Agnes* by Uhlman [p. 129] is one of the most appealing and memorable lithographs of not just the 1951 series but of the whole scheme.

However, along with Ayrton, Collins, Minton and Rogers, Uhlman did not auto-lithograph his print. While all of these artists were undoubtedly more than capable of employing the medium, in reality they were probably selected more because Beddington saw an existing example of their work which in some way captured 'British scenes and the British way of life'.[11]

Artists were still encouraged to make suggestions for the content of the lithographs, but, unlike with the 1947 series, their ideas were not always accepted. As a way of avoiding any 'trouble' concerning subject-matter (such as that he encountered with Hooper's and Kessell's lithographs from the first series), this time Beddington compiled a list of suitable topics, such as 'Taxi Man' and 'Inside a Corner House'. In the end, in its depiction of a London square only *Roosevelt Memorial, Grosvenor Square* [p. 109] by Peter Collins bore any relation to these initial suggestions, but in comparison with the hotchpotch of subjects covered in the first prints, the 1951 lithographs are a much more cohesive group, more or less united by a common theme.

11. Letter from Jack Beddington to Barnett Freedman, 13 June 1950 (Lyons Lithograph Archive, Towner Art Gallery).

The Cricket Match [p. 115] by Gross, *Henley* [p. 123] by Mozley and *Yeoman Warders* by Scanlon, for instance, all illustrate quintessentially British characters and activities. *Fishing at Marlow* [p. 117] by La Dell, *The Shire Hall* by Lamb, *Apple Orchard, Kent* [p. 121] by Minton, *River Buses at Putney Bridge* [p. 125] by Rogers and *The Lighthouse of St Agnes* by Uhlman then present a gentle overview of 'the British scene'.

In relation to these examples, in its more everyday subject matter *The Fishmonger's Shop* [p. 111] by Darwin is the broadest interpretation of the British theme, while *The Spectators* [p. 107] by Ayrton and *Music – Still Life* by Freedman abandon it altogether and, in their focus on entertainment, are perhaps more pertinent to the Festival itself.

Publicity

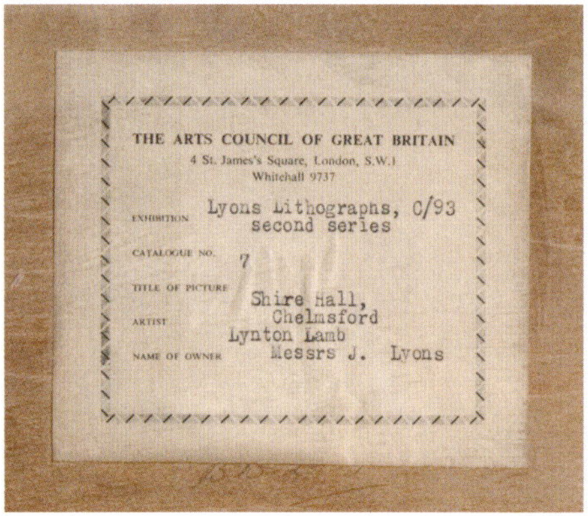

An Arts Council exhibition label preserved on the reverse of the original oil painting of *The Shire Hall* by Lynton Lamb.

No plans were made to launch the second series at the Trocadero, because the Salmons were determined that the prints would, at the very least, be officially publicised through the Festival. As a result, undeterred by Barry's original rejection, between September 1950 and February 1951, Julian negotiated his way, somewhat belligerently, to not only a Festival-related exhibition in London, but also a touring show of the prints that was endorsed and coordinated by the Arts Council.

Julian stood his ground on every point concerning an exhibition of the lithographs, and did not accept the conciliatory suggestion from the Festival authorities that they would 'be very pleased to hang them in the press rooms and some of the administrative offices',[12] finding it an altogether 'depressing'[13] offer.

Everything Julian saw as features of particular note about the scheme, Philip James, Director of Art for the Arts Council, cited as presenting 'certain difficulties'.[14] Julian, for example, believed that showing the twenty-eight lithographs plus all the originals from both series would be of 'great interest to the general public';[15] but the Panel did not think it necessary to 'pad the exhibition … with preliminary drawings'[16] and were against including 'the first sixteen lithographs which have been so widely distributed, and are now well known'.[17]

12. Letter from Gabriel White to Julian Salmon, 9 October 1950 (Barnett Freedman Archive, Manchester Metropolitan University Special Collections, FRE/1/1/251).
13. Letter from Julian Salmon to Gabriel White, 16 October 1950 (Barnett Freedman Archive, Manchester Metropolitan University Special Collections, FRE/1/1/251).
14. Letter from Philip James to Julian Salmon, 30 September 1950 (Barnett Freedman Archive, Manchester Metropolitan University Special Collections, FRE/1/1/251).
15. Letter from Salmon to White, 16 October 1950.
16. Letter from James to Salmon, 30 September 1950.
17. ibid.

Eventually, after a number of letters rejecting and accepting various proposals, Lyons were granted an official exhibition, but this was staged at the headquarters of the Arts Council, in St James's Square, and not on the South Bank, the preferred and more high-profile location. The show opened with a press and private view on 1 August, at the height of the Festival, and remained open to the public until 1 September. It was billed as *Lithographs by Contemporary Artists – First and Second Series* and eventually comprised the sixteen originals purchased for the first series, alongside the lithographs and originals from the second.

The exhibition was accompanied by a catalogue [right] produced by the Arts Council and containing a foreword written by Philip James, in which he highlighted how the scheme was 'a most commendable effort by Big Business to play its part as a patron of living art'.[18] He also took the opportunity, however, to make it clear that the lithographs were different from much of the visual art that had been officially commissioned for the Festival by mentioning, perhaps somewhat condescendingly, that they were 'something more modest … not for the great public forums but for the home'.[19]

The tour then got underway, and despite there being some doubt that more than one provincial showing could be arranged 'because … it will be very difficult to find galleries with vacant dates at … short notice',[20] the exhibition was displayed at venues in both Southampton and Leicester.

The lithographs were, of course, also displayed in the teashops, alongside prints from the first series. Lyons were always eager that the project was seen as a progressive undertaking, and were keen to reinforce this by showing the two series together not only in an official exhibition but also in the cafés.

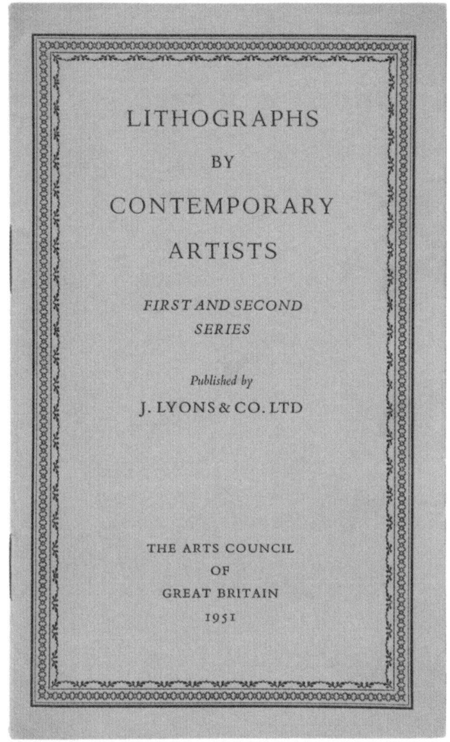

The front cover of the 1951 exhibition catalogue, designed by Barnett Freedman and printed at the Curwen Press.

18. James, *Lithographs by Contemporary Artists*, p. 3
19. ibid.
20. Letter from Philip James to Julian Salmon, 13 February 1951 (Barnett Freedman Archive, Manchester Metropolitan University Special Collections, FRE/1/1/251).

Again, the Salmons encouraged institutions and public organisations to purchase copies of the lithographs, and despite having 'done quite well initially'[21] with sales in America, Julian was anxious that, this time, they contact 'potential institutional buyers, such as schools, offices, Government Depts etc.'.[22]

In this, Julian clearly exerted his personal influence on the scheme. Having been appointed managing director of Lyons in 1949, he decided to do everything in his power to ensure that a second series of the Lyons lithographs was successfully published to coincide with the Festival of Britain.

21. Letter from Julian Salmon to Barnett Freedman, 5 September 1951 (Barnett Freedman Archive, Manchester Metropolitan University Special Collections, FRE/1/1/251).
22. ibid.

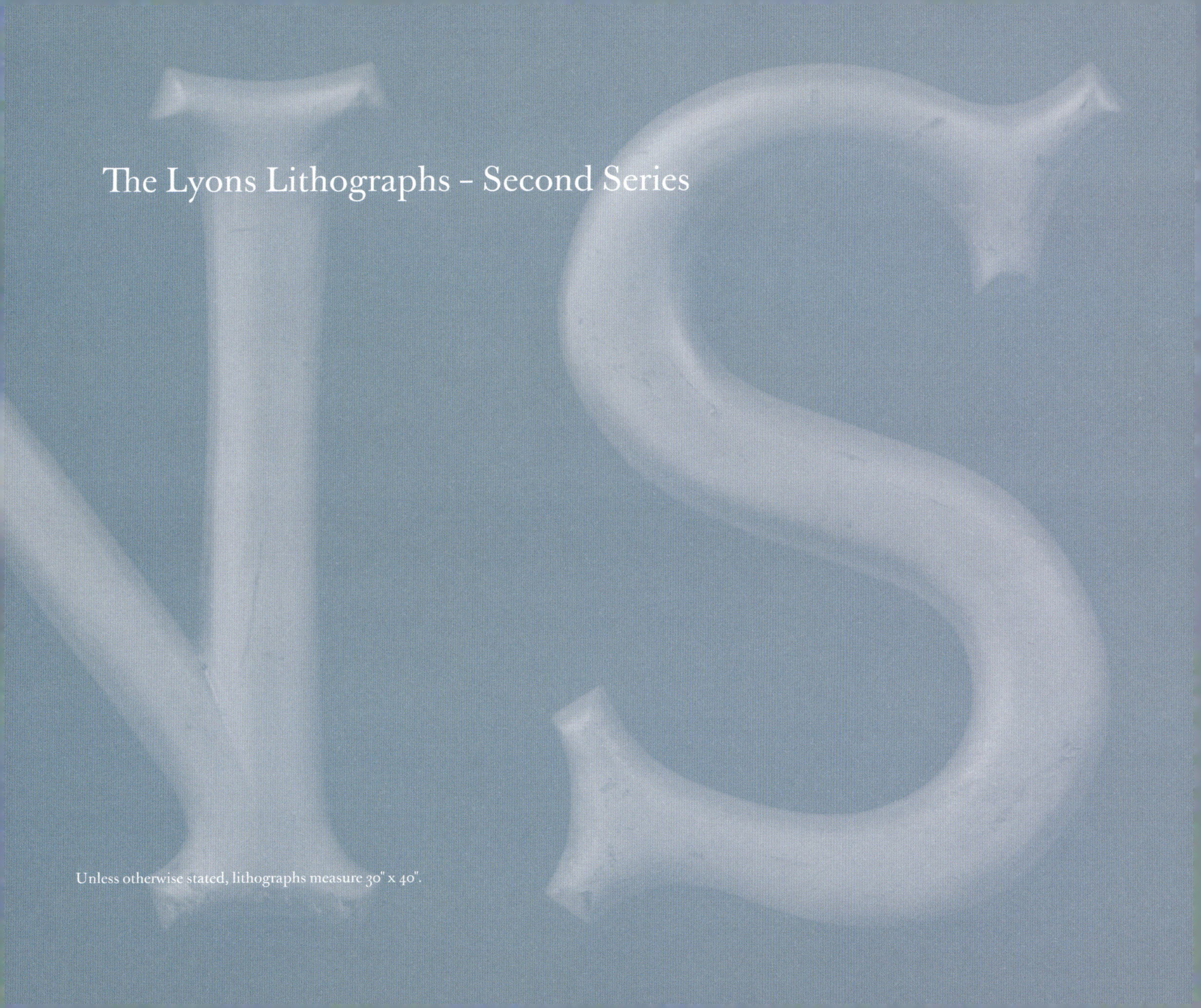

The Lyons Lithographs - Second Series

Unless otherwise stated, lithographs measure 30" x 40".

1. The Spectators

Painted by Michael Ayrton (20" x 30")

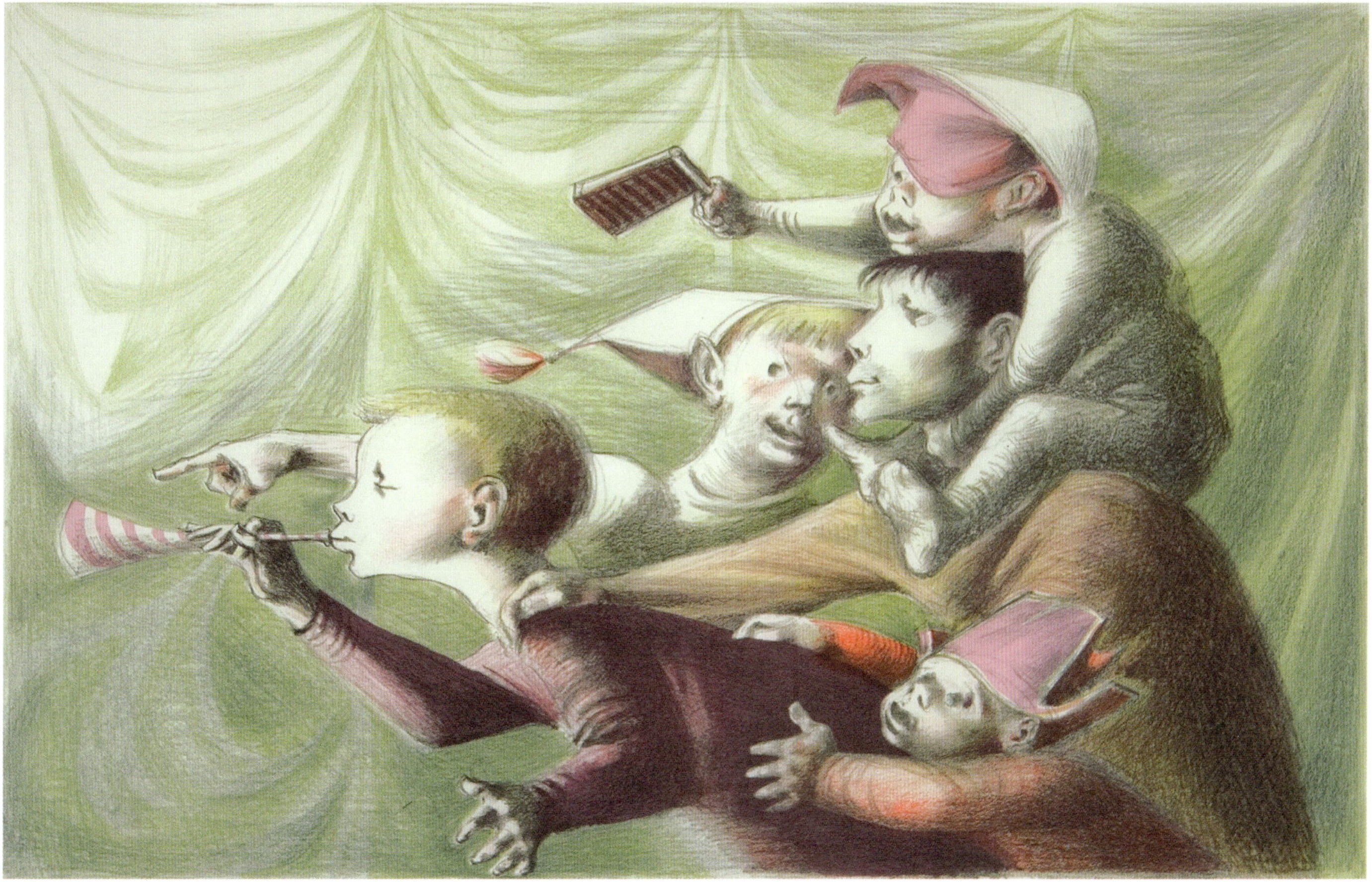

2. Roosevelt Memorial, Grosvenor Square

Painted by Peter Collins (20" x 30")

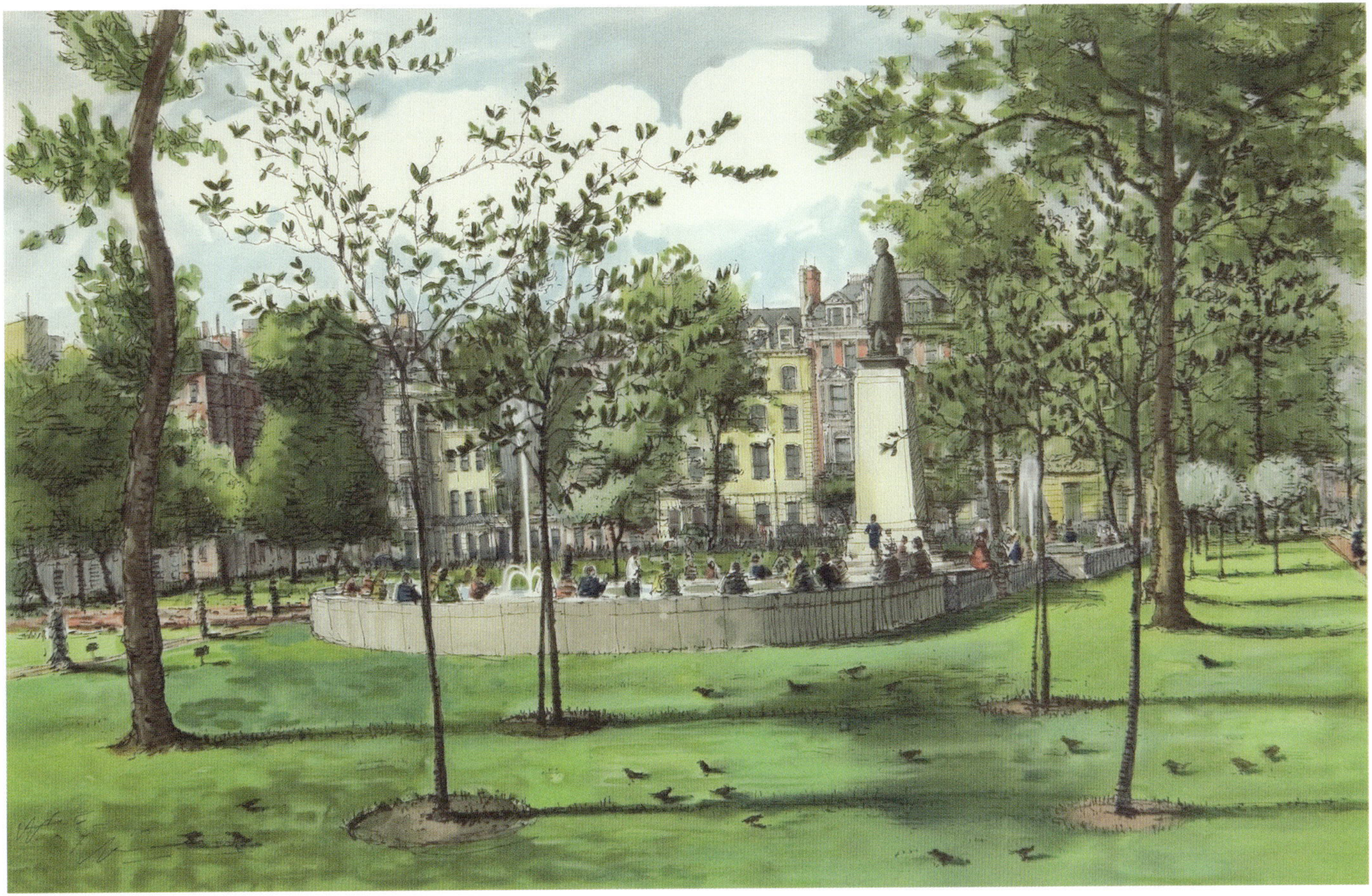

3. The Fishmonger's Shop

Designed and lithographed by Robin Darwin

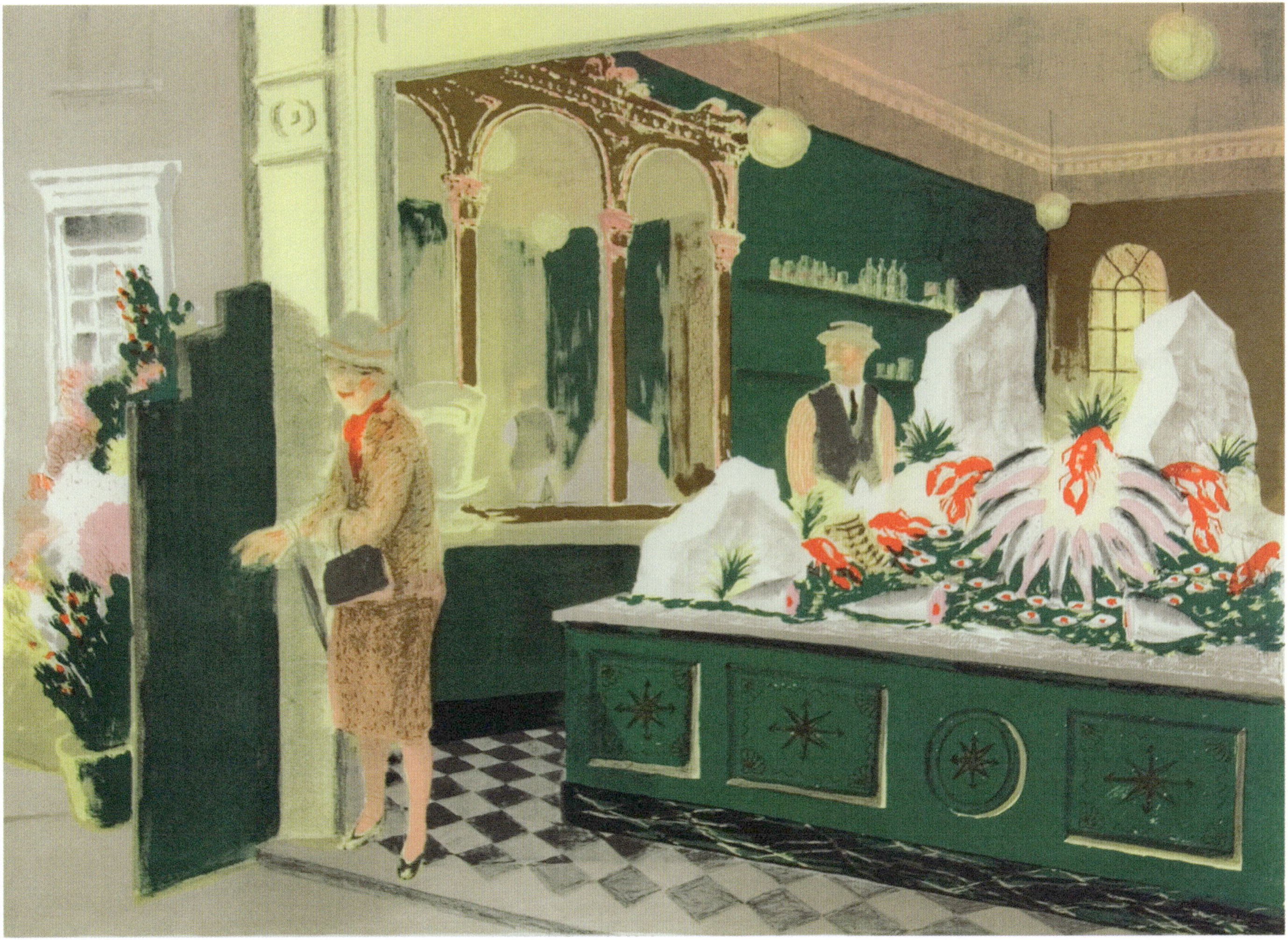

4. Music – Still Life

Designed and lithographed by Barnett Freedman

Freedman received all manner of praise for this lithograph. Lamb, for instance, said it 'scores on every count. It is a proper masterpiece'.* Being so close in detail to the original sketch, the print bears testament to Freedman's skill as an autolithographer. Felix even said, 'I could not imagine when I saw the sketch that it could be improved on it was so good, but this is the best ever.'†

In 1951 Freedman adapted the composition of the lithograph in an oil painting entitled *Music*. In 1953, J. Lyons & Co. presented this painting to the Tate.

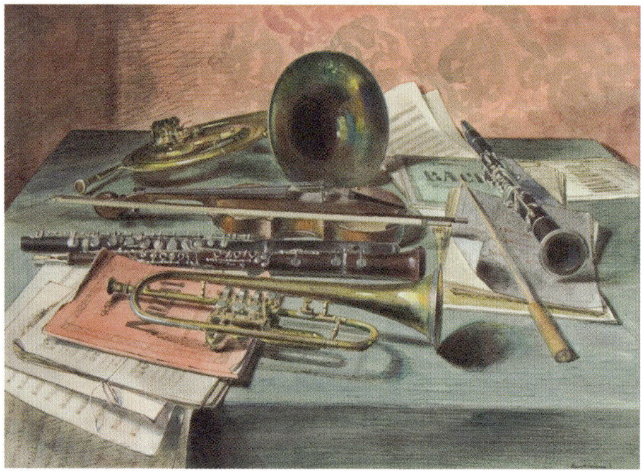

Barnett Freedman, *Music – Still Life*, 1951 (original), pen, ink, watercolour and gouache, 35.5 cm x 48.2 cm.

* Letter from Lynton Lamb to Barnett Freedman, 4 August 1951 (Barnett Freedman Archive, Manchester Metropolitan University Special Collections, FRE/1/1/226).
† Letter from Felix Salmon to Barnett Freedman, 3 July 1951 (Barnett Freedman Archive, Manchester Metropolitan University Special Collections, FRE/1/1/251).

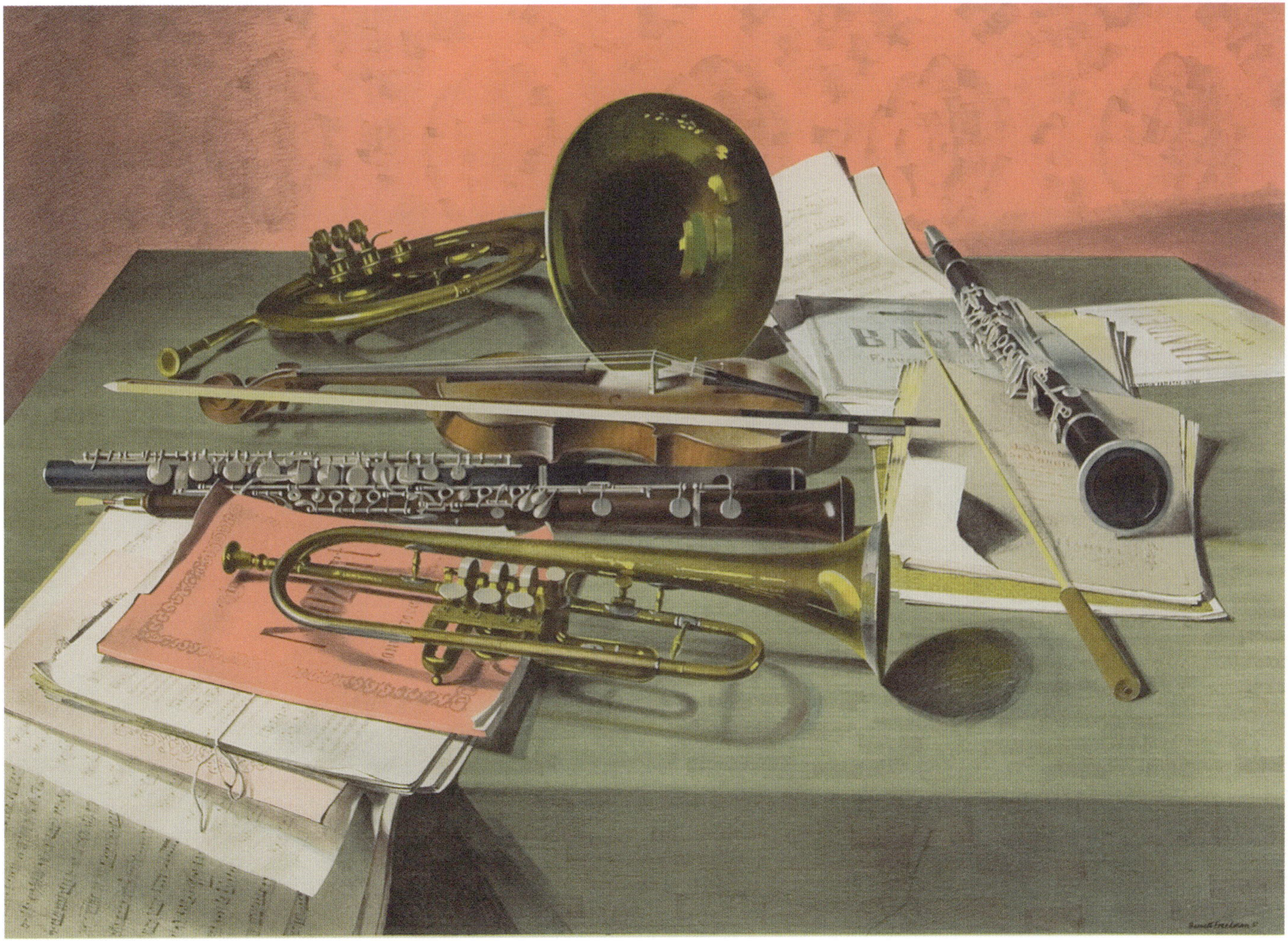

5. *The Cricket Match*

Designed and lithographed by Anthony Gross

Oppenheimer ensured that the production of each lithograph was 'just right'. On hearing, for instance, that Gross had found it difficult to obtain the exact colours for *Herne Bay Pier* (his first lithograph), for *The Cricket Match* Oppenheimer arranged for him to send details of the colours he intended to use to Chromoworks. In response, they sent him the nearest match and even purchased special inks to achieve his desired result. Oppenheimer believed this was the best option because the 'extra trouble and cost … should be less than the cost of the time otherwise spent on the machine in trying to match colours, so we should get a better result at less cost and less trouble'.*

* Letter from Frank Oppenheimer to Barnett Freedman, 22 November 1950 (Barnett Freedman Archive, Manchester Metropolitan University Special Collections, FRE/1/1/87).

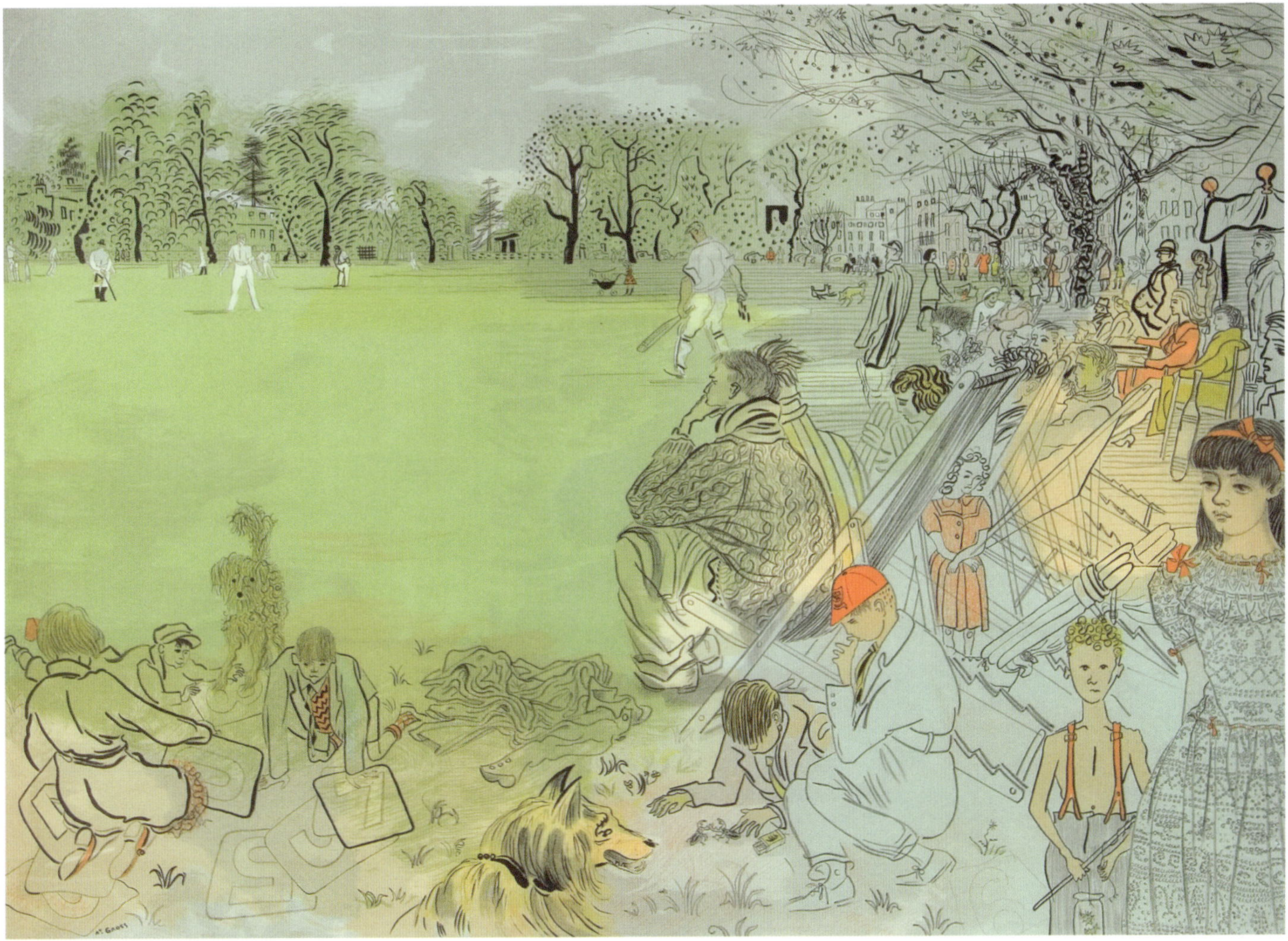

6. Fishing at Marlow

Designed and lithographed by Edwin La Dell

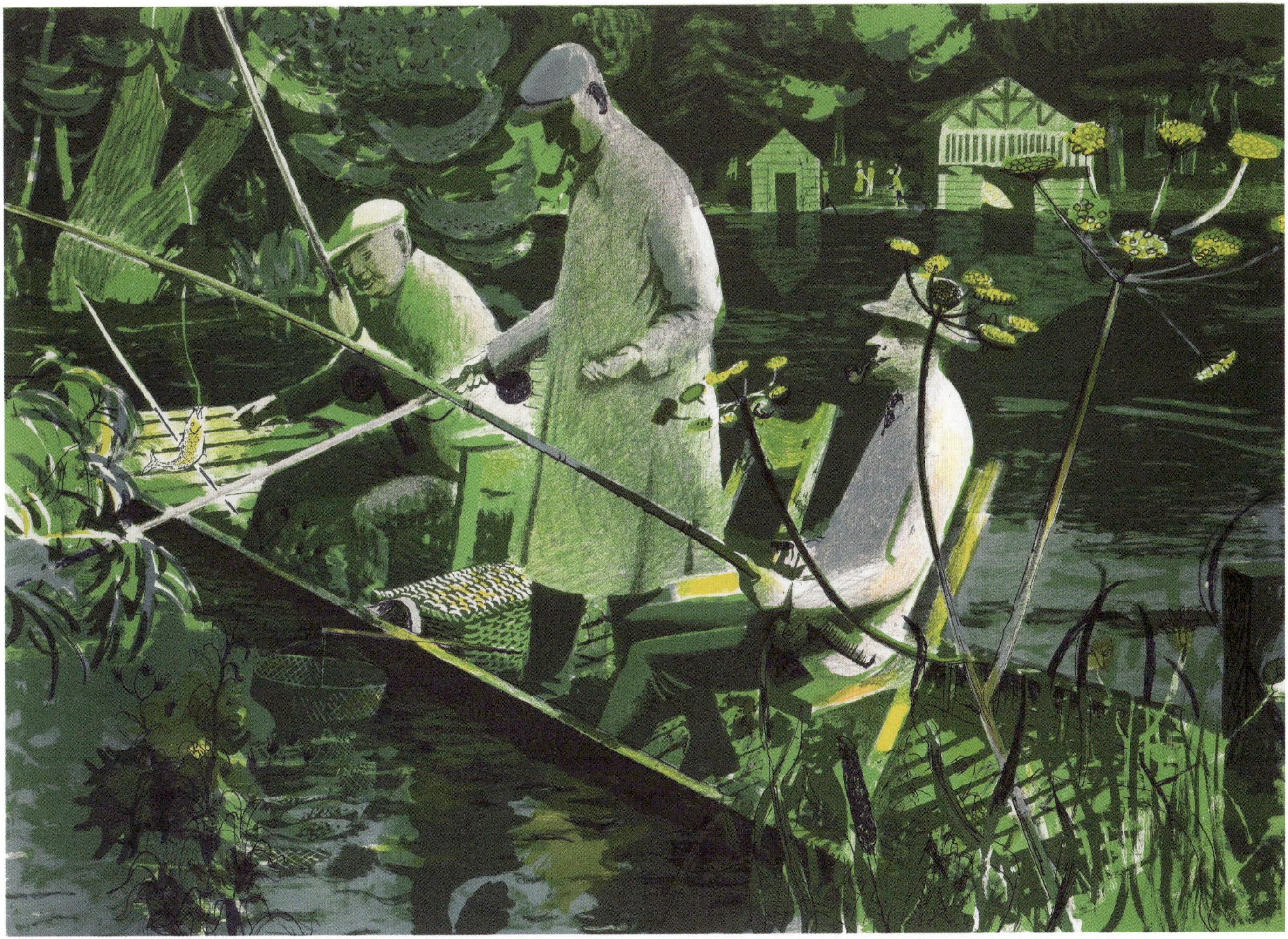

7. The Shire Hall

Designed and lithographed by Lynton Lamb (20" x 30")

Although Lamb auto-lithographed his work for the teashops, the finished lithograph was printed the wrong way round because of a mix-up concerning the practicalities of offset lithography. A flurry of letters subsequently passed between Lamb, Oppenheimer and Freedman; Lamb firmly laying the blame with Oppenheimer and Oppenheimer stating that Lamb had 'misdirected himself'.* Freedman was thus somewhat caught in the middle. Lamb did, however, concede that in the end it was only 'a small matter' and that it did not matter 'being the wrong way round, except locally'.†

Lynton Lamb, *The Shire Hall - Chelmsford*, c. 1950–51 (original), oil on board, 35 cm x 48.2 cm.

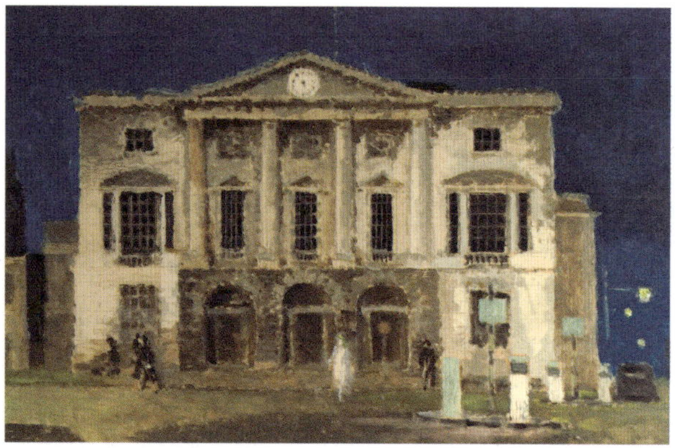

* Letter from Frank Oppenheimer to Barnett Freedman, 5 April 1951 (Barnett Freedman Archive, Manchester Metropolitan University Special Collections, FRE/1/1/87).

† Letter from Lynton Lamb to Barnett Freedman, 30 March 1951 (Barnett Freedman Archive, Manchester Metropolitan University Special Collections, FRE/1/1/87).

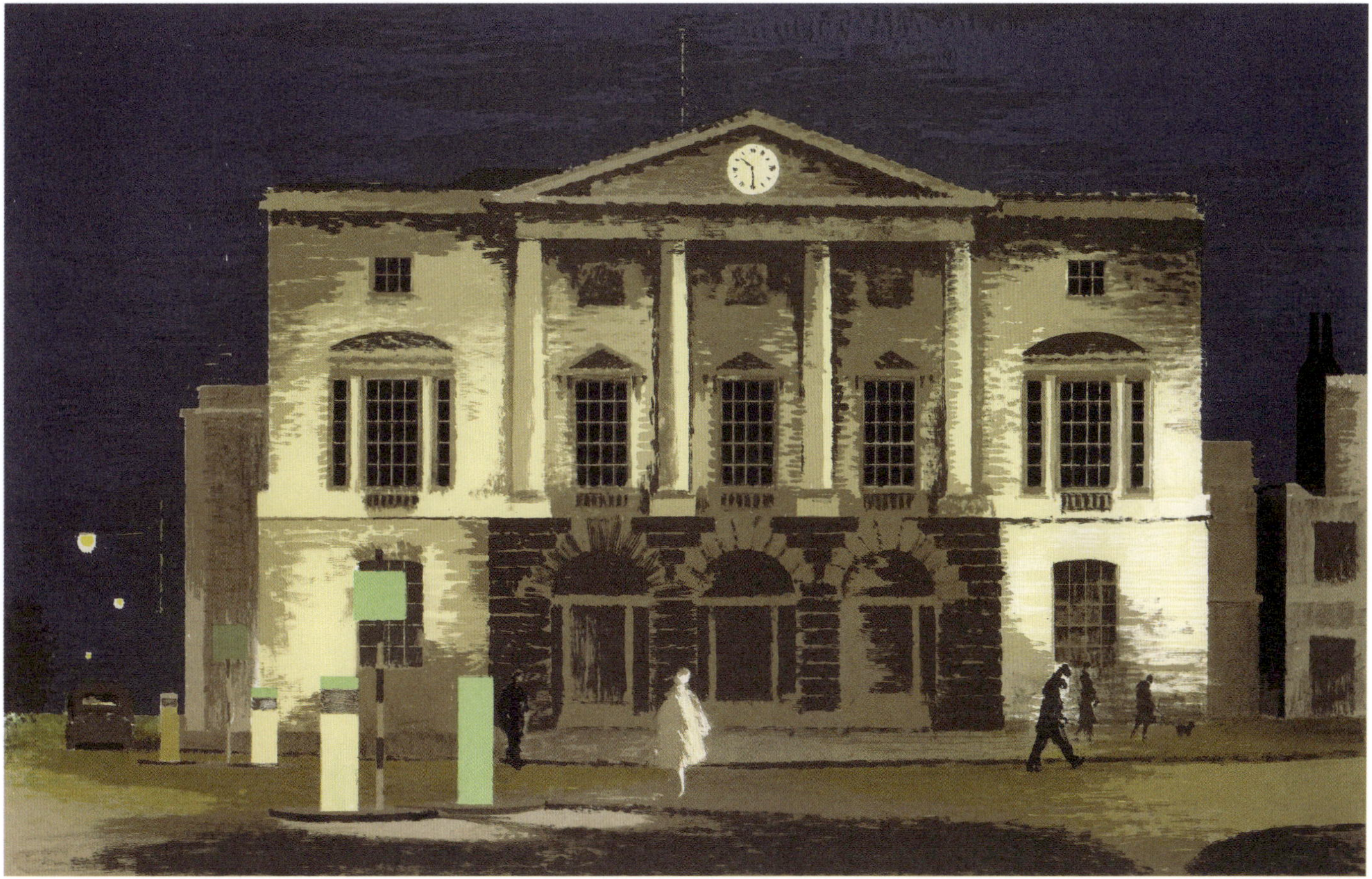

8. Apple Orchard, Kent

Painted by John Minton (20" x 30")

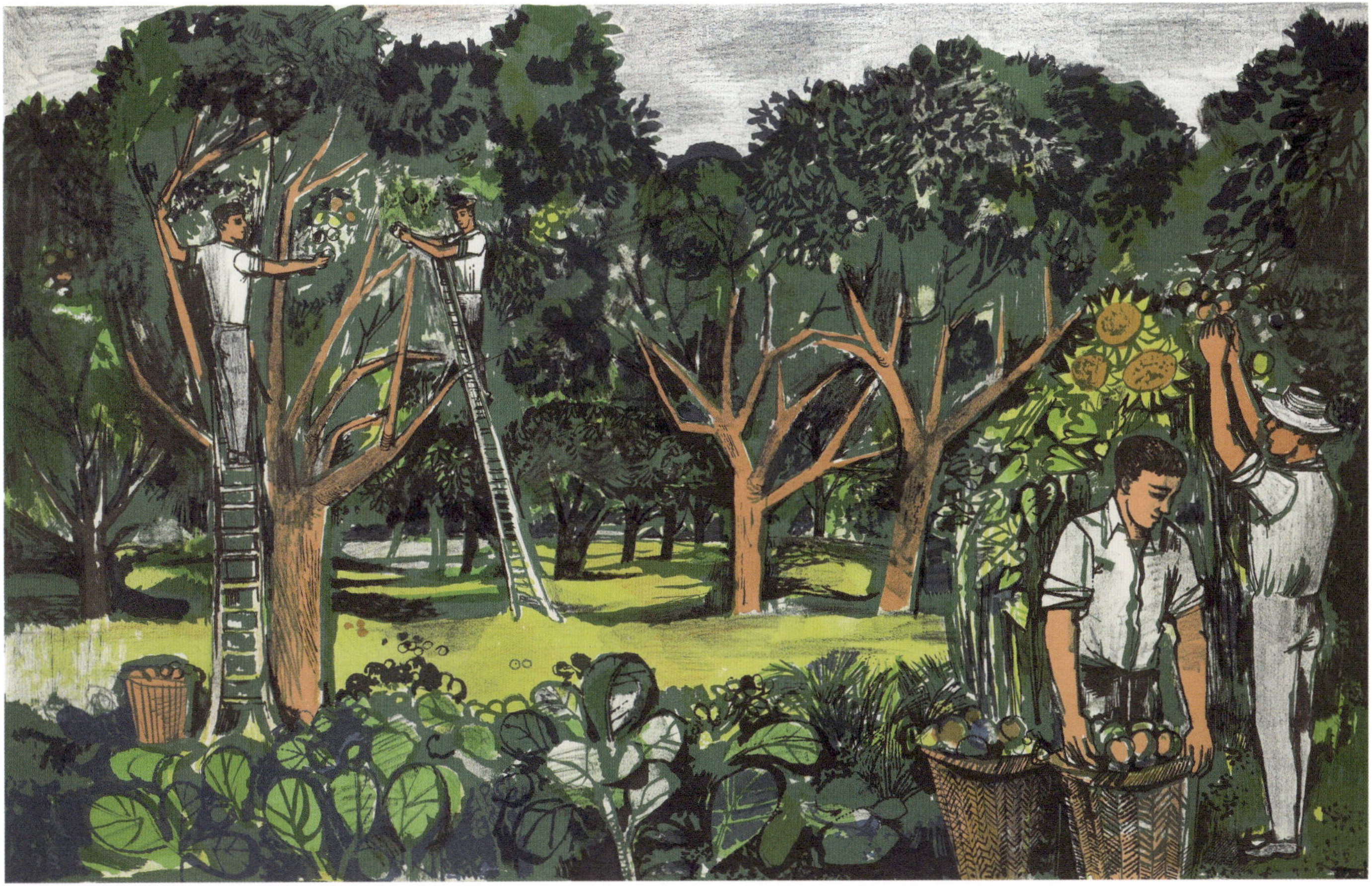

9. Henley

Designed and lithographed by Charles Mozley

When Oppenheimer saw the early pulls of *Henley* he wrote to Freedman stating that he thought it should be reprinted. He felt the distortion of the figures had become too pronounced, and because the print bore the Chromoworks name he was concerned that 'most people … will probably think the defect is due to bad printing', rather than a reflection of Mozley's artistic intention. He did, however, close his letter by saying, 'do not think I am prejudiced about this lithograph; on the contrary, I admire a lot of it enormously.'*

* Letter from Frank Oppenheimer to Barnett Freedman, 3 May 1951 (Barnett Freedman Archive, Manchester Metropolitan University Special Collections, FRE/1/1/87).

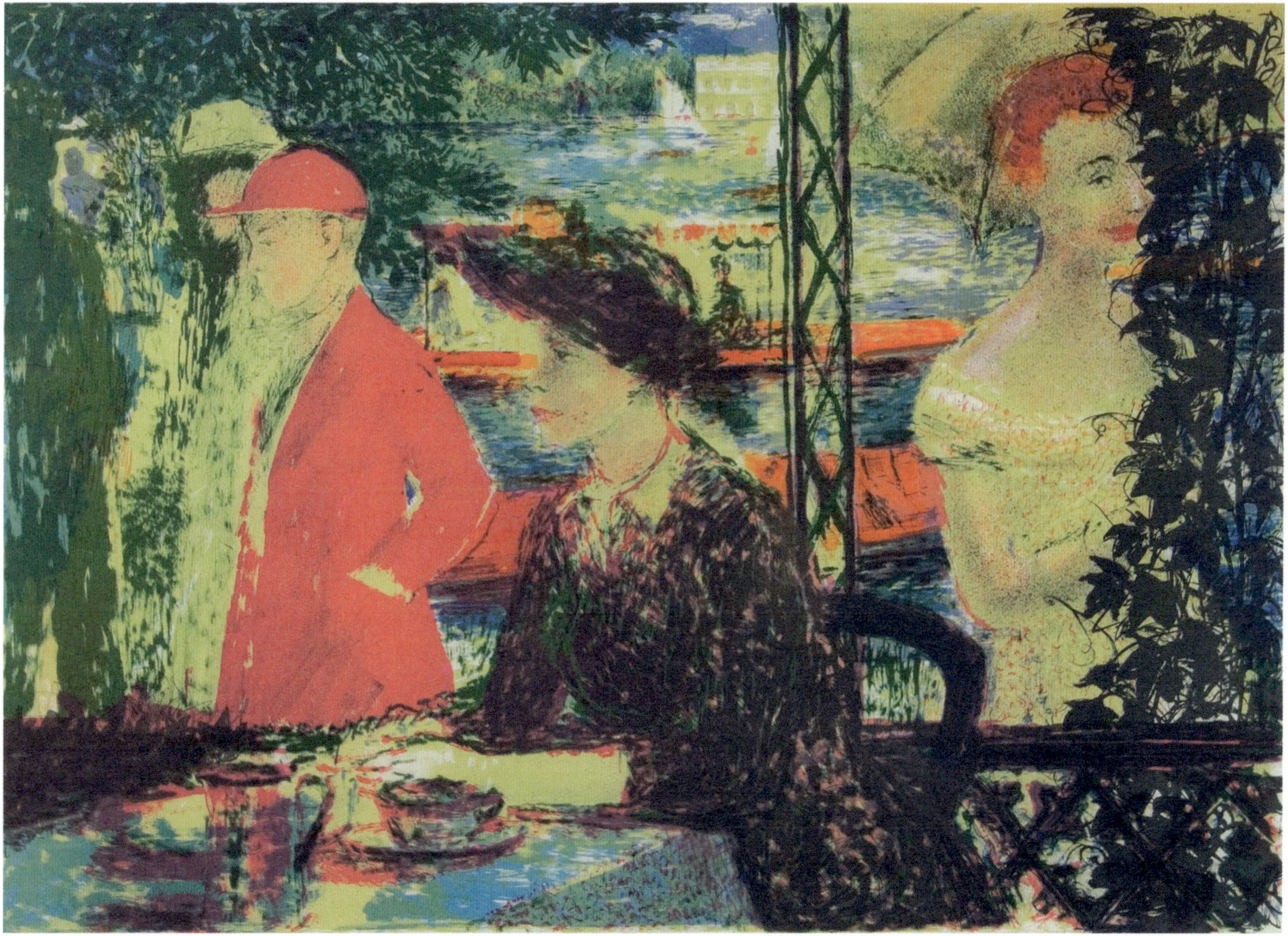

10. *River Buses at Putney Bridge*

Painted by Claude Rogers (20" x 30")

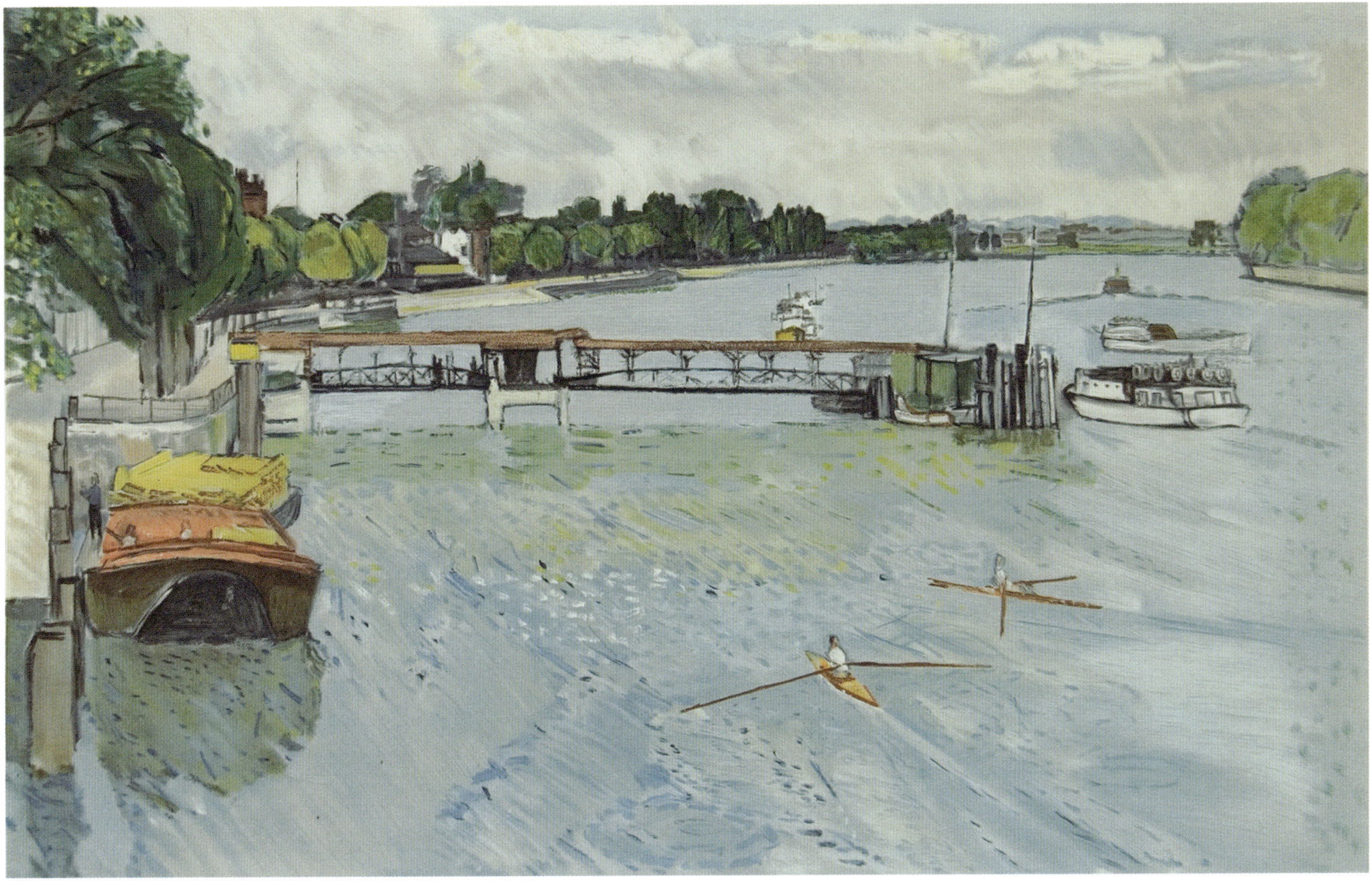

11. *Yeoman Warders*

Designed and lithographed by Robert Scanlon

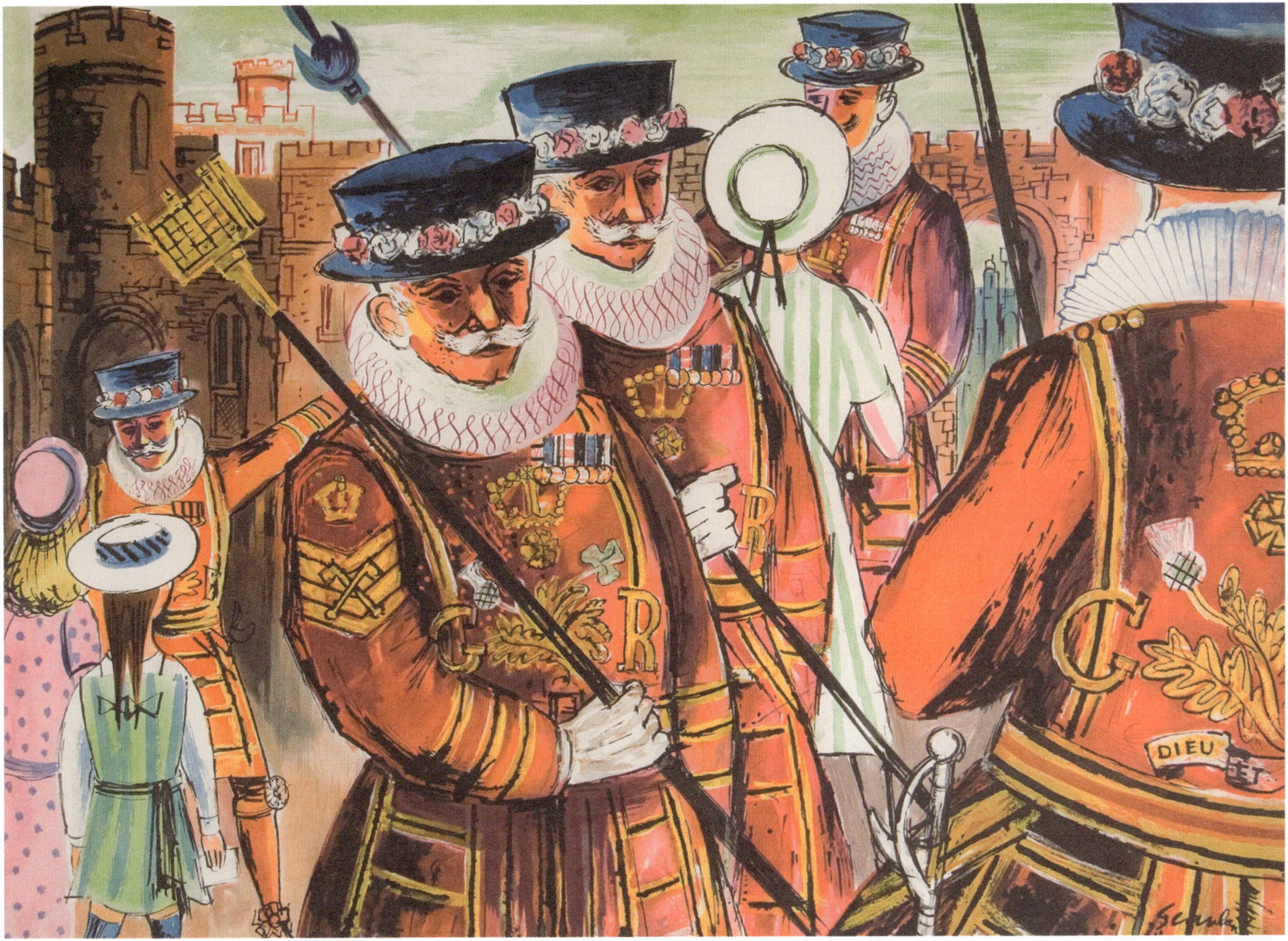
DIEU

12. The Lighthouse of St Agnes

Painted by Fred Uhlman (20" x 30")

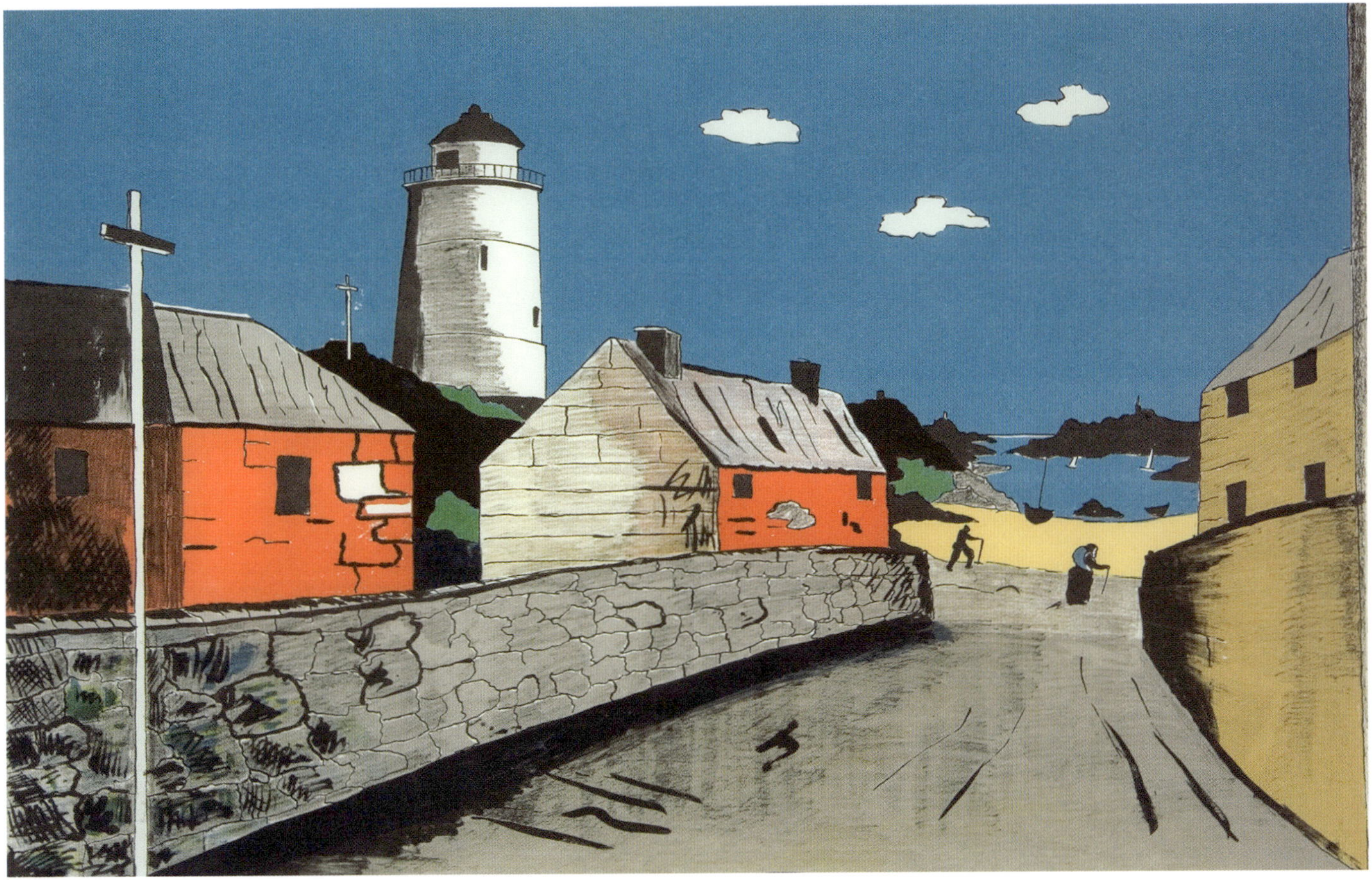

The Third Series, 1953–1955

Between 1953 and 1955 J. Lyons & Co. produced the last of their lithographs for the teashops, although there was no particular need to publish another series other than to bring the total number of prints to a rather satisfying forty.

Beddington made his first recommendations for the series in July 1953, proposing that a further twelve lithographs should be produced, a mixture of 20" x 30" and 30" x 40" prints, that the artists' fees should largely remain the same, and that a sixpence royalty should be paid as usual for every print sold.[1]

Artists and Treatment

Of the twelve artsists selected for the third series, Elinor Bellingham-Smith, David Gentleman (b. 1930), Edward Middleditch (1923-1987), John Piper and Sam Rabin (1903-1991) were new contributors to the scheme. Yet although the inclusion of Freedman, Gross and La Dell indicates that Beddington's artistic pool was becoming ever smaller, eight of the final series were auto-lithographed. This was more than in any of the previous series and reflects a conscious decision to employ artists who were already happy to use the medium and who understood what this particular job entailed. The inclusion of Piper, who was in his fifties, alongside Gentleman, who was twenty-four, demonstrates that Beddington was still determined to

1. Letter from Jack Beddington to Julian Salmon, 16 July 1953 (Barnett Freedman Archive, Manchester Metropolitan University Special Collections, FRE/1/1/251).

commission both established and emerging artists. Piper was by then an experienced practitioner, but Gentleman had only recently graduated from the Royal College of Art. *Cornish Pilchard Boat* [p. 157] was just his third lithograph, and his first 'big job'[2] as a professional artist.

With two thirds of the works being auto-lithographed, Beddington still had some leeway to include artists who, for a number of reasons, did not employ the auto-lithographic process. He asked Ayrton, for instance, to do an oil painting. This suited the artist because he was 'so pressed', and in order to create a suitable work he asked Freedman for 'any tips as to painting with litho reproduction in mind'.[3]

Although Ayrton sought this advice, *Still Life in Autumn* [p. 155] is one of the least successful of the four lithographs that were copied from a painting at the printers, owing to its sketchy treatment of detail. Likewise, *River Meadows, Pulborough* [p. 153] by Bellingham-Smith, also produced by Chromoworks from an original painting, while being a typical example of the artist's gentle style, makes for a rather 'soft' lithograph. *The River Rother at Rye* by Frith [p. 159], however, with its blocks of colour and simple composition, was translated from 'a carefully considered study'.[4]

These three works reflect the landscape theme that Beddington had loosely imposed on the series. In its depiction of a boxing match, Rabin's *Last Round* [p. 151], the other lithograph transferred at the printers, is markedly different. None the less, it is an appealing inclusion in both the series and the scheme, being similar in sentiment to Spear's less than genteel *Billiards Saloon* [p. 89] and as interesting, in terms of composition, as *The Dolls at Home* by Bawden [p. 63].

[opposite] David Gentleman, sketches from '*Mevagissey Sketchbook*', 1953. 'The sketches … were done while I was preparing to do the lithograph; though they aren't really studies for it in terms of compositions, they certainly had a bearing on it in terms of boat details and scribbles of fishermen standing around, plus the quayside buildings.' (Letter from David Gentleman to the author, 3 January 2005 (Lyons Lithograph Archive, Towner Art Gallery).)

2. David Gentleman, opening address for the exhibition *Tea and a Slice of Art – Commercial Lithographs Published by J. Lyons & Co., 1947–1955*, 24 July 2004, at the Towner Art Gallery, Eastbourne (Lyons Lithograph Archive, Towner Art Gallery). See *Appendix 2* for the full speech.

3. Letter from Michael Ayrton to Barnett Freedman, undated (Barnett Freedman Archive, Manchester Metropolitan University Special Collections, FRE/1/1/251).

4. E-mail from Clifford Frith to Ruth Artmonsky, 29 January 2005 (Lyons Lithograph Archive, Towner Art Gallery).

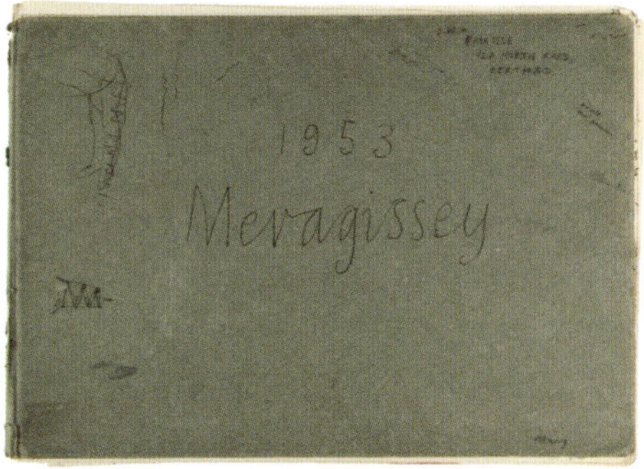
1953
Mevagissey

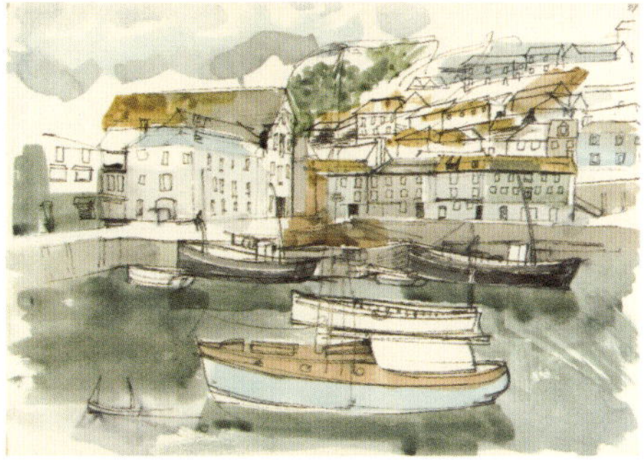

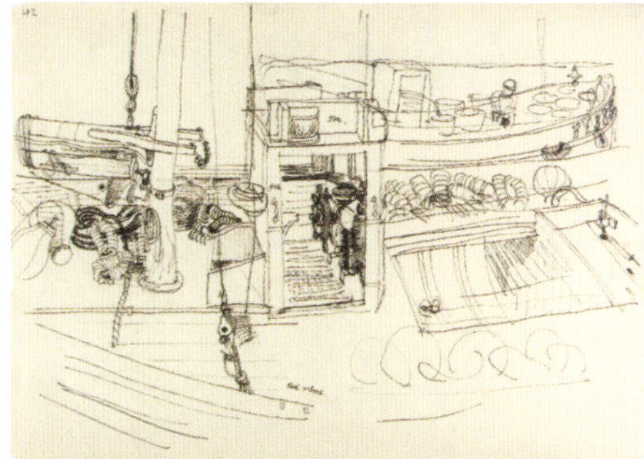

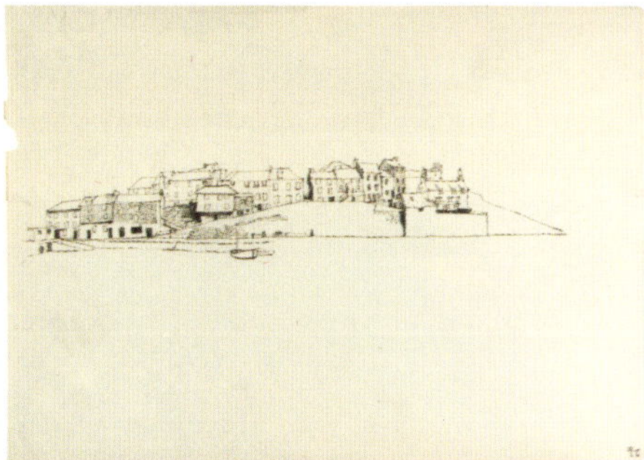

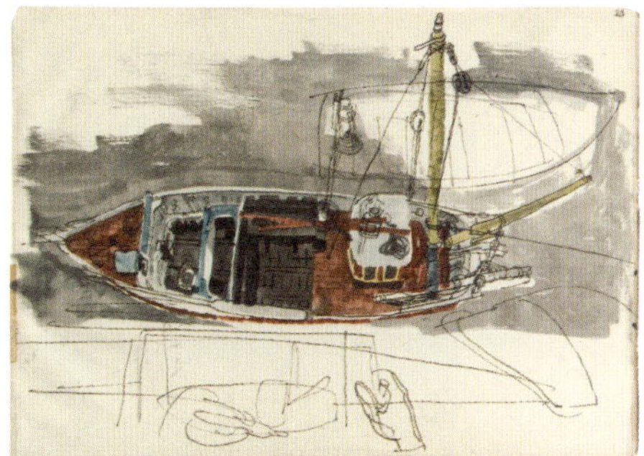

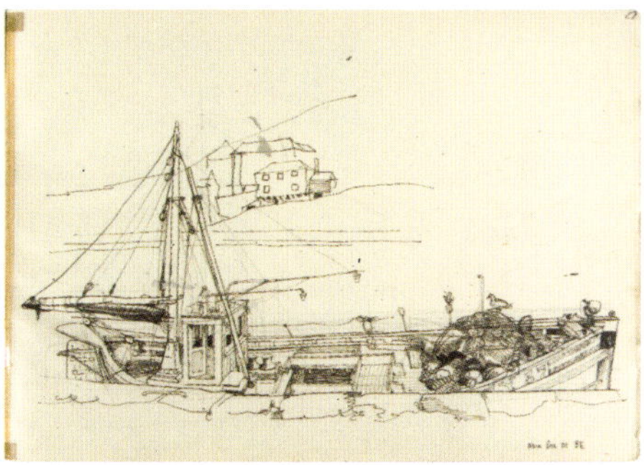

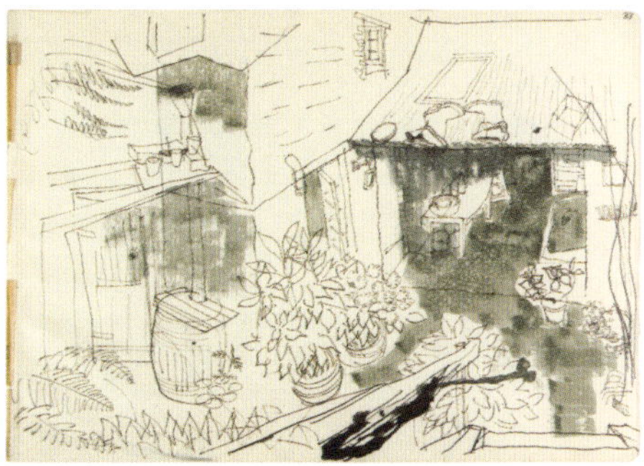

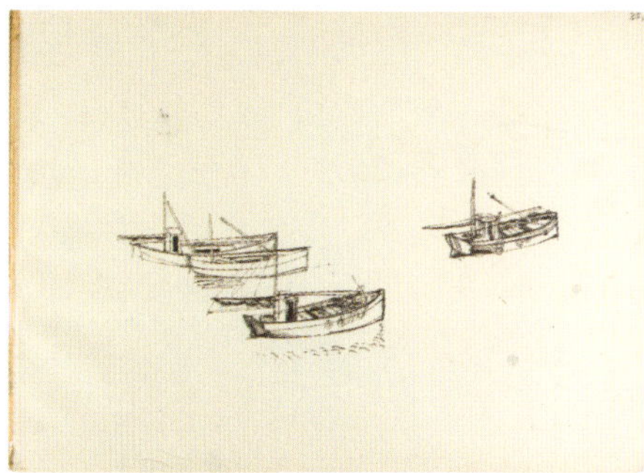

The success or otherwise of each of these four prints had little to do with Chromoworks, and depended solely on Beddington selecting, and the artists submitting, works which could function successfully both on canvas and as a lithograph. It was not just a case of direct transposition from one medium to another. Between 1953 and 1954, for instance, Freedman experimented several times in different media with the subject of figures at an open window. Choosing to re-work the idea for his third lithograph, *The Window Box* [p. 165], he modified the composition and detail to suit the medium, creating a work which Oppenheimer later said was, from a technical point of view, 'really first-class'.[5]

Incidentally, it was not a foregone conclusion that Chromoworks would print the 1955 lithographs. As the Salmons were keen to keep the cost of the series as low as possible, this time the job was also put out to tender to the Curwen Press and Vincent Brooks Ltd. Chromoworks were able to see off the competition.

5. Letter from Frank Oppenheimer to Barnett Freedman, 19 July 1954 (Barnett Freedman Archive, Manchester Metropolitan University Special Collections, no ref.).

Publicity

With the publication of the 1955 series there was a sense that the project had reached its culmination. In total, forty individual prints had been produced, and the Salmons (always keen to stress the cumulative nature of the project) chose to stage an exhibition of the three series together.

Freedman arranged the exhibition at the Tea Centre on Regent Street, and also designed a catalogue [right], poster [p. 138] and invitation for the private view [p. 139]. Beddington used his contacts to attract the attention of the great and the good; and although Kenneth Clark had made it 'an absolute rule not to open exhibitions' he was 'prepared to break a rule for an old friend'.[6]

Beddington was also quick to highlight the strengths of the scheme. Knowing, for instance, that the MP David Eccles had an interest in the Royal College of Art, he asked him to write a foreword for the catalogue, pointing out that 'many of the artists were there or are now … teachers and professors there'.[7] The foreword was, however, eventually written by the art critic and curator James Laver, who stated that the lithographs represented a 'real picture-gallery for Everyman'.[8]

Beddington ensured that the exhibition received attention in the press, and favourable reviews appeared in a wide variety of publications. The *Jewish Chronicle*, for example, declared the exhibition would 'do more good than any Bond Street

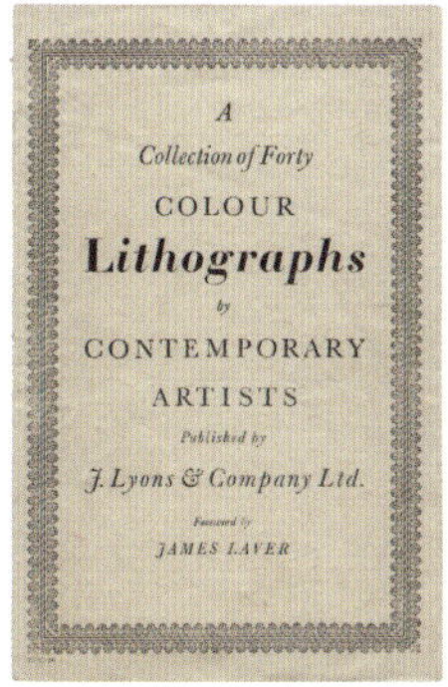

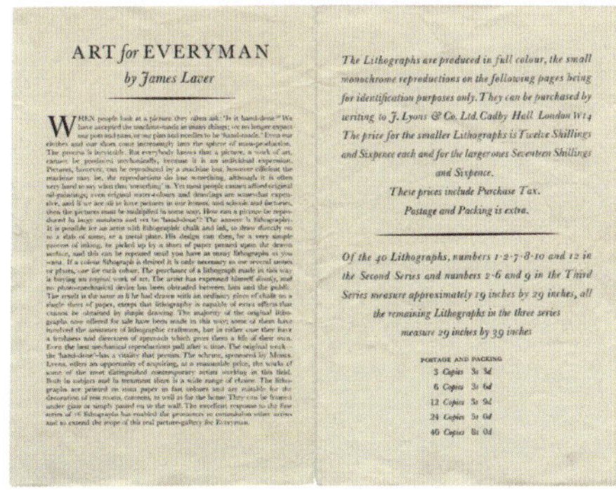

The front cover and interior of the 1955 exhibition catalogue.

6. Letter from Kenneth Clark to Jack Beddington, 10 November 1954 (Barnett Freedman Archive, Manchester Metropolitan University Special Collections, FRE/1/1/251).
7. Letter from Jack Beddington to David Eccles, MP, 23 November 1954 (Barnett Freedman Archive, Manchester Metropolitan University Special Collections, FRE/1/1/251).
8. J. Laver, Foreword to *A Collection of Forty Colour Lithographs by Contemporary Artists* (London, J. Lyons & Co., 1955), p. 1.

show … open during working hours',[9] and the *Scotsman* stated that, 'This kind of cooperation between large concerns and the crowded world of artists is admirable. It introduces art to a public which seldom ventures into the art galleries of London.'[10]

Appreciative reviews also appeared in the specialist art press, with Pierre Rouve decisively concluding in *Art News & Review* that 'the informal atmosphere of a tea shop is much more effective than the solemn impressiveness of the museums.'[11]

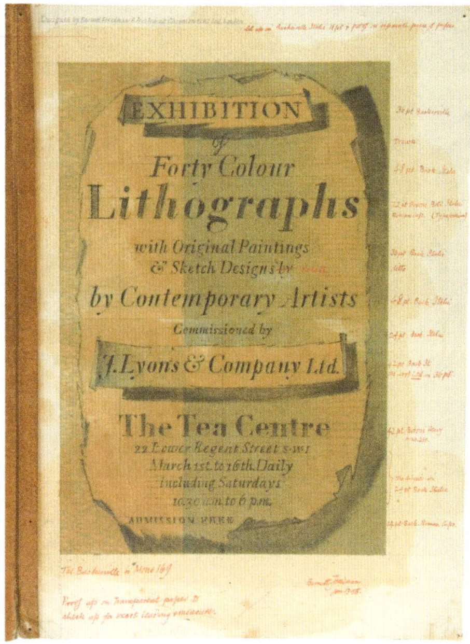

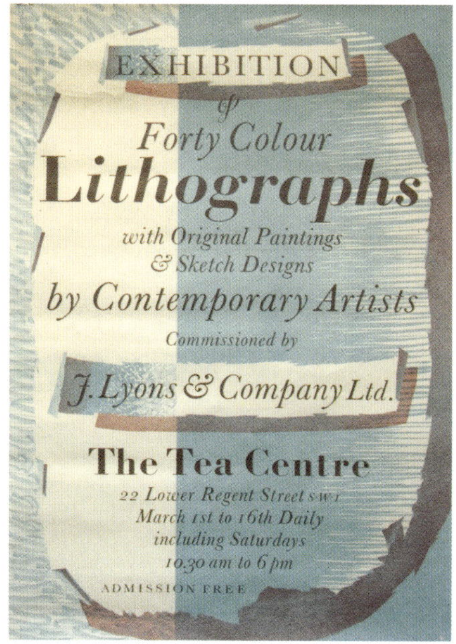

[right] Original design for the 1955 exhibition poster, showing Barnett Freedman's hand-written annotations.

[far right] The 1955 exhibition poster.

9. *Jewish Chronicle*, 11 March 1955 (J. Lyons & Co. Archive at the London Metropolitan Archives, ACC/3527).
10. *Scotsman*, 2 March 1955 (J. Lyons & Co. Archive at the London Metropolitan Archives, ACC/3527).
11. *Art News & Review*, 5 March 1955 (J. Lyons & Co. Archive at the London Metropolitan Archives, ACC/3527).

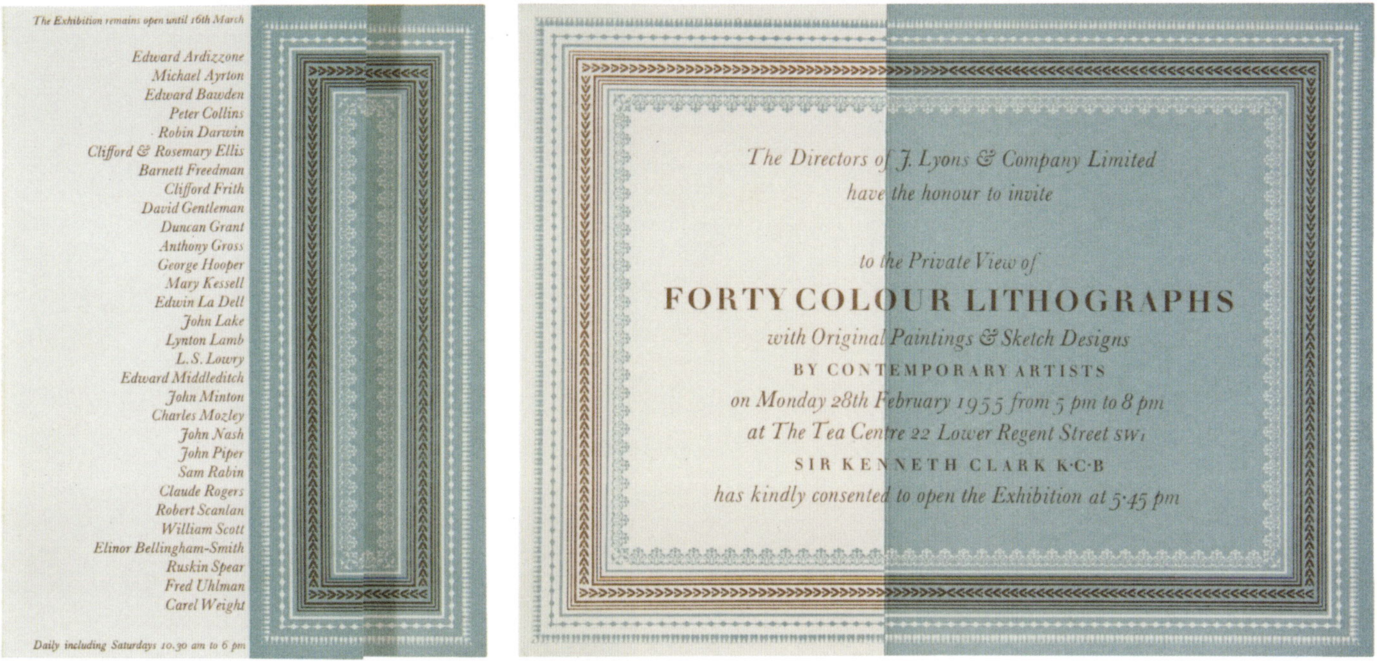

Invitation to the private view of the 1955 exhibition at the Tea Centre.

The Lyons Lithographs - Third Series

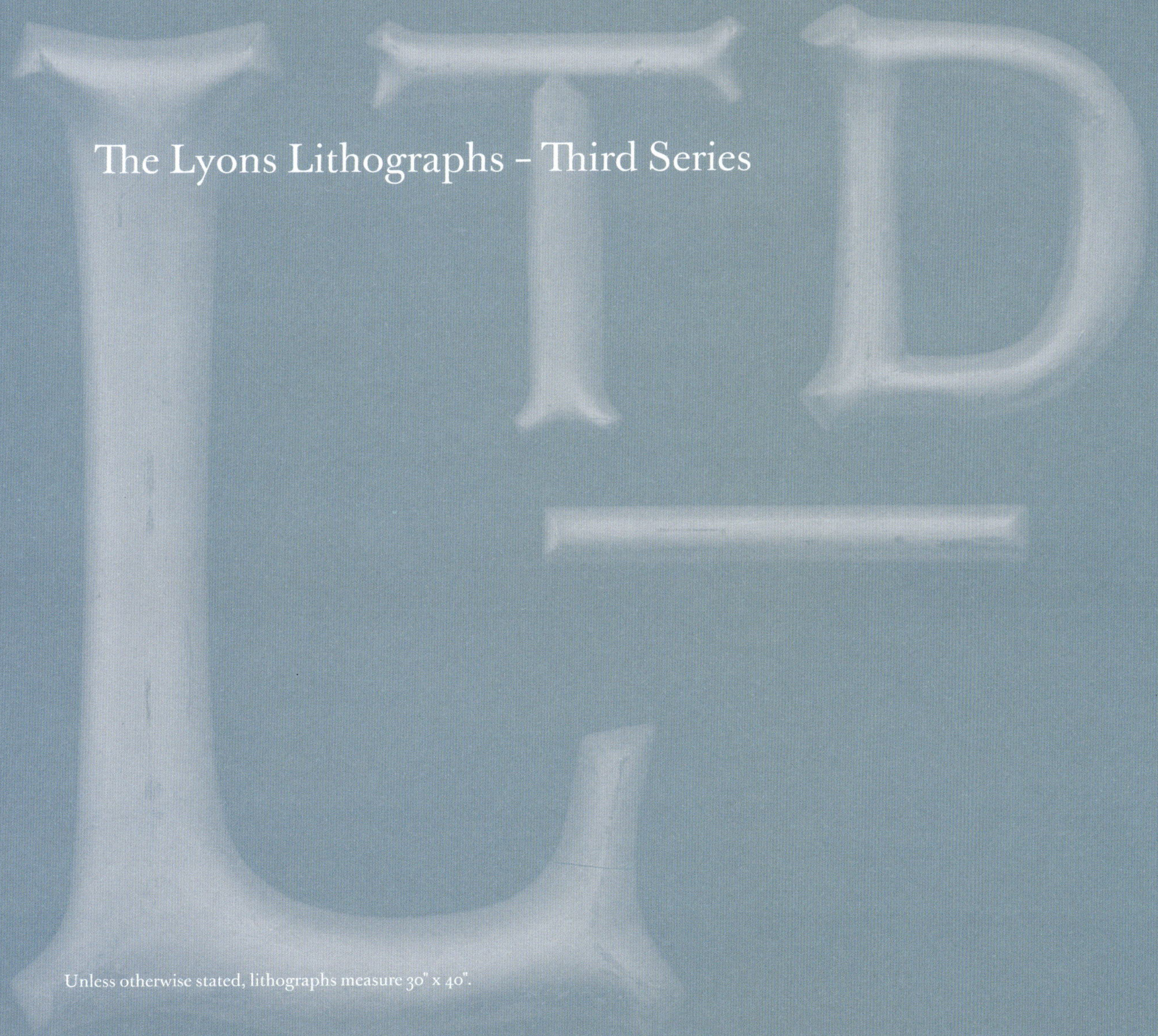

Unless otherwise stated, lithographs measure 30" x 40".

1. Shopping at Mysore

Designed and lithographed by Edward Ardizzone

In November 1952, Ardizzone embarked on a six-month visit to India, spending three months in Delhi and three months in Bombay. He had been invited by UNESCO to take part in their 'Seminar for the Production of Audio-Visual Aids for Fundamental Education'. Throughout the trip he kept a written and illustrated diary, in which he refers to making trips to Mysore to shop and eat. On 2 April 1953, for example, he states, 'Most of the day spent in Mysore shopping, on the whole successfully.'*

* Edward Ardizzone, *Indian Diary 1952–53* (London, The Bodley Head, 1984), p. 128.

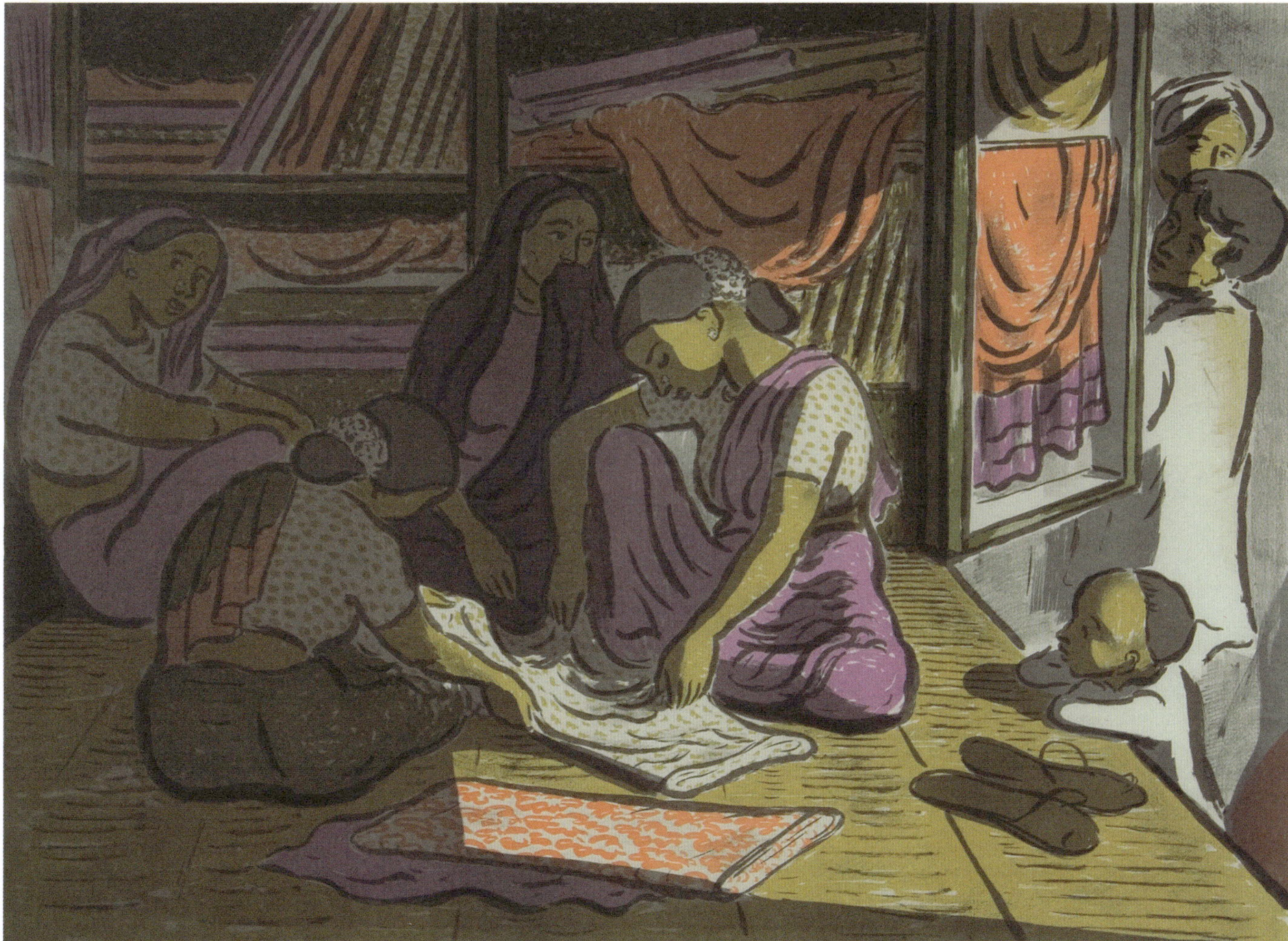

2. *Louisiana Landscape*

Designed and lithographed by Anthony Gross (20" x 30")

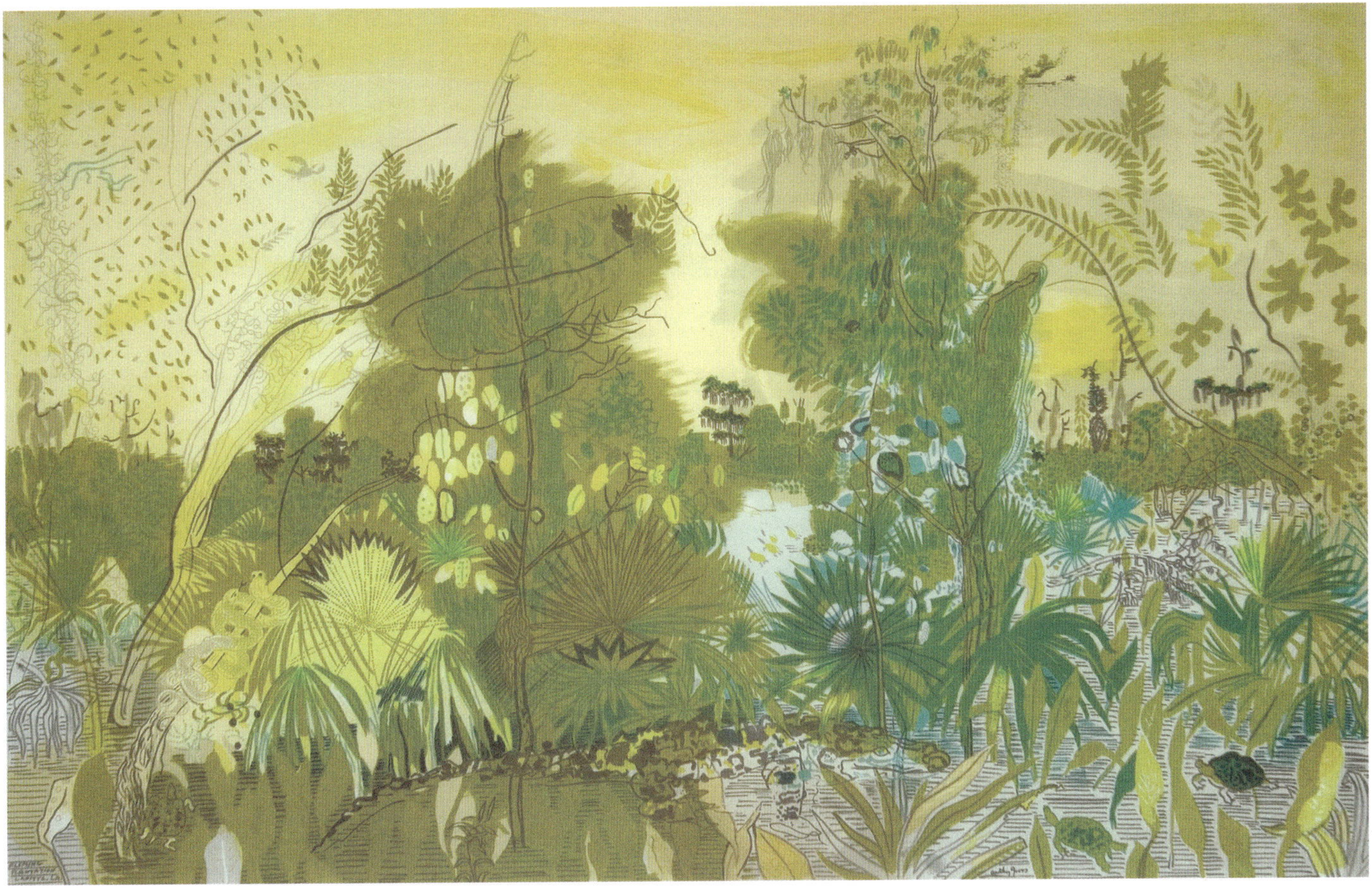

3. Trees, Kensington Gardens

Designed and lithographed by Edward Middleditch

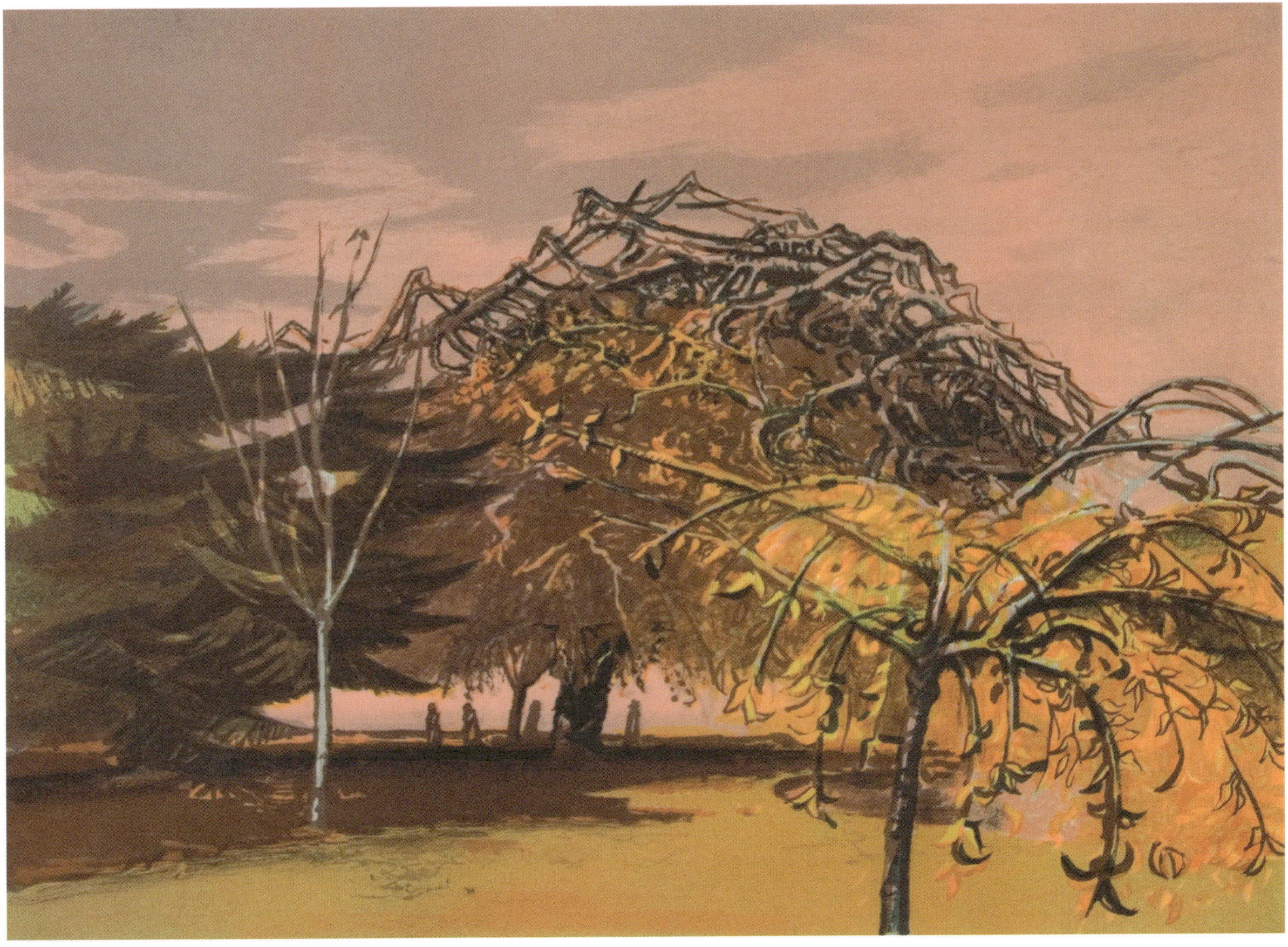

4. Clare Bridge, Cambridge

Designed and lithographed by Edwin La Dell

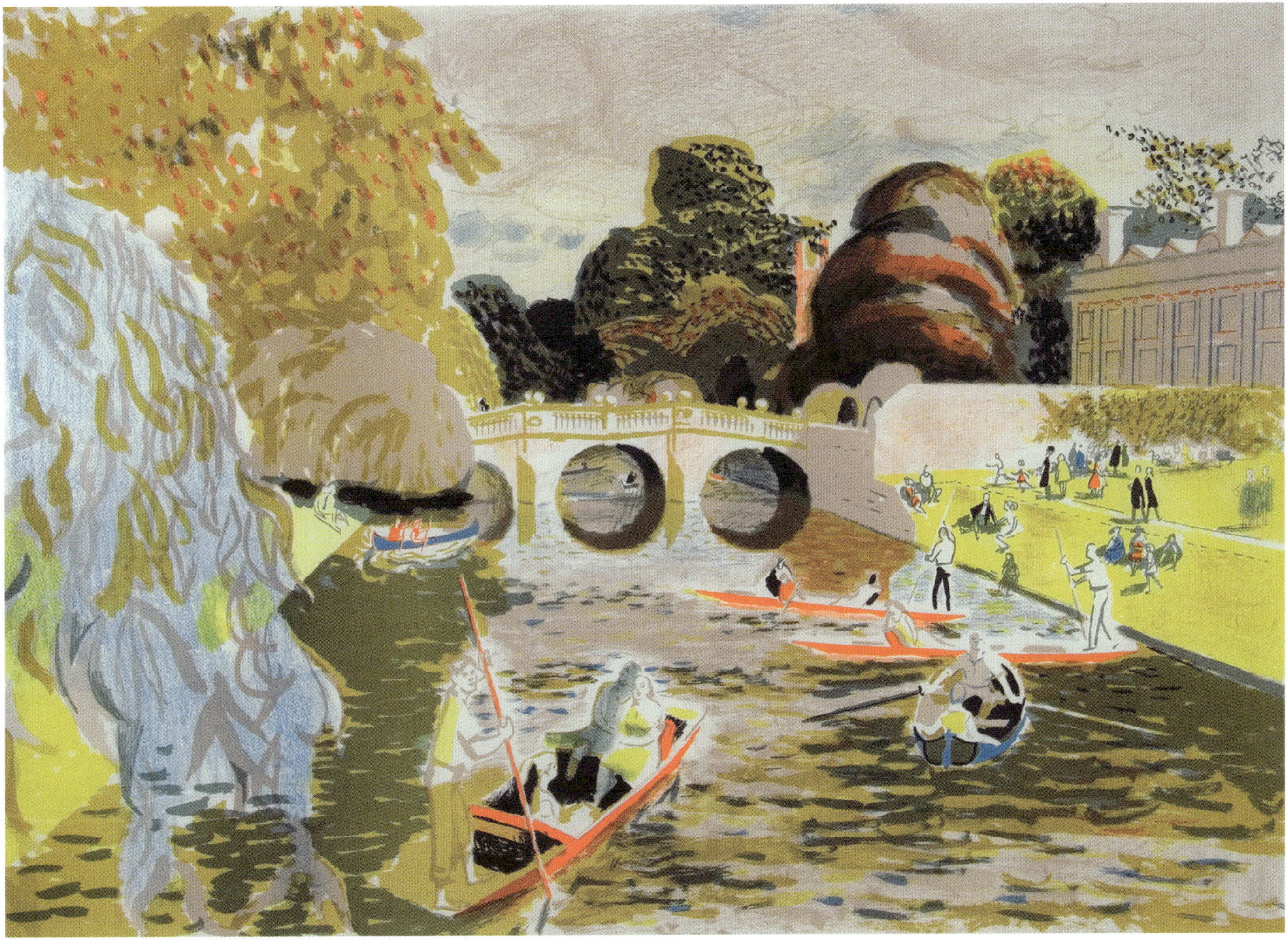

5. *Last Round*

Painted by Sam Rabin

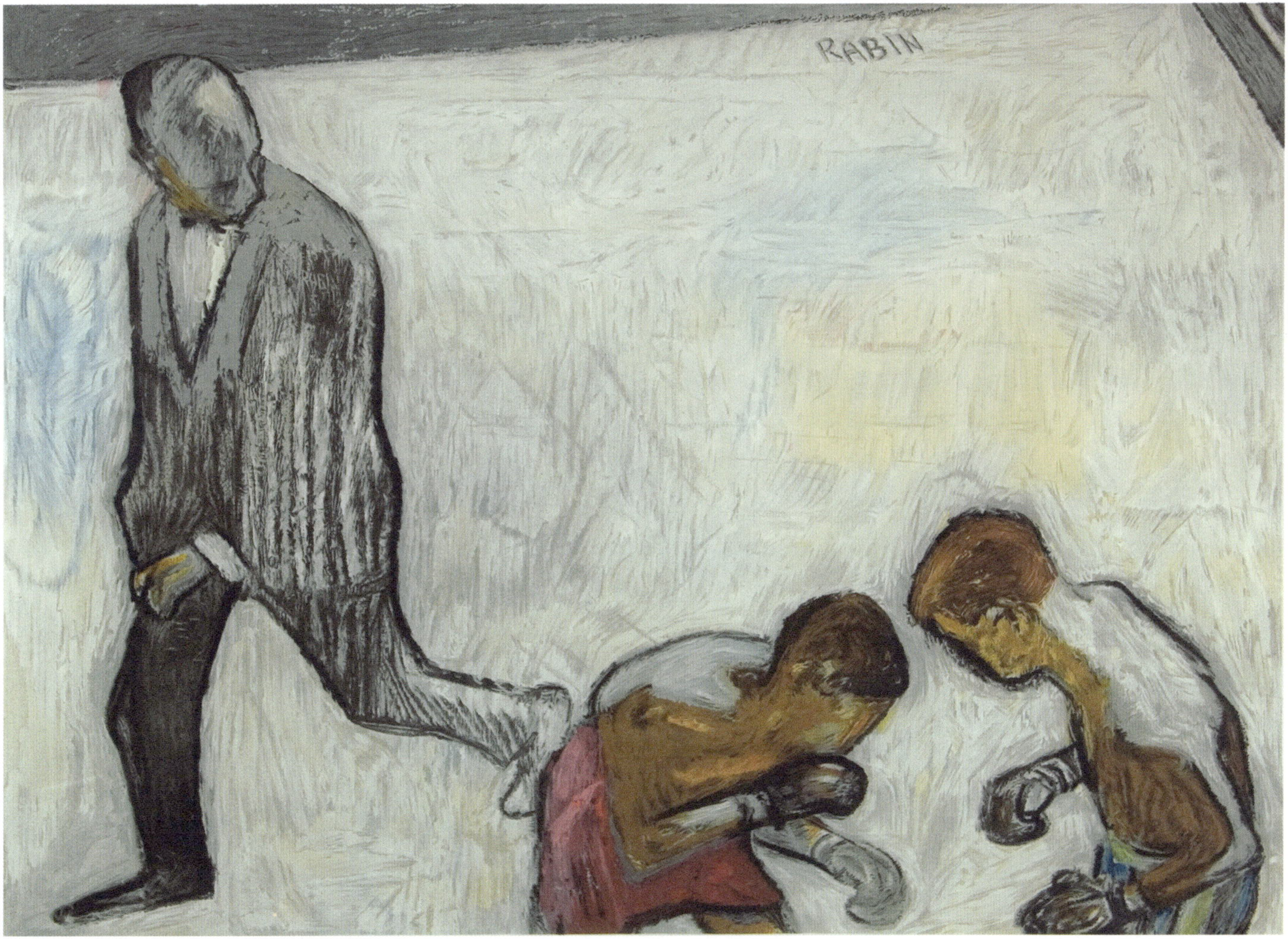
RABIN

6. River Meadows, Pulborough

Painted by Elinor Bellingham-Smith (20" x 30")

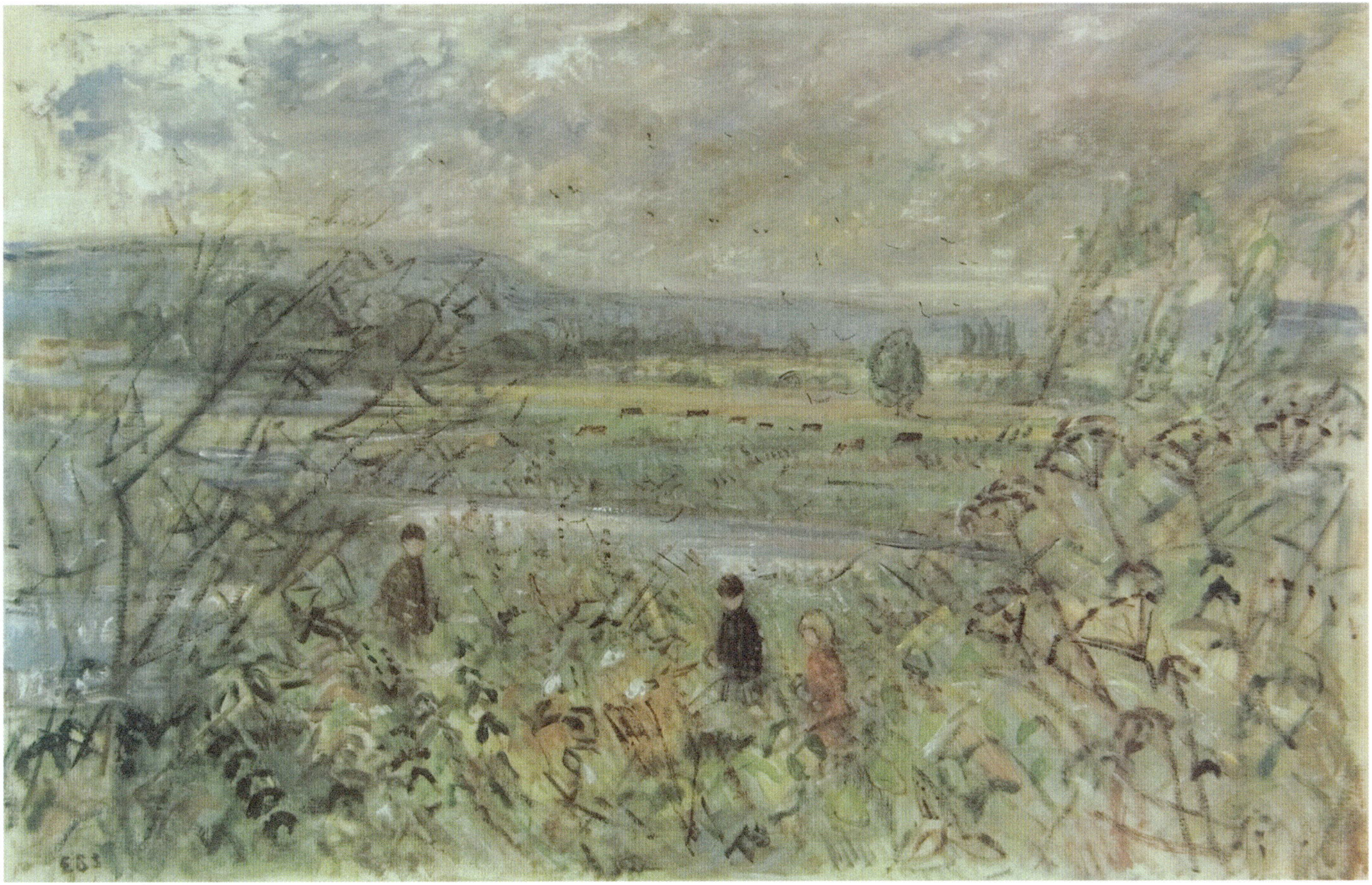

7. Still Life in Autumn

Painted by Michael Ayrton

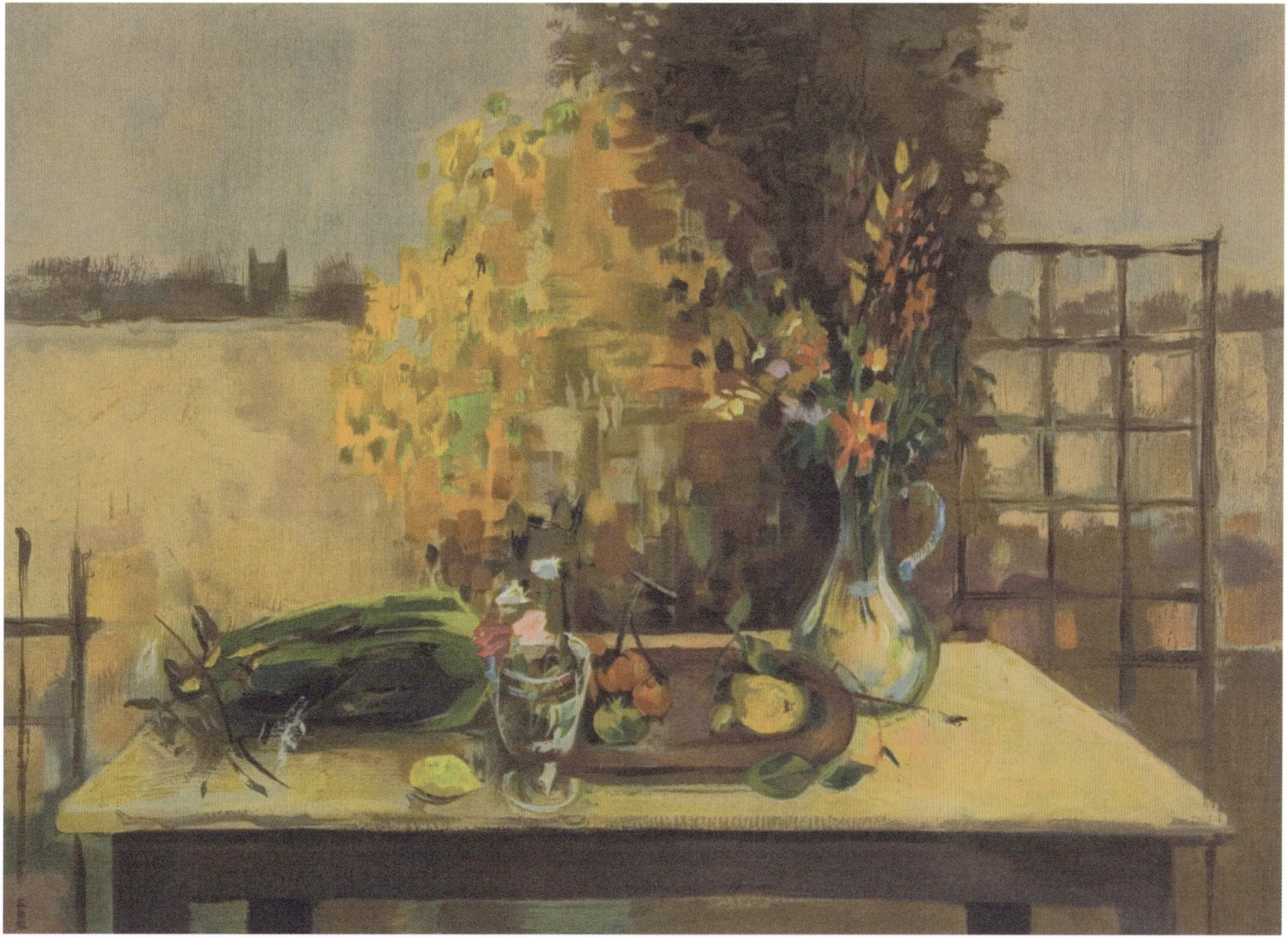

8. Cornish Pilchard Boat

Designed and lithographed by David Gentleman

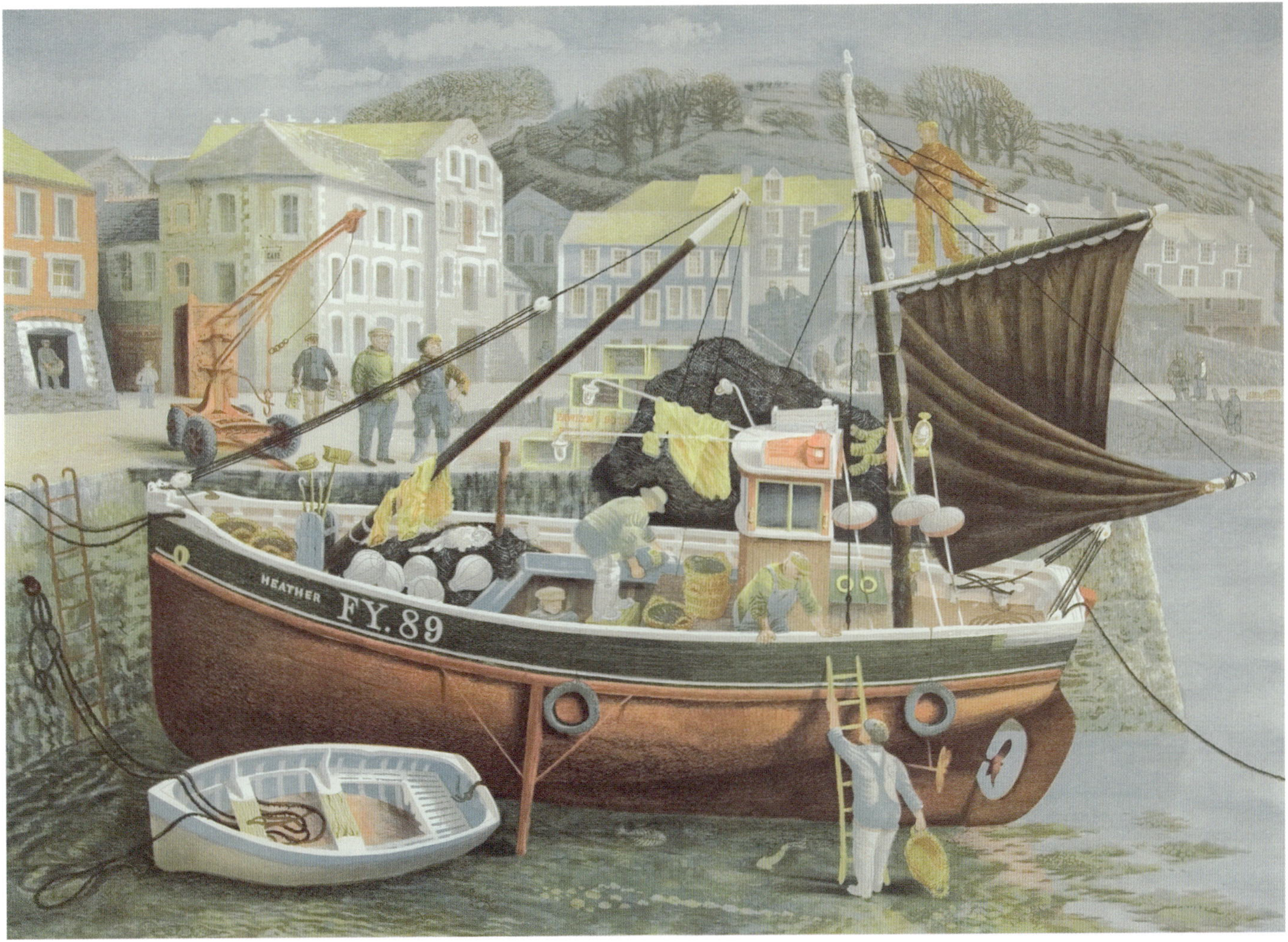
HEATHER
FY. 89

9. The River Rother at Rye

Painted by Clifford Frith (20" x 30")

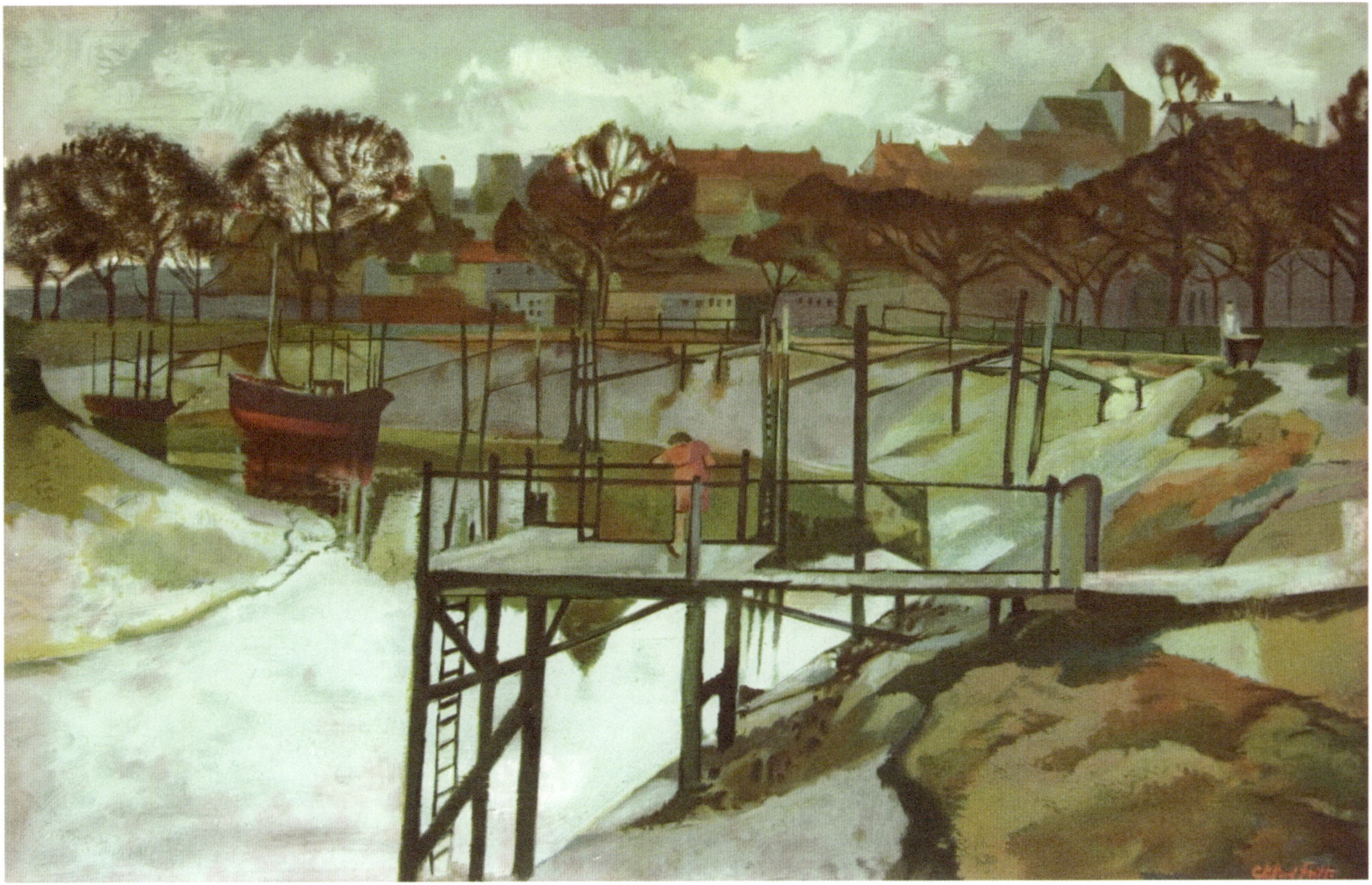

10. Children's Music

Designed and lithographed by Charles Mozley

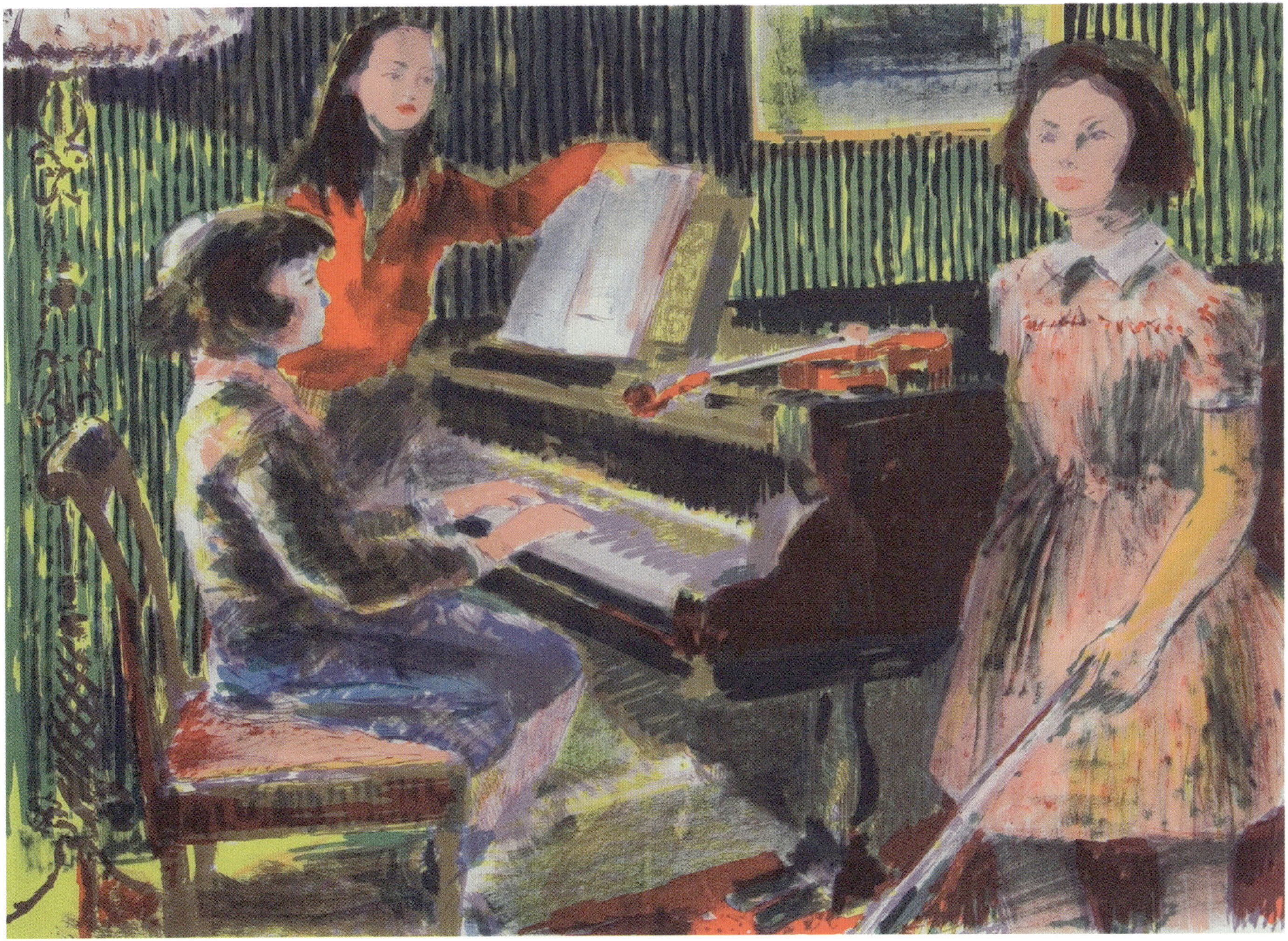

11. *Elizabethan Dance*

Designed and lithographed by John Piper

In 1953 Piper designed the stage sets and costumes for Benjamin Britten's new opera *Gloriana*, a work examining the relationship between Elizabeth I and the Earl of Essex, which was commissioned to mark the forthcoming coronation of Elizabeth II. This image thus draws heavily on those theatrical designs.

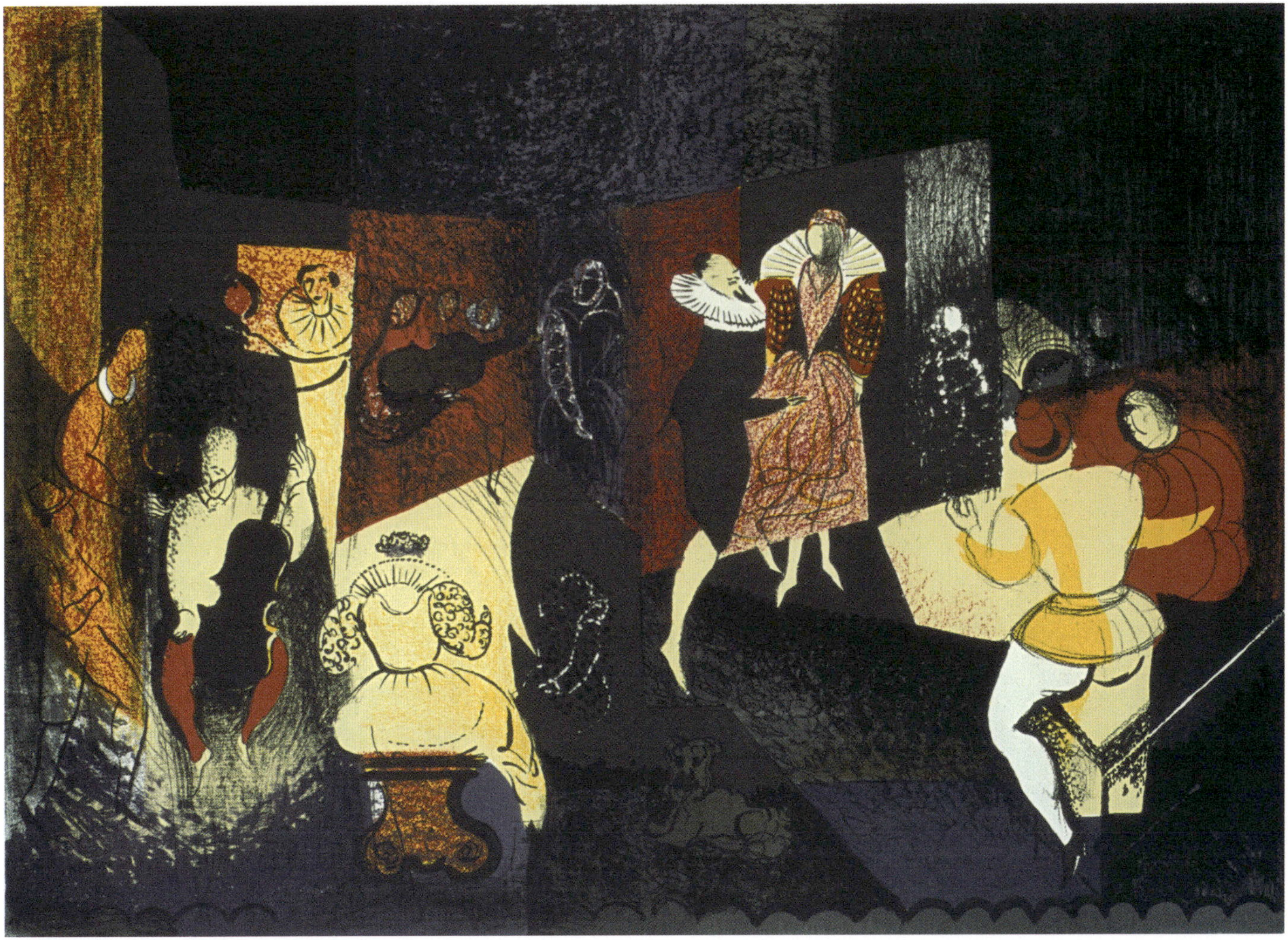

12. *The Window Box*

Designed and lithographed by Barnett Freedman

The two girls pictured in this print are actually Mozley's daughters, Elizabeth and Juliet. The girls also appear in *Children's Music* - Mozley's own auto-lithograph for the third series.

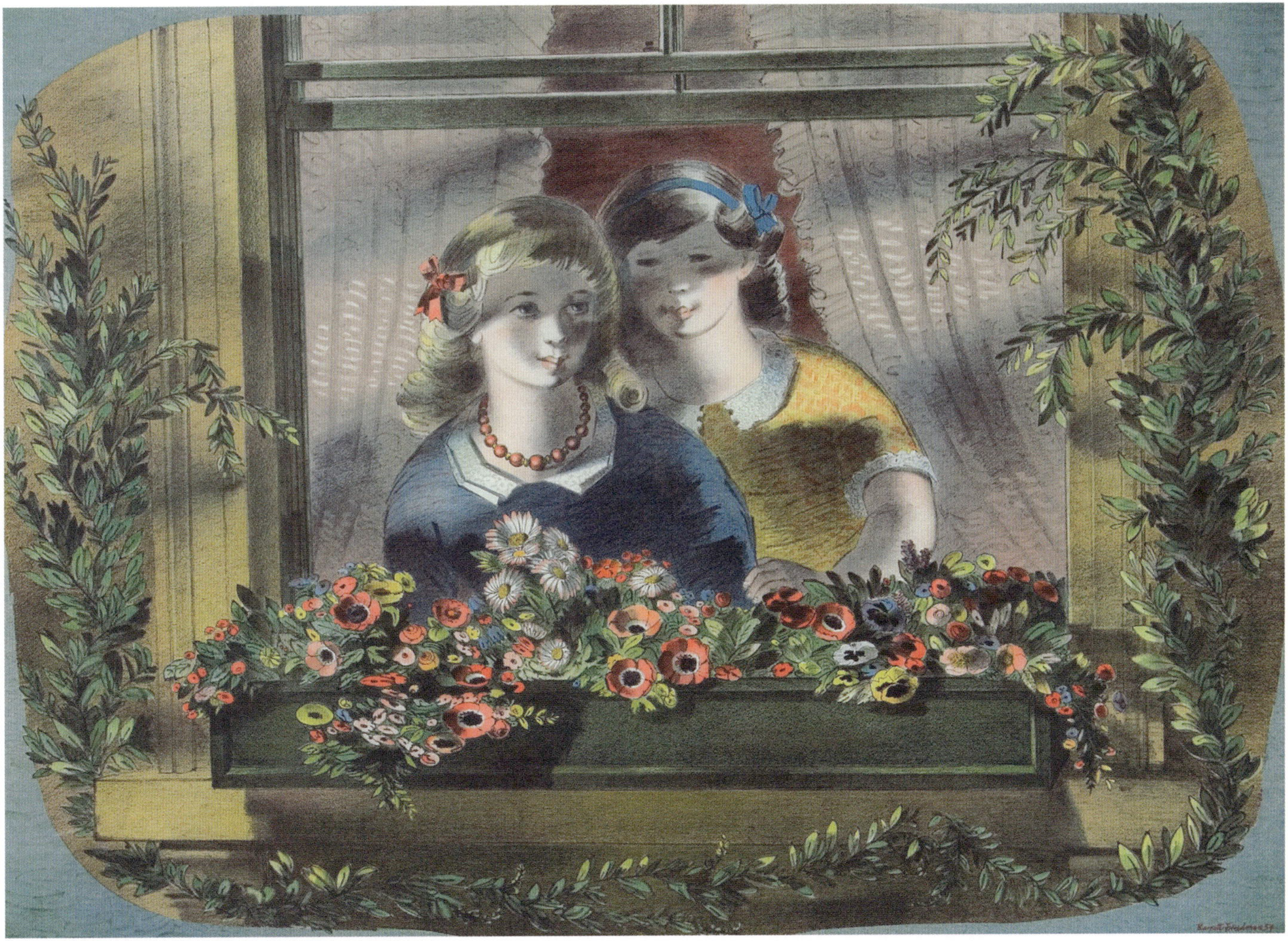

The Aftermath

The Lyons lithographs were displayed continuously in the teashops until the cafés closed in the 1960s, although by that time long-term exposure had somewhat blunted their impact and their familiarity had, for the public at large, reduced them to mere wallpaper. Copies also remained on show alongside the originals in the Lyons headquarters at Cadby Hall in Hammersmith.

In 1974 the company decided to dispose of their collection. Some of the originals, including *Music – Still Life* and *Herne Bay Pier* were purchased by the directors, but most, including *The Dolls at Home* and *The Bird Cage*, were sold at a Christie's auction of 'Modern British Paintings, Drawings and Sculpture' on 28 February 1975.

In June 1977, the South London Art Gallery staged an exhibition of *The Lyons Restaurant Lithographs* to mark the thirtieth anniversary of their first appearance and to recognise 'one of the most enterprising examples of patronage in British art in recent years'.[1] For this, a number of the originals were displayed alongside the lithographs, because, just as the Salmons had once felt, the gallery believed the exhibition would be considerably enhanced by their juxtaposition.

After the exhibition, in 1981 tentative plans were made to produce special editions of Spear's *Billiards Saloon* and Ardizzone's *The Railway Station* at Chromoworks. The following year it was reported that Lyons still held copies of the 1947–55 lithographs but the subsequent disposal of these finally brought the scheme to an end for the company.

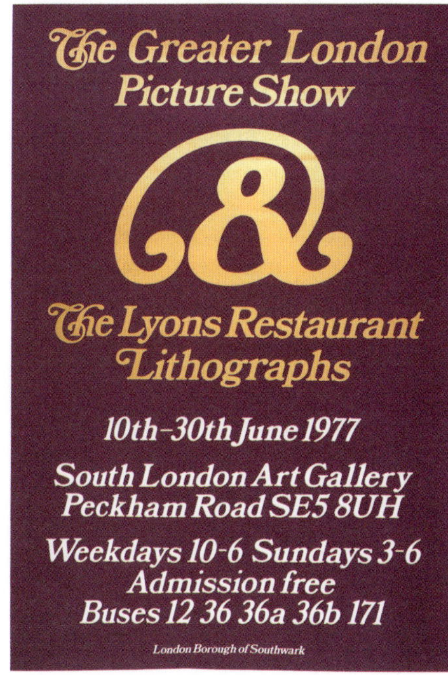

The poster for the exhibition at the South London Art Gallery, June 1977.

1. Letter from South London Art Gallery to J. Lyons & Co., 1977 (J. Lyons & Co. Archive at the London Metropolitan Archives, ACC/3527/245).

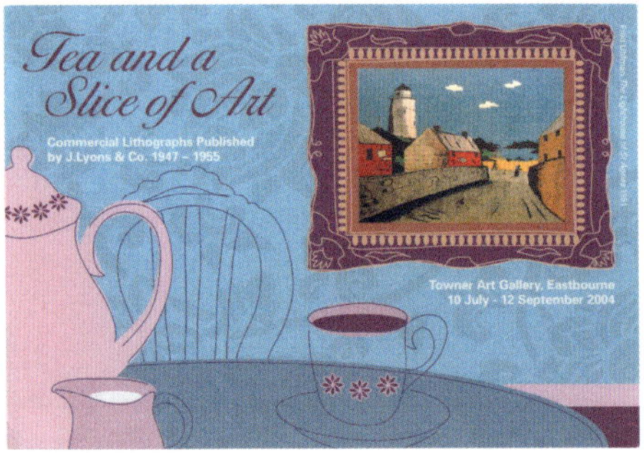

A flyer for *Tea and a Slice of Art*.

In 1988 complete sets of the first two series were donated to the British Museum by a former Lyons employee. Scholarly articles about the subject appeared in journals such as *Antique Collecting* (1993) and *Matrix* (1999). It is thought that the teashop prints were then not seen *en masse* in a public setting until the Towner Art Gallery staged *Tea and a Slice of Art* in 2004.

Beyond this, the prints have long since been consigned to the dark recesses of people's attics or have simply been lost. Occasional flurries of interest have brought copies onto the commercial market, but despite the prints being produced in fairly large editions, it is difficult to know just how many survive.

What have survived, however, are people's memories of the lithographs, hanging not only in the teashops but in their own homes. One reader of *The Times*, for example, wrote,

> The Stygian basement of our Victorian house ... was transformed by these lithographs - *Fishing at Marlow* with its marvellous greens lit up the passage, we played music under Barnett Freedman's *Music - Still Life*, cooked under the *Trees, Kensington Gardens* and shared our living room with one of Lowry's delightful industrial scenes.[2]

Despite positive statements like this, it is almost impossible to measure the success of the Lyons lithographs. Without doubt, the prints did brighten up the teashops, and customers described the enterprise as 'a life-enhancing experience within reach of all'.[3] To that extent, at least, J. Lyons & Co. achieved what they had set out to do.

2. Letter from J. Plowman to *The Times*, 16 August 2004, p. 17.
3. ibid.

'An Eyeful As Well As a Mouthful'

Between 1946 and 1955 J. Lyons & Co. developed and realised an artistic enterprise which produced forty decorative lithographs; quite an achievement at a time of widespread austerity, and a substantial return on what was originally just an ambitious idea discussed between acquaintances over lunch.

However, despite the fact that a number of significant British artists and respected professionals were involved with the project, it has taken some time for the teashop scheme to be recognised as a fascinating instance of well-organised corporate patronage and, perhaps more importantly, as a notable example of post-war British printmaking. There are a number of reasons for this, but close physical study of the prints can only have been hampered, rather than encouraged, by the fact that the majority of the lithographs which were once displayed in the teashops were discarded, and thus lost, when the cafés closed.

Perspicacious thinking by the Salmons (and by Julian in particular) meant that copies of the lithographs have, of course, found their way into a number of public and private collections. However, while this has ensured that examples of the prints have been preserved, few organisations or individuals hold complete sets of forty, and without these it is difficult to grasp the full scale and scope of the scheme.

Further to this, because the lithographs were often treated as ephemeral objects and pinned directly to the wall, copies which have come to light are frequently in some state of disrepair. Others have also been trimmed and no longer bear the imprint on the bottom edge, and this must have hindered the identification and correct attribution of the prints on more than one occasion.

Even J. Lyons & Co. themselves only retained a handful of copies of each work, and while a diligent company archivist did, in later years, gather together some relevant information about the scheme, no 'official' document offering the firm's perspective on the project was ever published. It was perhaps felt that the prints, exhibitions and catalogues were record enough, but it did mean that when the enterprise came to an end many of the finer details were forgotten.

A complete set of the prints once owned by the company are now held at the London Metropolitan Archive (LMA), along with an assortment of letters, memos and other documentation relating to the scheme. Yet, unlike Shell and London Transport, which continue to fund archives with a remit to research and promote the substantial volume of art they once commissioned, given the 'one-off' nature of the teashop project, until recently no such provision had been made for the Lyons lithographs.[4] The LMA copies are, therefore, just one inclusion in a larger body of information about J. Lyons & Co. and, as such, it is easy to understand why they have often been overlooked, rather than embraced as the results of an interesting and self-contained enterprise which successfully took the firm beyond their usual field of operation.

Publishing a series of fine art prints was, of course, an unusual activity for the company to undertake, but it is not surprising that they actually achieved what they set out to do, and with some panache. They had, after all, always possessed a 'can-do' approach to business and were in a position to employ leading professionals to deliver a quality product on their behalf. With the likes of Beddington and Freedman working on the project, it is then both interesting and important to note just what an active role the Salmons chose to play, as patrons, in the development of the scheme.

4. Since 2004 'The Lyons Lithograph Archive' has been steadily building alongside the Towner Collection. As well as original examples of all three exhibition catalogues and various other documentation, at the time of writing the archive holds copies of all but four of the lithographs, and there are serious ambitions to complete the set.

As directors of the company, it was natural for Felix and Julian to want to keep a tight reign on the project, in order to protect the established commercial interests of the teashops. It is, therefore, not surprising that they did not let George Hooper depict the workings of a pub in his 1947 lithograph; an 'error' that was more to do with Beddington's initial image selection than a lack of judgement by Hooper. However, while this action is not overly significant in itself, it did represent the first (but not the last) time the Salmons exerted demonstrable and significant editorial influence on the scheme.

The Lyons lithographs were certainly not overt commercial advertising in the same vein as the graphic posters produced by companies such as Shell-Mex or the General Post Office. Yet because Julian so fiercely sought to market the second series of teashop prints, the scheme quickly became a vehicle for the visible promotion of not only J. Lyons & Co. 'the corporate patron', but of J. Lyons & Co. 'the brand', making the lithographs no longer just decorative objects but strategic tools.

If the first series was defined by the technical expertise of Barnett Freedman, genuine altruism and a sense of controlled accident and experimentation, in sharp contrast, the second series was consciously published to coincide with the Festival of Britain and organised to achieve maximum corporate gain. Beddington and Freedman, of course, continued to carry out their respective roles, but in truth no one had a greater effect on the development and dissemination of the 1951 series than Julian himself. This influence was, in a number of ways, far less pronounced in the 1955 series, because, with eight of the twelve prints being auto-lithographed, it was this, and the artists themselves, which really defined the third and final series.

By so actively promoting their artistic enterprise the Salmons thus clearly wanted to personally ensure that the prints had a presence beyond the teashops, although, in reality, it was Jack Beddington who actually wove the artists, the subjects and the three series together and made the enterprise a credible stand-alone creative project.

In spite of this, as an artistic publishing scheme, the Lyons lithographs are a somewhat curious entity, being neither an absolute ally of the posters published by other commercial giants, nor a carbon copy of the prints produced for any of the other so called 'Art By Stealth'[5] schemes, such as *School Prints*. None of these schemes were, for example, sustained for particularly lengthy periods, because of problems with the supply of paper, distribution and consumer demand; but because the Lyons prints were always destined for the teashops (despite whatever other ambitions the Salmons may have had for them), distribution was never a particular problem. The supply of paper eased with the publication of each series and public demand for copies was something of a bonus, rather than an absolute necessity. Yet it is perhaps only because research and knowledge about the characteristics and role of these other, more commercial schemes has emerged first that the Lyons lithographs have been able to find a life outside of the teashops, a role beyond decoration and a place in the history of British printmaking.

With the scheme thus free of the shackles that brought about the demise of other similar undertakings, the teashop lithographs could never actually have been a failure (commercial or otherwise), but, even with this safety-net, it is difficult to know just how the artists initially responded to being commissioned to design a print for the Lyons teashops. In truth, few of the published prints can be judged as 'works on which reputations hang'[6] and, as a consequence, 'the job' is very often not discussed at any length in the wider context of the artists' creative output. Nevertheless, the scheme did unite the work of a number of significant and versatile professional artists who were working in post-war Britain, and, as David Gentleman remembers, overall the undertaking was regarded as,

5. P. Clayton, 'Joe's Arts', *Sunday Telegraph*, 12 June 1977, p. 15 (J. Lyons & Co. Archive at the London Metropolitan Archives, ACC/3527/245).
6. P. Rennie, 'The Lyons Lithographs', *Antique Collecting*, April 1993, p. 16.

> a lively and imaginative venture – a bit of enlightened patronage, more in the honourable tradition of the pre-war London Transport than of the ad agency, giving people of all sorts something decent to look at as they spooned up their bowls of tomato soup or ate vast platefuls from the Salad Bowl counter or drank their cups of Lyons tea. I'm glad I was one of the artists involved.[7]

While much has been made of the Salmons and their desire to attach various corporate agendas to the lithographs, it is important to emphasise that the company did genuinely want to offer worthwhile support for British artists through the scheme, their respect for the professional status of those commissioned perhaps being best reflected in the decision to pay generous fees as well as royalties for every print that was sold.

In the period immediately after the Second World War, lavishing both time and money on an artistic project, in many ways, seems somewhat incongruous with the pressing concerns of the time. Indeed, when looking at the gentle scenes of fun fairs and people fishing which are captured in the teashop lithographs, it is difficult to perceive that they were created when Britain was recovering from a war, locked in a substantial programme of physical, economic and social rebuilding.

Aesthetically, the teashop prints thus do have something of a timeless quality although, inversely, the scheme itself is actually a pertinent document of the times in which it was conceived. The introduction of new trends from Europe and America coupled with events such as the Festival of Britain, for instance, all helped to boost the morale and invigorate the visual tastes of an increasingly consumer-orientated society, and this made hanging artist-designed prints in the teashops and offering them for sale an altogether acceptable, rather than outlandish,

7. David Gentleman, opening address for the exhibition *Tea and a Slice of Art – Commercial Lithographs Published by J. Lyons & Co. 1947–1955*, 24 July 2004, at the Towner Art Gallery, Eastbourne. (See Appendix 2.)

practice. Likewise, the horizons of the British art world were beginning to change, and while exhibitions of often controversial work by European and American artists, such as those staged at the Institute of Contemporary Art and the Whitechapel Art Gallery, did not have a particularly noticeable impact on the Lyons lithographs, the drive for people to have access to a broad range of art, and in the widest possible context, certainly did have a bearing on the nature and overall success of the scheme.

The Lyons lithographs will not, therefore, be remembered as avant-garde examples of modern British art, but they should be remembered for their functional elegance, which, in the difficult aftermath of the Second World War, helped J. Lyons & Co. to serve '...an eyeful as well as a mouthful...'[8] in their famous teashops.

8. Sir Kenneth Clark quoted in the *Jewish Chronicle*, 11 March 1955 (press cuttings held in the J. Lyons & Co. archive at the London Metropolitan Archives, ACC/3527/245).

Appendix 1

The Lyons lithographs

D+L = designed and lithographed by   PTD = painted by

First Series – 1947

The Railway Station	Edward Ardizzone	D+L
The Dolls at Home	Edward Bawden	D+L
Teignmouth	Clifford & Rosemary Ellis	PTD
People	Barnett Freedman	D+L
Fun Fair	Clifford Frith	PTD
Still Life	Duncan Grant	PTD
Herne Bay Pier	Anthony Gross	D+L
Hotel Entrance	George Hooper	PTD
Flight into Egypt	Mary Kessell	PTD
Hastings	Edwin La Dell	D+L
Les Lecques Bay	John Lake	PTD
Industrial Scene	L. S. Lowry	PTD
Landscape with Bathers	John Nash	D+L
The Bird Cage	William Scott	D+L
Billiards Saloon	Ruskin Spear	PTD
Albert Bridge	Carel Weight	PTD

Second Series – 1951

The Spectators	Michael Ayrton	PTD
Roosevelt Memorial, Grosvenor Square	Peter Collins	PTD
The Fishmonger's Shop	Robin Darwin	D+L
Music – Still Life	Barnett Freedman	D+L
The Cricket Match	Anthony Gross	D+L
Fishing at Marlow	Edwin La Dell	D+L
The Shire Hall	Lynton Lamb	D+L
Apple Orchard, Kent	John Minton	PTD
Henley	Charles Mozley	D+L
River Buses at Putney Bridge	Claude Rogers	PTD
Yeoman Warders	Robert Scanlon	D+L
The Lighthouse of St Agnes	Fred Uhlman	PTD

Third Series – 1955

Shopping at Mysore	Edward Ardizzone	D+L
Louisiana Landscape	Anthony Gross	D+L
Trees, Kensington Gardens	Edward Middleditch	D+L
Clare Bridge, Cambridge	Edwin La Dell	D+L
Last Round	Sam Rabin	PTD
River Meadows, Pulborough	Elinor Bellingham-Smith	PTD
Still Life in Autumn	Michael Ayrton	PTD
Cornish Pilchard Boat	David Gentleman	D+L
The River Rother at Rye	Clifford Frith	PTD
Children's Music	Charles Mozley	D+L
Elizabethan Dance	John Piper	D+L
The Window Box	Barnett Freedman	D+L

Appendix 2

Address presented by David Gentleman at the opening of the exhibition Tea and a Slice of Art *at the Towner Art Gallery, 24 July 2004.*

Thank you Matthew for your kind introduction.

I'm very pleased to be here today, even though I suspect it's really because, as one of the few surviving Lyons lithograph artists, I must have unwittingly become one of the exhibits - a curiosity, a veteran, a sort of artistic Chelsea Pensioner, remarkable merely because I've survived at all. These prints were all done roughly - or in my case exactly - fifty years ago, when I was 24. It was only my third lithograph and the commission was my first big job, so I was naturally excited and on my mettle.

The Lyons corner houses, Joe Lyons for short, were then a national institution - a big chain of hundreds of teashops and restaurants, somewhere between Starbucks and Conran - and publishing these lithographs, which were hung on the teashop mirrors, was an ambitious project. It was the idea of the Salmon brothers, who owned Lyons, and the legendary Jack Beddington, who before the war had commissioned the famous Shell posters. And the artist who looked after the practical side was the distinguished lithographer Barnett Freedman.

My father had worked with Beddington at Shell, and knew Barnett Freedman well, so they must have liked him and been well disposed to me. Perhaps that's why I got the job. Also, I'd just finished studying illustration at the Royal College of Art, where I'd been taught by John Nash, Edward Bawden, Edward Ardizzone, John Minton, Barnett Freedman and Edwin La Dell, all of whom did Lyons prints - Edwin La Dell's was of Eastbourne, though it's not included here today.[9]

9. In fact, the La Dell lithograph is of Hastings.

All the artists commissioned were figurative – most of the others, at least, were well known, respected, what we now call 'accessible' – in other words, comprehensible – their work wasn't hard to understand: it needed no elucidation. That still seems to me to be quite a virtue. The nearest the Lyons list got to the avant garde was the discreetly formalised pots and pans of William Scott.

I'm probably biased, but I think that after fifty years the list of artists chosen has worn reasonably well. Several of them, like Bawden, belonged in that hard-to-categorise but in my view fruitful limbo somewhere between painter, illustrator and designer, a group that also included my hero, the Eastbourne-educated war artist Eric Ravilious. If he'd survived the war he'd surely have been on the list too; but he didn't.

The fishing boat in my lithograph was like those I'd seen at Mevagissey during my National Service in Cornwall. I went back there to make the drawings and studies for this print, but because the litho plates were too big to work on in my tiny flat in Battersea, I drew them in my new studio at the Royal College, where I'd just returned as a sort of usher.

Most of the lithographs were drawn to plate by the artists: each colour drawn by hand on separate zinc plates, which were then proofed and printed by Chromoworks at Willesden. This firm also printed posters, and the Heinz Baked Beans tin labels – I remember great vats of Baked Beans Blue printing ink standing by the presses. The young man in charge of production, Richard Russell, here today, was friendly, unflappable, supportive and encouraging. He had to be. Normally you complete the proofing of a print, altering the colours as necessary in relation to each other, *before* you print the final edition. But on this occasion, making the task unusually nightmarish, there was no separate proofing process. As soon as you thought you'd probably got each colour right, the whole edition of 1500 was run off; no second thoughts were possible. I've made about seventy lithos since then, but never again had that grisly experience. It was nerve-wracking. But once each day's proofing was done, Richard Russell would send me back to the Royal College in the Chromoworks limo, and I'd feel very grown-up and grand.

This exhibition's invitation card calls the Lyons series 'commercial lithographs'. But I'm not sure what that means: any prints that get published at all are commercial. Other people have apparently dismissed the Lyons lithographs as mere advertising. I think that denigrates them unjustly, and cheapens the whole project. The prints weren't ads. They said nothing about Lyons or its products; they didn't even try to get one into the teashops – by the time you saw them, you were inside already. But they certainly gave the teashops colour, interest and a sense of style; they weren't dumbed-down; they were original prints, good of their kind by the standards of the day; and if you wanted you could buy any of them for almost nothing. And they didn't put you off your meal; imagine having to eat your ham salad today under a BritArt sliced cow.

So I think that the scheme was a lively and imaginative venture – a bit of enlightened patronage, more in the honourable tradition of the pre-war London Transport than of the ad agency, giving people of all sorts something decent to look at as they spooned up their bowls of tomato soup or ate vast platefuls from the Salad Bowl counter or drank their cups of Lyons tea. I'm glad I was one of the artists involved, glad that the Towner Art Gallery has honoured all of them with this splendid exhibition, and delighted still to be here today in my survivor's get-up to pay it my respects.

Appendix 3

Artist Biographies
Compiled by Ruth Artmonsky

Edward Ardizzone

born 16 October 1900, Haiphong, Vietnam
died 8 November 1979, Rodmersham, Kent

Studied part-time at Westminster School of Art from 1920, under Bernard Meninsky. A full-time artist from 1926.

First solo exhibition held at the Bloomsbury Gallery, 1930.

A major illustrator of books (*c.* 180) – illustrating his own and designing book jackets. First book commission in 1926, his last in 1978, with some works published posthumously.

Undertook numerous illustrative commissions for magazines and for advertising, e.g. Guinness.

Taught at Camberwell College of Art (1948–51) and the Royal College of Art (RCA) (*c.* 1952–65).

WWII Official War Artist, attaching himself to fighting units in Europe, across North Africa and with the Allied invasion of Italy.

EXHIBITIONS:

V&A (1974), Scottish Arts Council (1979–80), Camberwell (1999), Ashmolean (2000)

HONOURS:

Elected RA (1970), RDI (1974)

REFERENCES:

1979, *Edward Ardizzone: Artist and Illustrator*, Gabriel White, Bodley Head
2000, *Edward Ardizzone's World: The Etchings and Lithographs*, Nicholas Ardizzone, Unicorn Press
2003 *Edward Ardizzone: A Bibliographic Commentary*, Brian Alderson, Private Library Association

Michael Ayrton

born 20 February 1921, London
died 16 November 1975, London

Little formal art training – a short spell at Heatherley's School of Fine Art (1935) and in de Chirico's studio in Paris. A precocious talent: by the age of 25 he had carried out theatrical designs (inc. for Gielgud and Constant Lambert), taught theatrical design at Camberwell (1942–4), and was art critic for the *Spectator*.

Career as an artist interspersed with writing (art criticism, art history, novels) and for a time with film-making. By 1951 he had become a high-profile broadcaster and 'public personality'.

As an artist he was serially absorbed in 'themes' – the circus, the bull ring, bones, and, in the 1950s, Daedelus, Icarus, the Minotaur and mazes; designing the Arkville Maze in 1969.

By the late 1950s he was also undertaking sculpture, and was a considerable etcher and occasional portraitist.

EXHIBITIONS:

Wakefield Art Gallery (1949), Whitechapel Art Gallery (1955)

PUBLIC COLLECTIONS:

Inc. British Museum, National Portrait Gallery, Tate

REFERENCES:

1978, *Michael Ayrton: An Illustrated Commentary*, Peter Cannon-Brookes, Birmingham Museum and Art Gallery
1994, *Michael Ayrton: A Biography*, Justine Hopkins, André Deutsch

Edward Bawden

born 10 March 1903, Braintree, Essex
died 21 November 1989, Saffron Walden, Essex

Studied at Cambridge School of Art (part-time 1918, full-time 1919), scholarship to the RCA (1922–5), where he studied with Paul Nash. Whilst a student won commissions from the Curwen Press and London Underground.

A major illustrator of books/book jackets (*c.* 140). Also designed wallpapers, textiles, ceramics, advertising materials and murals. A considerable watercolourist and lino-cutter.

First solo exhibition held at the Zwemmer Gallery, 1933.

Taught variously at the RCA (1930–46, excluding the war), the Royal Academy Schools and Leicester College of Art and Design.

An Official War Artist (1940–45) in the Middle East and the Western Desert.

EXHIBITIONS:
Minories, Colchester (1983), Imperial War Museum (1984), V&A (1989)

PUBLIC COLLECTIONS:
Inc. Imperial War Museum, Tate, V&A

HONOURS:
CBE (1946), RDI (1949), Trustee, Tate Gallery (1951), RA (1956), Honorary Fellow, RCA (1963), Honorary Doctorate, Essex University (1974)

REFERENCES:
1950, *Edward Bawden*, R. Harling, Art & Technics
1979, *Edward Bawden*, Douglas Percy Bliss, Pendomer Press
1988, *Edward Bawden: A Retrospective Survey*, Justin Howes, Combined Arts
2005, *Edward Bawden and His Circle*, Malcolm Yorke, Fleece Press
2005, *Edward Bawden: The Editioned Prints*, Jeremy Greenwood, Wood Lea Press

Elinor Bellingham-Smith

born 1906, London
died 1988, Ipswich, Suffolk

Studied at the Slade School of Fine Art (1929–31).

Married Rodrigo Moynihan in 1931. Her wit and zest for life made their Chelsea home a haven for artist friends. On their separation in 1957 she moved to Bildeston, near Ipswich.

First showed at the RA in 1947 and then through to 1988. From 1948, had seven solo exhibitions at the Leicester Galleries. Member of the London Group.

The Island won one of five prizes awarded in the Festival of Britain exhibition *Sixty Paintings for '51*.

A landscape painter of strong, often bleak scenes, particularly of East Anglia and the Fens.

Some commissioned work, e.g. for Shell Chemicals and *Harper's Bazaar*.

PUBLIC COLLECTIONS:
Inc. Arts Council, Tate

REFERENCES:
1989, *Elinor Bellingham-Smith, Memorial Exhibition* (cat.), New Grafton Gallery

Peter Collins

born 1923, London

Part-time student at Willesden School of Art and Hornsey School of Art.

Studied at the RCA from 1946 under Spear. Taught at St Martins School of Art.

Advertising work for British Rail and British European Airways.

Ran, and exhibited at, the Balcombe Galleries.

PUBLIC COLLECTIONS:
Leicester Education Authority

Robin Darwin

born 7 May 1910, London
died 20 January 1974

After Eton College, studied briefly at Cambridge and then 'slightly less briefly' at the Slade (1929). Art master at Eton College (1933–8).

First solo exhibition at the Redfern Gallery, 1933.

Worked for the Ministry of Home Security (1939–44), Secretary of the Camouflage Directorate (1946–7).

Director of the King Edward VII School of Art and Professor of Fine Art at Durham University.

Worked for the Council of Industrial Design preparing a report on 'The Training of the Industrial Designer', proposing curriculum changes at the RCA. In 1948 appointed Principal of the RCA – known as the 'Darwin Era'. Transformed the college by making it independent of the Ministry of Education and saw it through to university status. Restructured the departments, relating them more closely to industrial needs and appointed staff of status. Also saw the college into its new building (now known as the Darwin Building). He retired as Rector in 1971.

PUBLIC COLLECTIONS:

Inc. Contemporary Art Society, Manchester City Art Gallery

HONOURS:

CBE (1954), knighted (1964), elected RA (1972)

REFERENCES:

1987, 'The Dodo and the Phoenix', in *The Royal College of Art: One Hundred and Fifty Years of Art and Design*, Christopher Frayling, Barrie & Jenkins

Clifford and Rosemary Ellis

Clifford:
born 1907, Bognor Regis, Sussex
died 19 March 1985

Rosemary:
born 1910, London
died 1998

Clifford attended St Martins (1923–4) and Regent Street Polytechnic (1924–7), taking his Teaching Certificate in 1928 and studying Art History at London University in 1929.

Rosemary studied at Regent Street Polytechnic (*c.* 1927–31), where Clifford taught (1928–36).

They married in 1931 and were working partners for the rest of their lives. In the 1930s they designed lorry bills and posters for Shell-Mex, BP, the Empire Marketing Board, the General Post Office and London Transport. The work was signed first by whoever had initiated the design.

During the 1930s they also worked on mosaics, and between 1943 and 1985 designed nearly 100 book covers for the New Naturalist series published by Collins.

In 1938 Clifford was appointed head of the Bath Academy of Art, which moved to Corsham Court in 1946, becoming the first residential art school. He built up a staff of major artistic talent, e.g. William Scott, Kenneth Armitage, Howard Hodgkin and Terry Frost. Rosemary was also a teacher at Corsham. Clifford retired in 1972.

REFERENCES:

1989, *Corsham, a Celebration: The Bath Academy of Art, 1946–72* (cat.), Michael Parkin Gallery

Barnett Freedman

born 19 May 1901, Stepney, London
died 4 January 1958, Kensington, London

Studied part-time at St Martins (1917–22) and (with a scholarship) at the RCA (1922–5).

Taught at the Ruskin School of Art (1930–46) and the RCA (*c.* 1929–47, excluding the war).

First major solo show at the Zwemmer Gallery, 1931.

By WWII was an established designer working on commissions for Shell-Mex (1932 onwards), London Passenger Transport Board (from 1936) and the General Post Office; in 1935 he designed the Silver Jubilee stamp.

WWII Official War Artist serving with the army and navy, earning distinction for portraying whole crews.

Most well known as book illustrator and book-jacket designer, particularly for Faber & Faber and the Limited Editions and Heritage Clubs of NY, e.g. *War and Peace* and *Anna Karenina*, earning recognition for his unique attention to the design of book spines.

He was the leading lithographer of his generation (advised by Harold Curwen and T. E. Griffits) and wrote on, and promoted, lithography. Frequently worked at the Curwen Press.

An occasional broadcaster between 1938 and 1954.

EXHIBITIONS:

Arts Council (1958), Manchester Polytechnic Library (1978 and 1990)

PUBLIC COLLECTIONS:

Inc. Imperial War Museum, V&A

HONOURS:

CBE (1946), RDI (1949), Honorary Fellow, RCA (1956)

REFERENCES:

1948, *Barnett Freedman*, Jonathan Mayne, Art & Technics

1958, *Barnett Freedman, 1901–1958: Catalogue of Paintings, Drawings and Graphic art*, Arts Council

1990, *Barnett Freedman: Painter, Draughtsman, Lithographer*, Rogerson and Hoskins, Manchester Polytechnic Library

2005, *The Graphic Art of Barnett Freedman*, Professor Ian Rogerson, Fleece Press

Clifford Frith

born 1 October 1924, London

Studied at Camberwell and St Martins (1938–42).

1942–72 worked as a fine artist and from 1942 taught at Camberwell and Goldsmiths College. Between 1959 and 1962 taught at Ahmadu Bello University in Nigeria and was then Head of Fine Art at Croydon College of Art.

Emigrated to Australia in 1972. Between 1972 and 1989 was Senior Lecturer at the South Australia School of Art in Adelaide.

From 1977 produced public sculpture, e.g. for commercial head offices of Adelaide University.

Retired in 1989 to become a full-time artist and sculptor.

Lives at Henley Beach in Adelaide with a studio at Burringbar: mainly paints the sea and varying effects of light but as a way of experimenting with paint rather than for the image itself.

EXHIBITIONS:

Artspace Adelaide Festival Centre (1995)

PUBLIC COLLECTIONS:

Inc. Parliament House (Canberra), National Gallery of Australia, Tate

David Gentleman

born 11 March 1930, Hertford

Studied at St Alban's School of Art (1947–8 and 1950) and the RCA (1950–53) – taught by Edward Ardizzone, Edward Bawden and John Nash.

National Service at the Army School of Education in Bodmin (1949).

Taught at the RCA (1953–5) and since then has worked as a freelance artist and designer.

Prolific designer/illustrator for newspapers (inc. *Sunday Times* and *Sunday Telegraph*), for advertising (inc. London Transport, Shell, the General Post Office and the National Trust) and for magazines (inc. *House & Garden*). Also created a large-scale mural for London Transport at Charing Cross underground station.

In 1962 began to design stamps for the Post Office, producing over 100 images in forty years of commissions; contributing radical design changes, such as where the Queen's head was placed.

A major book illustrator, designing, among other commissions, thirty-two covers for the Penguin Shakespeare series. Also writes books for children, and travel guides (inc. Paris and Italy).

HONOURS:

Honorary Doctorate, Kingston University

REFERENCES:

2000, *The Wood Engravings of David Gentleman*, Introduction by Fiona MacCarthy, David Esslemont

2002, *Artwork*, David Gentleman, Ebury Press

Duncan Grant

born 21 January 1885, Rothiemurchus, Scotland
died 9 May 1978, Aldermaston, Berkshire

Studied at Westminster School of Art (1902–4) and spent terms at the Slade during 1906 and 1908. Also studied at La Palette in Paris (1906–7), under Jacques-Émile Blanche.

A member of the Bloomsbury Group, influenced by the Post-Impressionists. In 1913 became co-director of the Omega Workshop, the beginning of a long career decorating and designing interiors, furniture, murals and sets for theatre, ballet, opera.

In WWI, as a conscientious objector, moved to Charleston in Sussex, a farmhouse he shared with the artist Vanessa Bell for the next forty years.

Unlike his decorative work, most of his landscapes, portraits, nudes and still lifes were drawn from life.

EXHIBITIONS:

Tate (1959 and 1975)

PUBLIC COLLECTIONS:

Inc. Tate, National Portrait Gallery, V&A

HONOURS:

Refused OBE (1953), Honorary Degree, RCA (1970), Honorary Degree, University of Sussex (1973)

REFERENCES:

1923, *Duncan Grant*, Introduction by Roger Fry, Hogarth Press

1959, *Duncan Grant: A Retrospective* (cat.), Tate

1990, *The Art of Duncan Grant*, Simon Watney, John Murray

1997, *Duncan Grant: A Biography*, Frances Spalding, Chatto & Windus

Anthony Gross

born 19 March 1905, London
died 8 September 1984, Le Boulvé, France

Short spells at various art schools, inc. the Slade (1923 and 1926), Académie Julian in Paris (1923–4) and (1925–6), and at schools in Madrid and Toulouse.

Lived in France (1926–39) making cartoon films and painting. From 1934 also had a base in London.

Art director of London Films (1936). From 1936 onwards also illustrated books.

WWII Official War Artist (1941–6) in the Middle and Far East and Africa.

Taught life drawing at Central School of Arts and Crafts (1948–54), and etching and engraving at the Slade (1954–71).

In 1970 wrote *Etching, Engraving and Intaglio Printing*, published by Oxford University Press.

John Read made the films *Anthony Gross: The Artist Speaks* (1960) and *A Printmaker's Workshop* (1971) for the BBC.

EXHIBITIONS:

V&A (1968), Ashmolean (1989)

HONOURS:

First President of the Printmakers' Council (1965), elected RA (1980), CBE (1982)

REFERENCES:

1950, 'The Graphic Work of Anthony Gross', Jonathan Mayne, *Image*, spring

1968, *The Etchings of Anthony Gross* (cat.), G. Reynolds, V&A

1989, *Anthony Gross: Paintings, Drawings, Prints*, J. Lee, Ashmolean

1991, *The Prints of Anthony Gross, Catalogue Raisonné*, Robin Herdman, Scolar Press

George Hooper

born 10 September 1910, Gorakhpur, India
died 18 July 1994, Reigate, Surrey

Studied at the Slade (1931–2). Also studied at the Royal Academy Schools (1932–7) and received the Gold Medal and the Edward Stott Travelling and Rome scholarships.

Unfit for military service during WWII but in ARP (1940–42) and sketched civil defence activities.

Was an enthusiastic and experimental teacher at Brighton College of Art and also taught WEA classes.

Worked for the *Recording Britain* scheme (1941–2), providing sixty images.

Commissions for Shell, Esso, British Rail and the Post Office.

EXHIBITIONS:

Charleston (1994), Michael Parkin Gallery (1995)

PUBLIC COLLECTIONS:

Inc. Brighton Museum & Art Gallery, British Museum, V&A

REFERENCES:

1995, *George Hooper*, James Beechey, Hooper Gallery

Mary Kessell

born 14 November 1914, London
died 1977

Studied at Clapham School of Art (1935–7) and at Central (1937–9). Married the artist Tom Eckersley.

Used literary sources as recurrent themes in her work – the Bible, seventeenth-century poets, Greek mythology and Chinese poetry.

First book commission, Osbert Sitwell's *Mrs Kimber* (1937). First solo exhibition at the Leicester Galleries (1950).

Designed murals for Westminster Hospital, ICI and Shell.

After the war worked for the Shell Studio. Also designed fabrics, costumes and jewellery, and painted for the Sadler's Wells Ballet. Produced illustrations for magazines, including *Vogue*.

In 1945 she was commissioned to record the plight of refugees moving through Europe, for which she visited Belsen and Berlin. *Cornhill* magazine published part of her German diary in 1946. In the 1960s she did a similar series of drawings in India, writing and illustrating *A Visit to India for Oxfam* in 1969.

Taught jewellery design at Central (1952–6), at Camberwell (1955–60) and drawing at the London College of Printing (1957–76).

EXHIBITIONS:
Camden Arts Centre (1980)

PUBLIC COLLECTIONS:
Inc. Imperial War Museum, Tate

REFERENCES:
1946, 'Mary Kessell', P. L. Heard, *The Arts*, No. 2

1980, *Mary Kessell, 1914–1977: Paintings, Drawings, Collages* (cat.), Camden Arts Centre

Edwin La Dell

born 7 January 1914, Coventry
died 27 June 1970

Studied at Sheffield School of Art (1930–35) and the RCA (1935–8) under Barnett Freedman, Percy Horton and John Nash. He also studied lithography at Central under James Fitton.

In 1939 he married Joan Kohn, Charles Mozley's sister-in-law.

In WWII he was attached to the Civil Defence Camouflage Establishment. His work was bought by the War Artists Advisory Committee.

Taught at Central, Camberwell (1946–8/9) and from 1948 at the RCA, becoming Head of the School of Engraving and Etching in 1950. He also set up the lithographic studio.

Seen as a leader in the movement to popularise colour lithography. Organised a series of lithographs for sale to coincide with the Coronation in 1953.

First solo exhibition at St George's Gallery, 1959. Illustrated books for the Folio Society and Faber & Faber and wrote *Your Book of Landscape Drawing*.

PUBLIC COLLECTIONS:
Inc. British Museum, Imperial War Museum, Tate

HONOURS:
Associate RA (1959)

REFERENCES:
1984, *Edwin La Dell ARA: Paintings, Watercolours, Lithographs and Etchings* (cat.), King Street Gallery

John Lake

born 1903
died 1975, Malaga, Spain

Studied at Eastbourne School of Art (1918–25) and the RCA (1925–9).

A landscape watercolourist painting in the south of France, in Kent and Sussex, and, on retirement, in Spain. After WWII also turned to avant-garde sculpture.

Exhibited at the Mayor Gallery, London.

During WWII served as a Camouflage Officer in the army (1939–45).

Taught at Brighton College of Art and was employed as Curator of the Towner Art Gallery between 1947 and 1958, enthusiastically reviving and developing it as an art centre.

Emigrated to Spain in 1958.

EXHIBITIONS:
Towner Art Gallery (1955 and 1976)

PUBLIC COLLECTIONS:
Inc. Arts Council, Towner Art Gallery

REFERENCES:
1976, *A Memorial and a Tribute to John Gascoyne Lake ARCA FRSA, 1903–75* (cat.), Towner Art Gallery

Lynton Lamb

born 15 April 1907, India
died 4 September 1977

Studied part-time at Camberwell and full-time at Central (1928–30) – taught lithography by A. S. Hartrick and wood engraving by Noel Rooke and R. J. Beedham.

During the 1930s shared a studio with Victor Pasmore and in 1940 moved to Sandon near Chelmsford.

First solo exhibition at the Storran Gallery, 1937.

Visiting tutor at Central until 1939, lecturer at the Slade (1950–71) and at the RCA (1956–71).

Book illustrator and typographer from 1939, initially working on bibles, prayer books and World's Classics for Oxford University Press. He also illustrated forty books for the Golden Cockerell Press, Shakespeare Head Press and Limited Editions Club, NY. Consultant typographer for Oxford University Press and Art Editor of the Oxford Illustrated Trollopes.

Wrote *The Purpose of Painting* and *Preparation for Painting* and contributed articles to *Signature*.

HONOURS:

President of Double Crown Club (1953), RDI (1974)

REFERENCES:

1978, *Lynton Lamb: Illustrator, 1907–77*, Introduction by George Mackie, Scolar Press

L. S. Lowry

born 1 November 1887, Manchester
died 23 February 1976, Mottram-in-Longendale, Cheshire
Studied at the Municipal School of Art, Manchester (1905–15) and the Salford School of Art (1915–25). Was an art student, both full- and part-time, for twenty years, but considered himself self-taught.

Lived in Salford (1909–48) then moved to Mottram. He rarely travelled far out of the area and worked as an insurance clerk, rising to Chief Cashier (*c.* 1910–52).

First solo exhibition at Reid & Lefevre, 1939.

From 1916 he focused on industrial landscapes of South Lancashire. By 1961 he had had seven solo exhibitions and turned to landscapes and seascapes (particularly the coastlines of Northumberland and Durham) and grotesques. He abandoned painting altogether in the 1960s.

EXHIBITIONS:

Salford (1951), Manchester City Art Gallery (1955), Tate (1966/7), RA (1971)

PUBLIC COLLECTIONS:

Inc. Arts Council, Tate, Lowry (Salford)

HONOURS:

Refused Knighthood and OBE
Elected RA (1962), awarded the Freedom of the City of Salford (1965) and three honorary doctorates. The General Post Office issued a Lowry stamp (1962)

REFERENCES:

1973, *The Drawings of L. S. Lowry*, Mervyn Levy, Jupiter Books

1977, *The Paintings of L. S. Lowry: Oils and Watercolours*, Mervyn Levy, Jupiter Books

1977, *Laurence Stephen Lowry, 1887–1976: A Catalogue of the Salford Collection*, F. Mullineux and S. Shaw

Edward Middleditch

born 23 March 1923, Chelmsford
died 29 June 1987

Served in the army (1942–7). Commissioned in the Middlesex Regiment (1944) and was on active service in France, Germany and Burma. Won the Military Cross.

Studied at Regent Street Polytechnic (1948) and the RCA (1949–52) using his ex-serviceman's grant. Considered to be Ruskin Spear's protégée.

Labelled as a member of the Kitchen Sink School.

Exhibited at the RA whilst still at the RCA. Included in *Artists of Fame and Promise* at the Leicester Galleries, 1951. First solo exhibition at Beaux Arts Gallery, 1954.

Painted a mural, with Derrick Greaves, for Nuffield College in 1956.

Represented Great Britain at the Venice Biennale, 1956.

Taught at Chelsea (1958–63), Regent Street Polytechnic (1960–61) and at Cambridge School of Art and St Martins.

Head of Fine Art at Norwich School of Art (1964–84), where he built up an atelier atmosphere with visiting artists.

Elected Keeper of the Royal Academy Schools in 1984. Resigned through ill-health in 1986.

EXHIBITION:

South Bank Centre (touring) (1987)

PUBLIC COLLECTIONS:

Inc. Arts Council, Tate

REFERENCES:

1987, *Edward Middleditch* (cat.), essay by Therese Lessore, South Bank Centre

John Minton

born 25 December 1917, Great Shelford, Cambridge
died 20 January 1957, London

Studied at St John's Wood School of Art (1935–8) and worked at Colarossi's Grande Chaumière (1939).

In 1940 registered as a conscientious objector but enlisted in the Pioneer Corps in 1941. Invalided out in 1943.

Shared a studio with Robert Colquhon and Robert MacBryde (1943–6), and with Keith Vaughan (1946–52).

Between 1945 and 1957 had seven solo exhibitions at the Lefevre Gallery.

A popular and legendary teacher at Camberwell (1943–6), Central (1946–8) and the RCA (1948–56).

Illustrated a dozen books, mainly for John Lehmann and Paul Elek. Undertook numerous illustrations for magazines, advertising and posters. Also designed wallpaper and did some theatrical work.

Committed suicide in 1957.

EXHIBITIONS:

Arts Council (touring) (1958–9), Reading Museum and Art Gallery (1974), Morley Gallery (touring) (1979), RCA (touring) (1994)

PUBLIC COLLECTIONS:

Inc. the British Council, Tate, V&A

REFERENCES:

1958, *John Minton, 1917–1957*, Arts Council
1991, *Dance Till the Stars Come Down: A Biography of John Minton*, Frances Spalding, John Curtis
1994, *John Minton, 1917–1957: A Selective Retrospective* (Oriel 31), RCA/Davies Memorial Gallery, Newtown

Charles Mozley

born 29 May 1914, Sheffield
died 1991, Kew, Surrey

Studied at Sheffield School of Arts and Crafts (1933), the RCA (1934–7). First solo exhibition whilst at Sheffield.

Served with the army in Camouflage and Intelligence (1939–45).

Worked as a freelance artist and graphic designer for, among others, London Transport, British Transport, film companies and Shell. During the 1950s he became particularly well known for his work with the wine trade and the City Music Society. Designed murals for the Festival of Britain.

Most distinguished as a book-jacket designer and illustrator. Used a variety of media, but was a specialist lithographer. Worked on over seventy books (thirty for children). Most closely associated with the Folio Society, Limited Editions Club, NY (1962–71), Chatto & Windus, Dent, and Franklin Watts, NY.

EXHIBITIONS:

Reading University Library (1996), Barbican Library Gallery (2002, 2005)

REFERENCES:

1996, *Charles Mozley, 1914–1991: Artist, Lithographer and Graphic Designer*, Reading University Library

John Nash

born 11 April 1893, London
died 29 September 1977, Colchester

No formal art training – his brother Paul advised against it.

In 1913 staged a joint exhibition with Paul at the Dorien Leigh Galleries.

Enlisted in the Artists' Rifles (1916), commissioned as an Official War Artist (1918). In WWII joined the Royal Observer Corps (1939). Appointed an Official War Artist attached to the Admiralty in 1940 and transferred to active service in the Royal Marines.

Became art critic of the *London Mercury* in 1919 and a member of the Society of Wood Engravers in 1920.

First solo exhibition at the Goupil Gallery, 1921.

Taught at the Ruskin School of Art (1922–7) and in the Design School at the RCA (1934–40) and (1945–57).

Moved to Wormingford in Essex in 1944, which remained his home for the rest of his life.

He was a prodigious book illustrator (the first in 1919): nearly fifty in total.

EXHIBITIONS:

Leicester Galleries (1954), RA (1967) – first living artist to be so honoured

PUBLIC COLLECTIONS:

Inc. Imperial War Museum, Tate

HONOURS:

Elected RA (1951), CBE (1964), Honorary Degree, University of Essex (1967)

REFERENCES:

1967, *John Nash CBE, RA* (cat.), Introduction by Frederick Gore, Tate

1978, *John Nash: The Painter as Illustrator*, J. Lewis, Pendover Press

1983, *John Nash*, Sir John Rothenstein, Macdonald & Co.

John Piper

born 13 December 1903, Epsom, Surrey
died 28 June 1992, Fawley Bottom, Oxfordshire

Studied at Richmond School of Art (1927–8) and the RCA (1928–9).

In the 1930s he experimented with abstraction, becoming Secretary of the Seven and Five Society in 1935 and producing *Axis* with Myfanwy Evans between 1935 and 1937. They moved to Fawley Bottom and married in 1937.

First solo exhibition at the London Gallery, 1938.

Co-editor of the Shell County Guides with John Betjeman. Contributed to the *Recording Britain* series and from 1940 served as an Official War Artist recording bomb-damaged buildings.

He also designed over twenty stage sets, many for Benjamin Britten's operas, and produced stained glass work for, among others, Coventry Cathedral (1958–62), Eton College (1958–63) and the Catholic Cathedral in Liverpool (1964–7).

EXHIBITIONS:

MOMA Oxford (1979), Tate (1983)

PUBLIC COLLECTIONS:

Inc. Arts Council, British Museum, Tate

HONOURS:

Trustee, Tate Gallery (1944), Companion of Honour (1972)

REFERENCES:

1979, *John Piper: 50 years of Work, Paintings, Drawings and Photographs, 1929–79* (cat.), MOMA Oxford

1979, *John Piper*, Anthony West, Secker & Warburg

1987, *John Piper: The Complete Graphic Works, 1923–83*, compiled by O. Levinson, Faber & Faber

2003, *John Piper in the 30s* (cat.), Jenkins and Spalding, Dulwich Picture Gallery

Sam Rabin

born (Rabinovitch) 20 June 1903, Manchester
died 1991, Poole, Dorset

Studied at Manchester School of Art from 1914 and at the Slade between 1920 and 1924 – an outstanding sculpture student.

Commissioned (with Henry Moore and Eric Gill etc.) to make *The Four Winds* for the headquarters of London Underground (1928) and *Past* and *Future* for the Daily Telegraph Building (1929).

During the late 1920s and early 1930s he funded his art by wrestling, having won a Bronze Medal in the 1928 Olympics. The 'ring' became the main focus for his work and he was painted fighting by William Roberts and Barnett Freedman. He also appeared in films as a fighter and in 1979 designed a memorial for the boxer Freddie Mills.

Singing provided additional income, working with the Army Classical Music Group during WWII and then for the BBC.

Taught drawing at Goldsmiths College (1949–65) and was also a visiting lecturer at

Camberwell, but became disillusioned with their emphasis on non-figurative work and moved to Bournemouth College of Art (1965–85).

REFERENCES:

1985, *Introducing Sam Rabin* (cat.), Dulwich Picture Gallery

Claude Rogers

born 24 January 1907, London
died 18 February 1979, London

Studied at the Slade (1925–8). Taught part-time at Raynes Park School (1935–8).

Founding member of the Euston Road School of Painting and Drawing, joining as a teacher in 1938.

Involved in the issue of the *Everyman Prints* in 1940 and in the same year held first solo exhibition at the Leicester Galleries.

In WWII enlisted in the Royal Engineers (1942) but was invalided out in 1943.

Enjoyed a distinguished career as teacher at Camberwell (1944–8), the Slade (1948–63), as Professor of Fine Art at the University of Reading (1963–72) and also as Professor Emeritus (1972).

Chairman of the Fine Arts Panel of the National Council for the Diploma in Art and Design.

EXHIBITIONS:

Hatton Gallery (1954), Whitechapel Art Gallery (1973)

PUBLIC COLLECTIONS:

Inc. Ashmolean, Tate

HONOURS:

President of the London Group (1952–65), OBE (1959)

REFERENCES:

1973, *Claude Rogers: Paintings and Drawings, 1927–1973* (cat.), Introduction by Andrew Forge, Whitechapel Art Gallery

1995, *The Affectionate Eye: The Life of Claude Rogers*, Jenny Pery, Sansom & Company

Robert Scanlon

born 15 February 1908, Cork
died 28 July 1997, Wimbledon

Studied for short periods in London, Paris, Spain and Romania.

Pre-WWII exhibited at the Leicester Galleries and in America.

During WWII served in the army but was released in 1942 to work as an Official War Artist in Malta.

Worked mainly as a commercial artist, having a contract with J. Walter Thompson (1935–70) and working, for example, as the art director for the UK launch of Kellogg's Special K and the Kellogg family on TV.

He also designed murals for *Britain Can Make It* and the Festival of Britain.

A cartoonist and illustrator for magazines and newspapers including *Lilliput*, *Night and Day*, the *Listener*, the *Strand* and *Harper's Bazaar*.

Designed posters for the General Post Office, the Central Office of Information and the London Passenger Transport Board – *Have You Seen your Picassos?* winning an award.

PUBLIC COLLECTIONS:

Inc. Imperial War Museum, Towner Art Gallery

William Scott

born 15 February 1913, Greenock, Scotland
died 28 December 1989, Coleford, Somerset

Funded to study at Belfast College of Art (1928–31) and the Royal Academy Schools (1931–5), where he won awards for both painting and sculpture.

In 1937 he married fellow student Mary Lucas, and set up a painting school in Brittany, returning to England 1939. In 1941 he moved to Hallatrow in Somerset.

He took a part-time teaching post at the Bath Academy of Art and returned as Senior Painting Master after serving in the Royal Engineers (1942–5). He left in 1956.

First solo show at the Leger Gallery, 1942.

Earned an international reputation from being included in a British Council overseas exhibition, teaching at Banff School of Fine Art at the University of Alberta and showing at the Venice Biennale in 1958.

Was in the inner circle of St Ives post-war painters and artistically experimented throughout working life using objects that were close at hand (e.g. saucepans).

EXHIBITIONS:
Tate (1972), Belfast (1986)
PUBLIC COLLECTIONS:
Inc. Brighton Museum & Art Gallery, Tate
HONOURS:
CBE (1966), Honorary Degrees from Belfast and Dublin universities
REFERENCES:
1963, *William Scott*, Ronald Alley, Methuen
1964, *William Scott*, Alan Bowness, Lund Humphries
1964, *William Scott: Paintings, Drawings and Gouaches, 1938–71* (cat.), ed. Alan Bowness, Tate
2004, *William Scott*, Norbert Lynton, Thames & Hudson

Ruskin Spear

born 30 June 1911, Hammersmith
died 1990, London

Studied at Hammersmith School of Art (1926) and the RCA (1930–34).

Taught at Croydon School of Art (1935 and 1941–3), St Martins and then Central (1945–8), the RCA (1948–77).

Exempt from war service because of polio.

Exhibited at the RA from 1932 onwards. First solo exhibition at the Leicester Galleries, 1951.

Painted the locality around Hammersmith and Fulham but was also a prolific portrait painter, e.g. Robin Darwin, Laurence Olivier and Harold Wilson.

Designed an altar piece for the RAF church, St Clement Danes, in 1958.

EXHIBITION:
RA (1980)
PUBLIC COLLECTIONS:
Inc. Arts Council, British Council, National Portrait Gallery, RA, Tate
HONOURS:
President of the London Group (1949), CBE (1979)
REFERENCES:
1980, *Ruskin Spear, RA: A Retrospective Exhibition* (cat.), RA
1985, *Ruskin Spear*, Mervyn Levy, Weidenfeld & Nicolson

Fred Uhlman

born 19 January 1901, Stuttgart, Germany
died April 1985, London

No formal art training. Trained as lawyer and practised as a barrister in Germany (1927–33). Moved to Paris (1933) and to London, where he married Diana Croft in 1936. Lived in Downshire Hill, Hampstead, which became a meeting place for artists, writers and academics, and helped refugee artists from Germany and Austria – the Kokoschka Group. Founded the Free German League of Culture.

First solo exhibition at Galerie Le Niveau, Paris, 1935. First UK exhibition at the Zwemmer Gallery, 1938, and then showed in various leading London galleries (1938–75).

Interned on the Isle of Man as enemy alien but released in December 1940. Produced many drawings during that time and in 1946 published *In Captivity*.

Wrote books, e.g. *Making of an Englishman* (1960) and *Reunion* (1970).

His unique collection of African sculpture was donated to the Hatton Gallery.

EXHIBITION:
Leighton House (1968)
PUBLIC COLLECTIONS:
Inc. British Museum, Fitzwilliam Museum, V&A

Carel Weight

born 10 September 1908, London
died 13 August 1997, London

Studied at Hammersmith School of Art (1928–30) and at Goldsmiths College (1930–33).

Exhibited regularly at the RA from 1931. First solo show at the Cooling Gallery (1933). Taught at Beckenham School of Art (1932–41).

Served in the army during WWII but not appointed an Official War Artist until 1945. Worked in Greece, Italy and Austria.

Tutor at the RCA (1947–57), Professor of Painting, RCA (1957–73). A distinguished teacher who particularly influenced the urban painting of John Bratby and Derrick Greaves.

Designed murals for the Festival of Britain (1951) and Manchester Cathedral (1963).

EXHIBITIONS:
RA (1982), Newport Museum (touring) (1993)

PUBLIC COLLECTIONS:
Inc. Ashmolean, Imperial War Museum, Tate

HONOURS:
CBE (1962), elected RA (1965), Companion of Honour (1995)

REFERENCES:
1982, *Carel Weight RA: A Retrospective Exhibition* (cat.), Royal Academy of Arts
1994, *A Haunted Imagination*, R.V. Weight, David & Charles

Appendix 4

References

Archives and Collections

The Barnett Freedman Archive, Manchester Metropolitan University Special Collections, All Saints Library.

The J. Lyons and Co. Archive at the London Metropolitan Archives (ACC/3527).

Examples of the Lyons lithographs are held in the collections of, among others, the Victoria & Albert Museum, the British Museum, the Scottish National Gallery of Modern Art, Brighton Museum & Art Gallery and the Towner Art Gallery. The London Metropolitan Archive holds a complete set.

Articles

N. Bentley, 'Lithographs for Lyons', *Alphabet and Image*, no. 7, May 1948, p. 54.

N. Carrington, 'Art in the Teashops', *Penrose Annual*, Vol. 47, 1950, pp. 50–52.

Barnett Freedman, 'Lithography: A Painter's Excursion', *Signature* (2), March 1936, pp. 1–14.

P. Rennie, 'The Lyons Lithographs', *Antique Collecting*, April 1993, pp. 13–16.

R. Russell, 'The Lyons Lithographs', *Matrix*, winter 1999, pp. 138–42.

G. S. Whittet, 'Teashop Lithographs', *The Studio*, September 1948, pp. 71–4.

Books and Catalogues

R. Artmonsky, *Jack Beddington: The Footnote Man* (London, Artmonsky Arts, 2006).

M. Banham and B. Hillier (eds.), *A Tonic to the Nation: The Festival of Britain 1951* (London, Thames & Hudson, 1976).

J. Beechey, *George Hooper* (London, Hooper Gallery, 1995).

J. Biggs, *Illustration and Reproduction* (London, Blandford Press, 1950).

P. Bird, *The First Food Empire: A History of J. Lyons & Co.* (Chichester, Phillimore, 2000).

F. Carey and A. Griffiths, *Avant-Garde British Printmaking 1914–1960* (London, British Museum Publications, 1990).

A. Delicata and B. Cole, *Speed to the West: Great Western Publicity and Posters, 1923–1947* (Harrow Weald (Middlesex), Capital Transport Publishing, 2000).

G. Ferry, *A Computer Called LEO – Lyons Teashops and the World's First Office Computer* (London, Fourth Estate, 2003).

J. Gardiner, *From the Bomb to the Beatles* (London, Collins & Brown, 1999).

R. Garton (ed.), *British Printmakers 1855–1955* (London, Garton & Co. in association with Scolar Press, 1992).

P. Gilmour, *Artists at Curwen* (London, Tate Gallery, 1977).

O. Green, *Underground Art*, 2nd edn (London, Laurence King, 2001).

P. Hendy, Foreword to *A Catalogue of Lithographs* (London, J. Lyons & Co., printed at the Shenval Press, 1947)

J. Hewitt, Introduction to *The Shell Poster Book* (London, Profile Books, 1998).

P. James, *Lithographs by Contemporary Artists – First and Second Series* (J. Lyons & Co. Ltd/ Arts Council of Great Britain, printed at the Curwen Press, 1951).

P. James, Foreword to *Sixty Paintings for '51* (London, Arts Council of Great Britain, 1951).

J. Laver, Foreword to *A Collection of Forty Colour Lithographs by Contemporary Artists* (London, J. Lyons & Co., 1955).

B. Miles, *At the Sign of the Rainbow: Margaret Calkin James, 1895–1985* (Alcester (Warwickshire), Felix Scribo, 2005).

A. Peat *et al.*, *Austerity to Affluence: British Art and Design 1945–1962* (London, Merrell Hoberton, 1977).

G. Smith, *Colour and Autolithography in the 20th Century* (Manchester, Special Collections, Manchester Metropolitan University, 2005).

F. Spalding, *British Art since 1900* (London, Thames & Hudson, 1988).